High Income Consulting

In memory of my father, Tom Lambert, who taught me, among many other things, that a man should always be prepared to buy his round and fight his corner.

And in respectful recognition of my debt to the late Howard Shenson, who taught the world about ethical consulting.

High Income Consulting

How to Build and Market Your Professional Practice

Second edition

Tom Lambert

NICHOLAS BREALEY
PUBLISHING
LONDON

This new edition first published by
Nicholas Brealey Publishing Limited in 1997

36 John Street
London
WC1A 2AT, UK
Tel: +44 (0)171 430 0224
Fax: +44 (0)171 404 8311

17470 Sonoma Highway
Sonoma
California 95476, USA
Tel: (707) 939 7570
Fax: (707) 938 3515

http://www.nbrealey-books.com

First published in hardback in 1993 and in paperback in 1995
(reprinted four times)

HB: ISBN 1-85788-1648
PB: ISBN 1-85788-1699

British Library Cataloguing in Publication Data
A catalogue record for this book is available from the British Library.

Printed in Finland by Werner Söderström Oy.

Contents

Preface to the Second Edition

Introduction   1
Confirms that consultancy is, and will continue to be, a growing market sector. Provides some basic information on current global trends and gives data on the consultancy profession. Most importantly, it provides all readers with realistic expectations of what this book will do for them.

PART I: BUILDING YOUR PRACTICE

1 To Be or Not To Be   15
Aimed exclusively at the reader who is considering setting up a practice. Gives advice on how to decide whether to go ahead. Also outlines the profession and its ups and downs from the beginner's point of view.

2 Beginners Only   42
Written with the sole intent of getting the beginner up and running, the only section of this chapter of interest to the grizzled professional is the speculative but well-founded consideration of the issue of liability – professional and product.

3 Consultancy at Work   56
The accent is still on the beginner's needs, but the established professional who believes that professional values are important will find food for thought.

4 Networking for Synergy   80
Most established professionals are committed to the concept of networking, but have had bad experiences. Establishes how to get the best out of networking.

**5 Business-Winning Proposals and Other Ways
of Getting Paid**   85
Even the most experienced find that too often they have given away valuable information with no hope of being compensated. This chapter ensures an appropriate return for your skills and knowledge.

6 Setting and Divulging Your Fees   100
The way professionals establish and divulge their fees can win (or lose) business. Explains how to meld professionalism with appropriate flexibility – and win business.

7 The Contract   115
The contract is an essential medium of communication which is too often underestimated as a marketing tool.

PART II: MARKETING YOUR PRACTICE

8 Tactical Marketing   128
The core of the book. The key difference between high earners and the rest lies in how they market their services – market the low-cost way and do it consistently and you will be a winner.

9 Making Your Brochure Work For You   155
More wasted dollars, pounds, francs and deutschmarks reside in filing cabinets than in consultants' pockets. This chapter will save you money and win you business.

10 Advertising for the Professions   164
In a world where the big guns enjoy the advantage of wasting money, the real professional needs to make advertising work. This chapter tells you how.

11 Referral Business Is Great Business   185
Referral and repeat business maximizes revenue, profit and personal income, but you only get what you know how to ask for.

12 Selling Your Skills   193
Psychological profiling shows that salespeople and consultants are different animals, but consultants must sell their services. This chapter explains ethical, professional and client-centred sales skills.

PART III: ADVANCED SKILLS

13 Consultancy Roles   222
We are now in the realm of advanced skills – beginners have an opportunity to fast-track and buyers of consultancy services have a rare opportunity to learn how to work with consultants.

14 Outline Strategies for Each Stage of the Assignment   231
Detailed information on managing the assignment, with the emphasis on client delight.

15 Avoiding Problems   249
How to avoid the most common pitfalls.

16 Loving Them to Death Is Not Enough   264
How to delight your clients consistently and continually.

PART IV: THE CONSULTANT'S TOOLKIT

Proven Tactics for Marketing Your Practice   285
An action-biased summary of the book.

Glossary   307
An annotated glossary of business and behavioural terms enabling busy professionals to focus their reading on the needs of the moment – lifelong learning: just in time.

Bibliography   331
*Extended and updated, a collection of books about tools of the trade,
new techniques and perspectives.*

Seminars for Professionals   337
*An unblushing indicator of a few of the learning opportunities which
I provide.*

High Income Consulting – Chapter Flow Chart

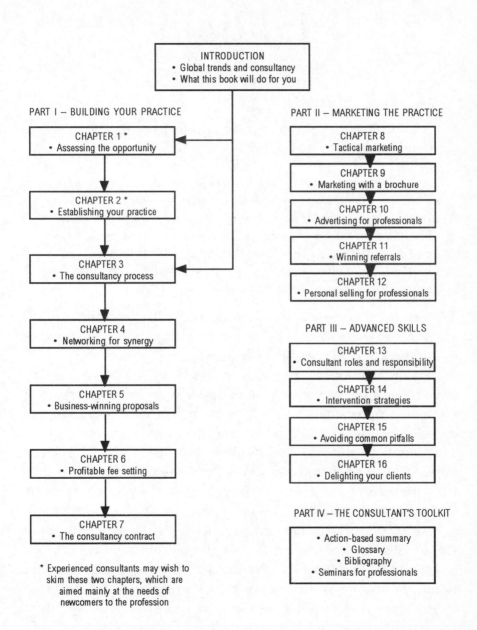

INTRODUCTION
- Global trends and consultancy
- What this book will do for you

PART I – BUILDING YOUR PRACTICE

CHAPTER 1 *
- Assessing the opportunity

CHAPTER 2 *
- Establishing your practice

CHAPTER 3
- The consultancy process

CHAPTER 4
- Networking for synergy

CHAPTER 5
- Business-winning proposals

CHAPTER 6
- Profitable fee setting

CHAPTER 7
- The consultancy contract

* Experienced consultants may wish to
skim these two chapters, which are
aimed mainly at the needs of
newcomers to the profession

PART II – MARKETING THE PRACTICE

CHAPTER 8
- Tactical marketing

CHAPTER 9
- Marketing with a brochure

CHAPTER 10
- Advertising for professionals

CHAPTER 11
- Winning referrals

CHAPTER 12
- Personal selling for professionals

PART III – ADVANCED SKILLS

CHAPTER 13
- Consultant roles and responsibility

CHAPTER 14
- Intervention strategies

CHAPTER 15
- Avoiding common pitfalls

CHAPTER 16
- Delighting your clients

PART IV – THE CONSULTANT'S TOOLKIT

- Action-based summary
- Glossary
- Bibliography
- Seminars for professionals

Preface to the Second Edition

IN THE INTRODUCTION TO THE FIRST EDITION OF *HIGH INCOME Consulting* I wrote:

> *This book is written with a straightforward purpose. It aims to help its readers to build and sustain very profitable high quality professional practices capable of providing excellent levels of secure income virtually regardless of the state of the economy. Aimed at the experienced professional as much as at the newcomer to the profession it is based on exhaustive research of what is actually done by the top earners on both sides of the Atlantic.*

The results of the research which drove the first edition have, if anything, been validated and strengthened by readers' acceptance of the book and further field experience.

The first edition, I am told almost daily by telephone, fax and sometimes, from the very ingenious (the first edition didn't give this information), by email, has become the most-thumbed reference of consultants from London to Dunedin. So why change now?

Richard Pascale said that 'nothing fails like success'. There is nothing more dangerous in a volatile business and social setting than the assumption that one has the formula which is certain to lead again and again to success.

Putting together a new edition helps me to avoid the ever-threatening rut and frees me from the unwarranted assumption that I said all that there was to be said on the subject the first time round. It also gives me a chance to sharpen some of my more turgid prose and introduce a few new tips and ideas. For these opportunities I am duly grateful. I hope that the result will be a stronger, tighter, better-focused and, above all, more useful book.

Introduction

'There is unlikely to be any business or institution which will escape radical change.'
          Sir John Harvey-Jones

'Tomorrow's effective organization will be conjured up anew each day.'
          Tom Peters

THE CORPORATE WORLD TODAY IS VERY DIFFERENT FROM THAT OF only a few years ago. Profits and share values are at record highs, yet 'downsizing' is still the holy grail of too many companies. Research and a growing number of customer complaints show that downsizing is all too frequently disastersizing, but it goes on. Even the merchant bank economists who cheered every swing of the axe are talking of 'hollow companies, bereft of the capacity for growth' (Roach, 1996). Most recent research indicates that downsizing, through the loss of experienced management and labour, leads to 'corporate amnesia' or worse, 'corporate Alzheimer's'.

In the United States downsizing is perhaps less a personal disaster than it is in Europe, because as jobs have disappeared others, sometimes of better quality, have been created and unemployment is being held at under 6 per cent. Europe, on the other hand, is experiencing at best sluggish growth and increasing unemployment exacerbated by falling investment.

The European Union has opened its internal borders and is now moving, much of the time unsteadily, towards monetary and possibly political union on an ambitious timetable.

Management fads have come and gone and some, in spite of their poor showing in the real world of work, have come and stayed. Corporations are still buying into process reengineering and the like in spite of an estimated 80 per cent failure rate. The bus queue syndrome of 'let this new idea slide, there'll be another one along any minute' is increasingly part of the spreading exhaustion which results from attempting to do more with fewer resources in less time and often for less pay.

Globalization, glocalization, empowerment and creating the future are more talked about than understood.

Yet with all this Western Europe and the US between them still account for almost 60 per cent of all world trade. That percentage will fall between now and the millennium, but that is not necessarily bad news. The chances are that it will fall only because world trade in total will expand at an accelerating rate. The US, which is between 90 and 95 per cent self-sufficient but produces a GDP so enormous that its meagre trade needs account for 17 per cent of the total world movement of goods and services into export markets, will continue to grow and prosper, as will Europe, but, on the basis of current projections, they will do so at different speeds.

Wisdom of the East

Meanwhile economies have continued to develop at a breakneck pace in South East Asia. Andy Grove, the CEO of Intel, expressed the view a few months ago that China would be the source of the greatest competition in the microchip industry within ten years. However, he now thinks that it will be there in just eight short years – or less.

Malaysia has grown its economy by an average of more than 8 per cent per annum for eight years now and predicts a similar level of growth every year to 2000. Myanmar, a name that is unfamiliar to many who still think of Burma, is taking strategic decisions which will boost it into the 'tiger' class within a few years unless its political problems trigger a commercial backlash. Vietnam is emerging from the political and economic wilderness.

Korea continues a customer-centred invasion of Europe and the US, offering not only new brand names and products but also new approaches to marketing and distribution. Taiwan has invented and is pursuing a new marketing concept of 'innovalue'. Its economic situation is enviable. GDP is growing at better than 5 per cent from a relatively sophisticated base and unlike its neighbours, of course always excluding Singapore, Taiwan appears to have inflation firmly under control.

Japan, in spite of having its funeral oration read *ad nauseam* by Western business and economic magazines and newspapers over the last 12 months, showed an annualized growth rate in GDP of 0.4 per cent in third quarter 1996, after having fallen 2.9 per cent the previous quarter. This was better than many economists expected. Equally importantly, this nation that so many have been sidelining as having 'run out of steam' is seeing a rapid return of consumer confidence.

Europe has its East too

The Czech and Slovak Republics, along with Hungary and Poland, are successfully rebuilding their business and industrial capacity to compete in the free markets of the free world. Czech output is rising at 5 per cent a year and Polish GDP is increasing at 7 per cent. Russia is still a major and terrifying questionmark, but it too has its occasional capitalist success stories.

The European Union is opening its arms and its markets increasingly to the newly thriving Eastern European industries, while the Eastern Europeans themselves are proactive in building strategic alliances in the Pacific Rim and elsewhere.

Africa after apartheid

South Africa, Namibia and Botswana as friendly neighbours are entering a great commercial, social and political adventure. Each has its unique landscape, customs, resources and ideas. Each is embracing the challenge of a rainbow society in a knowledge-driven world. Each, on a continent of despair, is a land of economic opportunity.

In summary, we have a rapidly changing world in which the only certainty is change. New ideas, new technologies and new rules to play by come thick and fast. The business cycle from formation to decline is more speedy than most of us can yet grasp. New markets emerge and old markets hold their own in spite of manifold difficulties. People are increasingly expected to do more with less for less and some believe that families and societies are falling apart as a result. It is a rich miscellany of good and bad, but it is a mixture with opportunities for the consultant. When the future for world trade has seldom been brighter, it's a good time to be in the business of supporting business.

What's in it for you?

Why have I taken the time and space to review, albeit superficially, so many apparently unconnected things that are happening in the world? I believe that these happenings and many more show why consultancy has been a good business to be in, why it will remain a good business wherever you choose to work, and why the demand for your services and mine will continue to grow.

Let me list just a few of the reasons that the growth of consultancy will outstrip the 20 per cent a year that it has averaged in the US and Western Europe over the last 20 or so years.

Good times: bring with them the problems of growth. Not just growth in general terms, but growth which avoids repeating the problems of the past. If you have the skills and knowledge to help organizations overcome these problems, you have a market.

ad times: where recession is still wreaking daily havoc there is a major market. Can you help businesses to survive? Can you advise governments or non-governmental agencies how to manage the social and political problems?

Fads, fallacies and foul-ups: the failure of such a high percentage of initiatives is not because the concepts themselves are faulty. Often they have been mistimed, implemented less than effectively or too many have been tried one after the other. Recently I heard an international consultant say, with apparent pride, 'We've reorganized their job. Of course we don't yet know whether they can work the new processes or whether we'll have to fire them all and start from scratch...' He doesn't just make a living, he's wealthy and verging on famous. Can you expect to do less well than someone to whom the real world of work appears to be a total stranger?

Emerging industrial nations: the perceived needs of countries from Eastern Europe to South East Asia to Southern Africa for external advice and guidance ensure that there are major markets for consultancy, conference speakers and trainers. Rates of exchange may mean that the pay is not always the highest, but job satisfaction is immense. Is this for you? If so, you have a market.

Global competition: the United States and other G7 countries have no hope of competing in price head to head against global competition. If a factory can hire 30 Filipinos for the wage of one American, there is little point in trying to compete by halving the American's wage. You're still more than 1000 per cent adrift. The US has moved faster and further than any other nation in developing service and high added-value industries. More needs to be done there and the rest of the 'developed' world has to catch up or, better yet, leapfrog global competition. If you have an idea or two that can help the real contenders, you have a market wherever you are.

The knowledge age: I recently met a consultant who specializes in database development. In my ignorance I assumed that databases were little more than lists of names and addresses to which we send mailshots. Wow, was I wrong! This guy has done everything from creating databases of footprints for the police to building all-singing, all-dancing, sound and vision interactive databases for historic buildings that would enable the silver spoon enthusiast to plan a visit to every stately home in the UK which has an impressive collection of silver spoons. If, like him, you can make information accessible to society, you have a market. If you can teach organizations to combine and use explicit information (facts, data) with tacit information (people's beliefs, values, hunches, guesses, concerns), you can play a key role in developing human resourcefulness, and the world is your oyster. If you can teach the world how to manage the human imagination without stifling it, I envy your earning potential.

Environmental and ethical concerns: we are beginning to realize, a little late in the day, that an ethical approach to business and concern for the environment are not optional extras. They are at the core of good business. But ethics is a tough area and what is good for the environment is not always obvious. Organizations are seriously seeking the best advice. If you can give that advice and make it work, you have a market.

New technology: no change is faster or more frightening to most of us than the growth of technology. We understand that with new technology come massive new opportunities but also new threats. If you can enable us painlessly to exploit the opportunities while protecting us from the threats, you have a market.

Training: someone once said that 'strategic planning, as it is carried out in most corporations, is the single biggest waste of corporate time'. He was wrong. Training is the biggest waste of time in any corporation. It simply doesn't work. Research by Bruce Joyce when he was at Columbia showed that the average attendee at a well-designed training seminar implemented between 5 and 11 per cent of what had been taught. Separate research by Xerox showed that, of what had been transferred to the workplace, 87.5 per cent was lost in the first three months. This grim combination gives about a 1 per cent return on the training budget. Yet in an age driven by knowledge effective training is essential. If you know how to make training work and you can share your knowledge economically, you have a market.

New legislation: even in the most liberal economic and political climate business is swamped by legislation and regulation. If you can ensure consistent compliance at low cost, you have a market.

This list is by no means exhaustive. If you are a scientist, philosopher or mathematician; if you are an economist, psychologist, sociologist, biologist or geologist; if you are an engineer, marketeer or business buccaneer; if you are an entrepreneur, an intrapreneur or a personal development guru – whatever your background and experience, your knowledge can find a market. The key to success is to be able to market your knowledge. This book will give you surefire, proven, at-the-coalface ways of doing just that.

Is the game worth the candle?

One of my colleagues, an alumnus of my High Income Consulting Masterclass, identified a niche market and has proved himself in it. In 1995 he recorded earnings of around $2 million. Sure, he's a person of remarkable talent, dedication and perseverance, but he does show what can be done – with talent, dedication and perseverance, and the confidence to take a substantial part of his earnings from success fees.

I would not be so impertinent as to come between a man and

the IRS, but I assume that top consultants like Tom Peters, Stephen Covey and Sir John Harvey Jones are a step or two removed from the breadline. As for me, I devote too much of my time to writing to be rich; publishers are notoriously parsimonious. But I get by.

Latest available figures for the bix six consultancies indicate the following billings for each consultant employed – down to the newest green bean:

McKinsey & Co	$469,000
Booz·Allen & Hamilton	$209,000
Ernst & Young	$149,000
Deloitte Touche Tohmatsu International	$144,000
Coopers & Lybrand	$142,000
Andersen Consulting	$125,000

It is a tough and more and more competitive world out there. It is also a rapidly growing market for increasingly essential services. There *is* a living to be made.

What this book will do for you

In the introduction to the first edition I said:

It is tempting to assert that the top earners are the best consultants. Tempting, but by no means necessarily true. Many of the highest earners show talents and skill far above the norm, but others would be little better than run of the mill were it not for their remarkable capacity to attract business and make money. Meanwhile an even larger number of first rate practitioners can do little more than get by. This book is designed to enable the capable but less successful to use their skills to optimize their personal incomes.

I see no reason to change my view. This book is still about developing and sustaining a high income professional practice. It is, however, about much more than that. It is about the tools of the trade and the ethics of the profession. It is about being a good consultant and a successful consultant for, believe me, it is dangerously easy to be only one of these in a world in which you increasingly need to be both.

I believe, as I believed four years ago, that the proclivity which too many of the larger consultancies demonstrate to send in inexperienced people with an off-the-shelf, one-size-fits-all solution is as venal as the one-man band who, driven by the need to get early bread on the table, takes any assignment offered whether they are qualified or not. The consultancy business is a goose all set to lay ever bigger golden eggs. I believe that it would be a tragedy for short-term greed or anxiety to kill that goose.

It isn't just a matter of economics – consultancy is a profession or it is nothing. Professions, to be worthy of the name, must walk the talk of their affirmed ethics.

Not only for consultants

I hope that this book, even more than its predecessor, will serve the needs of the buyer of consultancy services. It remains axiomatic that the buyer of consultancy is investing in something which is, in Churchill's phrase, a riddle wrapped in a mystery inside an enigma.

Consultants are brought in when the knowledge pool of the organization has run dry. In such a situation it is difficult to assess in advance whether the chosen outsider is right for the job. By developing an understanding of how the best and the most successful consultants work in practice, the buyer of consultancy can plan to maximize their chances of success.

To help with this I have added a new chapter on the ideal consultancy. We are creating the future and it works.

The promise of this book

This is a totally practical book. It contains no magic formulae. If you put into effect the ideas that you find between these covers you will succeed. If you read the book and put both it and its ideas to one side, you will gain nothing in return for your time and money.

The book contains the results of global research into what successful consultants do to build their reputation, their status, their practices and their incomes. It is a workbook which will work for you by enabling you to develop a comfortable and effective business strategy to attract and retain clients. It will assist you in maximizing your legitimate income and help you to avoid giving your valuable services away without payment.

The relevance of this book is not limited to management consultancy. My masterclasses have been attended by members and managers from all the professions. The book applies to members of any profession where the building and maintenance of business depend on the reputation and image of the people involved. It will work for those newly entering the profession and for those who, after years of experience, are still open to new ideas. Above all, it will work for people who are able to evaluate ideas, discard those which are not congruent with their aims or personality, and apply what remains with dedication, imagination and consistency. Please regard the contents of this book as if they were a menu. All of the dishes have been tasted by your fellow professionals and pronounced excellent. Select those which are most appropriate to your taste and they will enable you to achieve your goals.

Consultant, lawyer, accountant, doctor, psychologist, accountant or veterinarian – ask yourself four questions as you read:

❑ How does this relate to my specific situation?
❑ What can I use from this to build my practice and profit?
❑ To what degree is it consistent with my preferred behaviour and desired image?
❑ What can I do right now to apply and exploit my new knowledge?

When I wrote the first edition of *High Income Consulting* I held the naïve hope that I could persuade the world that books are not merely for reading: useful books are for writing in. The dialogue between author and reader is incomplete unless the reader interjects their comments and thoughts in a permanent form. I believe that reading is an activity which is most useful when the reader drives the relationship.

Please grab a pencil and as you read jot down comments, arguments, ideas and complaints about my style or the content. If you can't bear the idea of writing on the pristine pages of a book on which you have so recently spent some of your hard-earned dollars, fine. Have a block of Post-its or a yellow pad handy. But do ensure that you lose none of your good ideas.

Professional services have grown, are growing and their growth will accelerate as the demand for knowledge becomes more and more crucial in the Knowledge Age. With growth, however, comes increasing competition. There is a bigger cake, but those queuing for a slice increase in number every day. This book can and will give you the competitive edge that you need. But it has to be *your* edge: a personal advantage, chosen, adapted and implemented by you.

All that you need for success is in these pages. Those who will be best placed to exploit the coming opportunities will be the few or the many who have steadfastly worked to build their reputation and status without cutting either corners or prices. High income consulting is within your grasp. Go for it!

From time to time in this book 'Soap Boxes' will appear. They serve the dual purpose of giving business professionals something to think about and sometimes to exploit – they may even give me a chance to blow off steam! Above all, they enable me to include information and opinion without cluttering the main text with what I hope are useful but non-essential byways.

SOAP BOX

Nations and corporations alike are focusing on competitiveness. Sadly, politicians rarely understand that competitiveness when ascribed to countries is nothing like competitiveness between businesses. Business competition is a zero-sum game. I win, you lose. You get the assignment, therefore I don't. Economic competition between countries, on the other hand, is a non-zero-sum game. I am competitive and my economy grows, I can buy more of what I cannot make myself, and I buy it from you. Together we can spiral into major growth in trade and mutual prosperity. Concern rises, however, when a country slides down the competitiveness league table, or when the top performers begin to be heavily biased towards a new global area. According to the International Institute for Management Development (IMD), the United States is number one and has been in that exalted position for three years in succession. The World Economic Forum (WEF) sees things differently: its view is that the United States is slipping behind Singapore, Hong Kong and rising star New Zealand.

The world league tables for 1996 are as follows:

Competitiveness rankings 1996

Country	WEF	IMD	Country	WEF	IMD
Singapore	1	2	Denmark	11	5
Hong Kong	2	3	Australia	12	21
New Zealand	3	11	Japan	13	4
USA	4	1	Thailand	14	30
Luxembourg	5	8	UK	15	19
Switzerland	6	9	Finland	16	15
Norway	7	6	Netherlands	17	7
Canada	8	12	Chile	18	13
Taiwan	9	18	Austria	19	16
Malaysia	10	23	S Korea	20	27

In case you are wondering where some of the other big names of international trade are, the next five IMD places go to:

Sweden	21	14	Germany	22	10
France	23	20	Israel	24	24
Belgium	25	17			

Italy ranks 41 and 28 and Russia ranks bottom overall.

Note: The rankings are different because WEF excludes GDP growth, export sales and inward investment, arguing that these are the consequences, not the causes, of competitiveness.

The number of indicators included are WEF, 155 and IMD, 224.

There is a particularly strong correlation between GDP and export growth and the WEF ratings.

❑ What will those of you who are strategic consultants make of this information when talking to your clients or potential clients?

❑ Did you already know it? If not, why not?

❑ In the Knowledge Age, how can you increase your added value by being a constant and reliable source of added-value information?

❑ Are there ideas in this information that you can use to promote your services? There ought to be; but if you're in doubt right now, come back to this after you've read Chapter 8.

Part I

Building Your Practice

1

To Be or Not To Be

MANY PEOPLE WHO HAVE LOST THEIR JOB IN A PERIOD WHEN NEW jobs are hard to find very sensibly consider some form of consultancy as a means of putting bread on the table.

Considering consultancy is very sensible. Rushing into it without sufficient information with which to make an informed decision is less so. Let us look at some of the factors that should be taken into account.

Income

Consultancy is unlikely to make many of us millionaires. High incomes are perfectly possible, even likely, if the profession is approached in the right way, but they are by no means certain even for the most able.

The late Howard Shenson, who was for years the unchallenged authority on the subject, used to say that there are two kinds of consultant:

'good consultants and successful consultants. Sadly there are many more good ones than there are successful ones.'

If you want to make yourself really depressed, think about this: by no means all the successful consultants are good, so there must be a hell of a lot of excellent people out there just about getting by.

Recent research, completed during the deepest, longest lasting recession in living memory, gives a useful indication of how well the newcomer to the profession may expect to do in the first year or so. If you read this book and put its ideas into practice you will do better than the average newcomer.

New practices – first-year revenues (N=221)

Revenue higher than plan	38%
Revenue equal to plan	22%
Revenue less than plan	26%
No plan	14%
Profit higher than plan	28%
Profit equal to plan	28%
Profit less than plan	30%
No plan	14%

I am appalled that apparently more than one in ten people entering a profession in which they expect to have others pay for and follow their advice lacked the basic business knowledge to formulate even a simple business plan. Can these sort of statistics be taken at face value, or could they be distorted by exceptional circumstances?

There is an increasing tendency for large companies with imposed headcount restrictions to reduce their permanent staff and then to 'outsource'. Not surprisingly, those who have recently left are the best qualified to carry out the work, and come Monday morning, some who were bade a fond farewell on Friday are back at their old desks, now as self-employed 'consultants'.

Good luck to them, but it may distort the research a little. Revenues for some are artificially high in the first year because as part of a separation package they have been offered ongoing freelance work with their old employer, which has reduced the need to build new clients from scratch.

Worse results for profit than for revenue are in substantial part due to new consultants' inability to put a proper price on their services. There is also an element of underestimating overhead. (We will deal with both these potential minefields as the book unfolds.)

There is no way of assessing whether the plans of those new to the profession erred on the high or low side. To take revenue and profit figures in isolation is therefore potentially misleading. What counts is the number who derived sufficient income confidently to stay in the game. So what percentage of new entrants cease operation during the first year?

First, what looks like bad news. Approximately 20 per cent of those who offer their services as consultants go out of business at or before the end of their first year.

The good news is that almost 15 per cent do so because they have been offered employment as a result of contacts which they have made while marketing themselves to prospective clients. A further 3 per cent cease trading some time after they evaluate their first-year results. So a total of around 8 per cent of new entrants find the going too tough by the end of the first year. (It is certain, therefore, that even among those who are incapable of producing a plan for their own business, at least some survive to fight another day.) In summary, some 92 per cent either choose to continue on their own or are offered new job opportunities.

Consultancy is very much a field of birds of passage. Most experienced consultants, myself included, move in and out of private practice as other offers are made. Sometimes the move is into bigger practices which want to strengthen or develop their team. Often such appointments are limited in duration or ongoing satisfaction and the professional may return to private practice enriched, in both senses, by the experience.

Other considerations

Running their own practice usually means for ex-executives the novel experience of working alone. In the early stages most of us have to do everything alone. Strategic planning, typing, developing materials, answering the telephone, marketing, filing, writing articles, making tea, selling services, accounts – the list is endless and each responsibility ours alone.

Anyone who has spent much of their business life protected by secretaries and supported by staff may find the going tough and lonely.

If you are used to endless opportunities for bouncing ideas off colleagues in stimulating meetings before taking a decision, you can have real problems with no one to talk to but the cat. In my early days my telephone bill was inflated less by my committed search for business opportunities than by the need to hear another voice. Any other voice. I would call anyone on any pretext just to kid myself that I still had colleagues to talk to.

If I suggest that your spouse or lover may be of little help, I intend no impertinence. Your marriage partner is not necessarily your business partner. You need to talk 'shop': they have their own things to do and their own schedule to keep. You cannot call them to a meeting whenever it suits you and even if they try very hard to fill the void, there is an excellent chance that since you are, by definition, an expert, they will have little understanding of what you are talking about. Worse, they will not share your old employees' belief that it pays to agree with the boss. If I ask for my wife's opinion that is what she gives me and I have been known not to like it. For example, her comment on attempting loyally to read the first draft of *High Income Consulting* was, 'I'm sure it's in English, but what else do you expect me to say?'

So you have to be ready to work alone, take perhaps uncharacteristic risks, do all the menial tasks and almost certainly work seven days a week most weeks without receiving a pay cheque. If you can do all of that and deal constructively with rejection, frustration and stress, you will make a consultant. If you can also offer the market valued, flexible and infinitely transferable skills, you will make a good consultant. If you can market your skills effectively, you will make a successful consultant and probably become a rich one.

You have been warned about some of the drawbacks, but the rewards are worth considering in a little more detail.

Will you or won't you?

Income can be high. Job variety can be exciting. Job satisfaction can be incredible. The key to business decision making, however, always comes down in the last resort to the balance of opportunity against risk.

Consultancy is a multibillion dollar business which has been consistently growing at over 20 per cent a year for a decade, and in spite of some gloomy prognostications it looks as if it will continue to do so for the foreseeable future. Present difficulties and the growth of competitive tendering mean that the balance of market share is tilting toward the small firm and that is probably to your advantage.

The reputation of consultants and consultancy is not uniformly high, but if you can offer real added value and quality interventions your chances of success may be enhanced by the shortcomings of others. Some are working hard to raise professional standards, and this book will help you to join them.

There are risks, but this is one of the few professions where you can do well with virtually nothing more by way of assets than the pinky-grey jelly in your skull. You do not need fancy offices, expensive equipment and luxury transport to succeed. They are good to have, but you can do without them. It will be tough at times, but enthusiasm and creativity will take you a long way.

If you get depressed in the early stages when bills come in with regularity but cheques are noticeable by their absence, you may wish to remember a story told by Walt Disney. Walt's brother was company accountant, and whenever he sent for Walt that was a sure indication of money trouble. *Fantasia*, the follow-up to *Snow White*, was failing to draw the huge audiences predicted after an unprecedented investment. The studio was in hock. As Walt entered his brother's office he was greeted with:

'Walt, do you know we're in debt to the tune of twenty-five million dollars?'
'Wow, that's great. I can remember when no one would lend us twenty-five hundred.'

Unlike the film studio's, your risk is almost entirely controllable. The opportunities are as big as our imagination. But imagination alone is not enough.

Specialist or generalist?

It is essential that you position yourself clearly to avoid confusing your potential clientele. There is a healthy and often well-founded distrust of the 'Jack of all trades', so a decision has to be made. Will you offer yourself as a specialist or a generalist?

As a specialist you may choose to practise in one discipline or in a single industry. Many have built successful careers marketing in a single commercial sector. More of my professional life than I would wish has been committed to the automotive industry. That is where I am known and that is where it used to be particularly easy to attract assignments.

If you tie yourself to one industry, however, you may be particularly vulnerable to sector downturns.

The automotive industry was a happy hunting ground for specialist consultants until 1989, but when the downturn of 1990 became the slump of 1991, which in turn became the disaster of 1992, many projects which had been started were cancelled before completion. Consultants who continued to specialize fought for the small amount of business still available as budgets were slashed. As budgets were cut prices were slashed to match. Those who had either not foreseen trouble or, worse, having foreseen it ignored the signs and refused to approach other sectors, found themselves in serious difficulty.

But this is by no means unavoidable. Skilled marketing and an ability to identify and respond to the emerging needs of an industry, even one in decline, can pay off handsomely. One consultant I know has specialized throughout his professional life in an industry which many have written off as being in terminal decline. With very little competition for what others see as meagre business, he has done very well. He is now recognized as the industry guru and attracts good business from the few but now rapidly growing companies which dominate the sector.

You may choose to market yourself as a specialist in a single discipline. You could, for example, sell yourself as the expert in administering and analysing the results of just one psychometric test. Many do, and find that it has the advantage of ease of marketing which comes with having a product which can be promoted and sold as a simple package. It also carries the potential disadvantage that if the market turns against your product you are left with literally nothing of value to offer. By being flexible in your planning and adaptable in your approach, however, you can overcome the difficulty and extend the life of your product by constantly looking for new applications.

A bigger and more serious problem of narrow specialism is best encapsulated by Abraham Maslow's saying: 'If the only tool that you have is a hammer, you tend to treat everything as a nail'. Force-fitting the client's problems to whatever you are peddling is an example of the 'snake oil' which has done enormous disservice to the consultancy profession and to the clients it serves. If you look critically, however, at the real top earners – Tom Peters, Ken Blanchard, Stephen Covey, Anthony Robbins and the like – it is hard to resist the conclusion that they have a single product, flexibly applied and cleverly promoted.

You may decide that you are a generalist. That means you have a range of skills which are infinitely transferable across industrial and situational boundaries. Fine, but think about it for a moment. Remember that clients are simple people. They believe that an individual only has sufficient time to be a real expert in a limited field. What credibility will you or I have if we enter the marketplace saying, 'I can do just about anything: hire me'?

Confidence in even the most plausible renaissance man (or

woman) is flimsy. Widget manufacturers really do believe that there are key differences between green widgets and yellow widgets which only a dyed-in-the-wool green or yellow widget expert can understand. They are almost certainly wrong, but they do the hiring.

If you decide that you are truly a generalist, you may have to hide many of your lights under huge bushels and present yourself to each client as a narrow specialist in the area of greatest immediate need, introducing other skills as emerging situations dictate. In short, when it comes to marketing, promote yourself as a specialist and aim for a niche. Have a hundred specialisms and a hundred niches if you will, just offer them separately and sensitively to each prospective client.

In general, a specialist tends to be able to charge somewhat higher fees – and if you are hell bent on becoming famous, and I trust that you are, you will most easily become famous by consistently hammering away in, or about, a single field.

Operational or advisory?

When I was young and easy under the apple boughs there was only one kind of consultant. A consultant was, as Bob Townsend describes, one who borrows your watch, tells you the time and then pockets your watch with the fee. Perhaps it is my age, but I still think of them as good days when consultants advised and others did the work.

Today 90 per cent of consultants are operational. Not only do they recommend, they roll up their sleeves and play a major role in implementation. Without the ability of consultants to get things done, many highly desirable plans would moulder for lack of resources or skills to put them into effect.

If you believe that advisers advise and others 'do', you need to make a commitment. You must commit yourself to rising to the top of your profession. Only at the dizziest heights can you hope to avoid the need to get stuck in. Take heart. Those at the top of the profession earn the level of daily fee which makes up for having fewer opportunities to work. If you choose to limit your market to those who can implement your ideas without your further help, you are reducing it to a very small market indeed, so you must be sure that it is profitable.

Those who like the idea of seeing the job through to completion have two advantages. The time per assignment is obviously longer and earning potential higher in the longer term and, with the deskilling of industry and commerce which has taken place since the 1980s, opportunities for work are greater.

Personality traits and success

If you intend to be a successful consultant you must make up your mind to be directive, assertive and controlling. You will be dealing with clients who have only one justification for hiring you. There is an old business maxim that 'power flows to the one who knows' and as a consultant that is who you are. You need to consider at an early stage how comfortable you will be when exercising your power.

The client, not surprisingly, looks for signs of your credibility from the first meeting. Their confidence in hiring you will be largely determined not by your expertise – the client probably has no sound basis for judging that – but by your demeanour. Are you prepared to look, think and act the part of a successful professional all of the time? If not, this profession is not for you.

A number of studies conducted in the US and the UK identifying personality profiles which are indicative of success in consultancy careers have shown remarkably similar results. The following is a condensed version of the information they provide.

Most of the studies are published and in the public domain, others have been carried out for specific clients. You may find it interesting to compare your beliefs and values with those indicated by the research. Be clear, however, that the research neither shows that only those with the following traits are successful, nor that all who demonstrate these traits succeed regardless. However, the traits have been found, all other things being equal, to be reliable indicators of success potential.

Essential traits

Vocation
Effective consultants are strongly committed to the significance and purpose of the profession and the industries in which they work. Consultants with this trait demonstrate considerable pride in the outcomes to which their efforts lead. They are eager to show that their interventions make a significant difference to the lives of clients and colleagues through the further development of systems, solutions, product support and services. Above all, the concentration is on personal contribution rather than dependence on others outside the immediate team.

Growth
Consultants are expected to score high on this trait, both in their own development and in attracting and supporting talented others with whom to work. The focus is on using the strengths of others, particularly the client and the immediate team, to optimize profit opportunities. A significant negative indicator is if consultants make any statements which point to the strengths of others as being a threat to either their position or self-perception.

Affiliation
The ability to build rapport with associates and show empathy is, in the successful consultant, specifically directed at the attainment of objectives and not at the development of a cosy warmth within the team.

Affiliation is not a process of seeking to be loved by all. Effective consultants always show concern for people, but are able sensitively and strongly to put a case even where the truth as they see it may lead to a degree of unpopularity.

Focus
The development of specific rather than general objectives typifies effective consultants. They should show a clear ability to maintain direction in the face of difficulty. Typically consultants are keen to learn from the success of role models.

Power
The quintessential trait of the successful consultant is the sensitive use of power to get things done within the framework of the client's organizational culture.

This is the use of power in the institutional, rather than the personal, sense, and clear goal direction, based on the agreed needs of the client, dictates how and where power is applied. An inappropriate use of power is when the consultant relies on personal status and authority to get things done which do not attract the commitment of the client.

Subordinate traits

The following, although important, are recognized as being highly variable from individual to individual. Ideally the team of consultants and/or clients should be balanced to ensure that each trait is represented and applied appropriately.

Enthusiasm
The ability of the client to maintain improvements is frequently a function of the consultant's enthusiasm and confidence that the resulting tasks can be achieved.

Organization
Although there are examples of disorganized consultants who succeed in completing brilliant interventions on behalf of their clients, such people are usually highly specialized, technical experts. In general, effective consultants demonstrate an orderly and organized approach.

Achievement

Contrary to popular mythology, the effective consultant is an expert team player rather than a *prima donna*. In the most effective consultants a drive for achievement is normally moderate and directed towards client or team success.

When taken to excessive lengths, the desire for personal achievement gets in the way of developing the client towards autonomy and leads the consultant to seek and engineer ongoing dependence.

Stamina

The effective consultant works when necessary at a high tempo and with considerable endurance. The tenacious pursuit of goals over a long period is more characteristic of effective management than consultancy. Typically the consultant prefers high levels of activity for shorter periods.

Analysis

The ability to extract key factors from a situation and use them strategically in the future typifies many consultants. In excess, this trait denies real analysis by leading the consultant to react to insufficient evidence which suggests, but does not prove, a similarity to a previous experience. Many clients perceive as a major weakness of consultants a tendency to superficial analysis leading to an assumption that two situations which are in fact different are really the same.

Creativity

Only where a consultant is able to balance the ability to learn from the past and resist change for change's sake with a detailed analytic approach is the ideal client-serving combination found.

Sadly, most psychological studies indicate that no correlation appears to exist between true analytic skill and creativity. Consultants tested to date appear to have an unbalanced tendency to favour one, rather than a desirable approach incorporating both in equal measure. This frequently leads to force-fitting the client's problem to an established solution, or the promotion of novelty where tested and proven approaches are more appropriate.

Professionalism

In spite of the horrors some have perpetrated in its name, consultancy is a profession, and it must be a proud one. It is a profession in which individual reputation and image are the keys to success. Professionalism in everything that we do is vital.

I will have much to say on the subject as this book progresses, but for now let me discipline myself to one area. If you are new to the profession you will have a very reasonable wish to get 'bread on the table' from the earliest possible moment. An understandable aim; but there are dangers in accepting any assignment, or any client, just because they are there and you are hungry.

You will not, I assume, accept any assignment that you are not qualified to complete. This means that it is your responsibility to get to know your colleagues in the industry. When you are not the right person for the job you owe it to the client to introduce a specialist who is. If you take on work which you are unable to do to the standards required, you may get away with it in the sense that your fee will be paid and you will not be sued for malpractice. You will, of course, be unlikely to be assigned again by that client, but you may take the view, as many do, that there are plenty more where they came from. That view is as short-sighted as it is unethical.

Your reputation is your stock in trade. If you fail to perform effectively your reputation will be destroyed and without reputation you will cease to attract business. Worse, and more insidious, you will confirm the low opinion which some hold of consultants and you will have placed your own personal brick in the wall of mistrust and low expectation which can so easily constrain the market in which we all have to operate. If enough of us do that, we will all eventually go down.

One day, soon I hope, consultancy will be a fully certificated profession. Until then we all depend for our future on the professionalism of those, like you and me, who can without any restraint at present, enter the market and call ourselves 'consultants'.

I am making numerous assumptions on your behalf. For example, I assume that you would not accept an assignment which, if you carried it out as requested, would damage rather than support your client.

I have a valued client, let us call him Tony. Now Tony has one major shortcoming: he is a very easygoing and pleasant person. As is not unusual with nice people, there are times when others seek to take advantage. When working for Tony it is important that any consultant is unusually sensitive to the need not to usurp his position with his employees. I had been working with Tony and his team conducting some strategic planning and teambuilding workshops. As frequently happens when the consultant has control of process and is inputting a wide range of skills, my personal status within the group rose rapidly, sometimes to the detriment of the formal leader.

Having, in my early days inadvertently pulled the rug out from under the occasional boss, I now always try to be particularly careful to bolster the leader in the eyes of the group.

Groups enjoy novelty and if they see an informed and accessible consultant who seems to be full of ideas they are often tempted to try to push them into the leadership role. The facilitator must reject the overtures of the group to take over leadership and must build the status of the formal leader in the eyes of the group. Failure to build the relative status of the formal leader can create the danger that an informal leader will emerge and try their luck in a power struggle.

To avoid this I have developed approaches which are aimed at highlighting the formal leader's control, not only over the team but over me, the 'hired hand'. Something small, but significant, that I have found useful is to arrange covertly with the leader that, at a signal from me, they will interrupt me, apparently in full flow, and redirect me to an area or process that they (and I, as it happens) want to address.

As I said, Tony is a nice person and found it impossible publicly to assert himself over me, even at my instigation. His response to my suggestion was always some variant on, 'No. I am very happy with what you are doing, Tom. I'll leave it to you.'

A similar response was elicited by most of my other stratagems and I found myself, by default, increasingly perceived by the group as the 'real leader'.

Eventually I had my opportunity. It was essential that a key leadership task be undertaken and Tony asked me to do it for him. I refused. I coached him quickly and carefully in how to do it himself and walked away.

In the process I was walking away from a couple of days' work that I could ill afford to lose at that time. The coaching session had been short, less than half an hour, and I could hardly invoice for a few minutes, so I kicked myself as I walked back to my car.

The next morning I opened my mail anxiously looking for any positive response which could lead to an early assignment. There was a note from Tony which simply said 'thanks', attached to a cheque for a full two days of consultancy. Comparing the time taken to the value of the cheque, it was the best rate of pay I had ever received. As an emotional lift and reinforcement that the professional approach is always the right approach, it was priceless.

The undesirable client

Sometimes it pays to reject clients who do not meet the requirements of building your status and reputation.

Your choice of client has an effect on your perceived status. That is why most of us mention, without betraying professional confidence, our blue-chip clients at every opportunity.

In the early stages it is difficult to be choosy about the clients for whom you are prepared to work, but you need clients who do the following.

Pay their bills
Many don't and those who don't are known for it. It does as little for your reputation as for your bank balance if you are seen to be working for those who have a reputation for not paying. You

look either desperate or stupid, and neither builds your professional image.

Are ethical
Most clients are ethical, but those few who are not can destroy your reputation by association. If you have any doubts, steer clear.

Enhance your image
It is not only the blue-chip global enterprises which can enhance your reputation when you are seen to be working for them. In any industry there are opinion leaders and companies and individuals who have the respect of their peers. Seek them out and seek to serve them. It will repay your effort.

Have goals you can accomplish
Nothing succeeds like success. Be careful that a liking for challenge does not too often lead you to risk failure. You may be paid for your best efforts and not by results, but you will find that you are rehired strictly on the basis of your track record.

Will appreciate what you do
Referral business is the most economical, most profitable business. To get referrals you need to be proactive. We will discuss precisely how later. To win referrals you need something to work on and what you work on is a client who is delighted with what you have achieved together and is happy to tell the world.

Summary and action plan

❑ Consultancy is good business in good times and bad.
❑ The market is expected to grow at a compound rate of about 20 per cent.
❑ The balance of trade is shifting to the advantage of the small firm, at least in the short term.
❑ Building your reputation and status is the primary goal.

❏ Consultancy, as well as offering excellent income prospects in its own right, can be a stepping stone back into the world of paid employment for those who prefer that.

❏ One-man bands need to consider their ability to do everything themselves and withstand frustration and loneliness.

❏ Most newcomers stick it out and are more or less successful.

❏ Good consultants outnumber successful consultants. The purpose of this book is to help you to become or remain a successful consultant.

❏ To be successful you need to be clear about what it is you offer – particularly what you offer that others do not.

❏ Successful consultants build their credibility through assertive behaviour and by being selective in their choice of clients.

Before reading further, please take a few moments to consider:

❏ What are the full range of skills and knowledge which you can offer to the marketplace?

❏ Are you a generalist, or a specialist?

❏ Who specifically is likely to buy your skills and knowledge?

❏ How can you most quickly, cheaply and effectively contact potential buyers of your services?

❏ What are the unique features that you can offer?

> ❑ Is there a fashionable concept of the moment that you understand really well? (TQM, JIT, change, business process reengineering, empowerment, downsizing without tears, rightsizing, dominance strategies, outsourcing, environmental auditing.) I have purposely not explained any of the jargon or alphabet spaghetti. If you are not familiar with any of it, find out what it is. It could be a business opportunity.
>
> ❑ If you do know about something, do you have, or can you come up with, a new angle to it?
>
> ❑ **And, most importantly, what will you really feel comfortable and happy doing?**

Answer the above as fully as you can at present, but wait a little before you start to put together a detailed marketing plan. Have a piece of paper handy as well to jot down all of your other ideas. They are important: certainly important enough to demand that you stop reading and think for a while about your future.

Limit yourself for the moment to being sure that you know what you have to offer. Ensure that you believe there is a market for your skills. Most important of all, give some thought to what suits your personal style and preferences. Look for what is likely to reward you not just economically, but in terms of your quality of life. If consultancy or another profession which is built on personal reputation and status meets the bill for you, this book will help you to build your success.

More work for you

I warned you in the introduction that this is a workbook, and you are the worker. What I am going to ask you to do now that you have done some constructive thinking is to commit your thoughts more formally to paper as the basis of your business plan. Most of you will be familiar with SWOT analysis and so this is the tool that I would like you to use. But 'use' is the essential word, so I have redesigned an old tool to ensure use rather than mere completion. A brief word or so of explanation is possibly called for.

Strengths

Rather than simply listing your strengths (and please include everything that you can think of – that is important), I want you to consider from the beginning how your strengths relate to potential success in your chosen profession. Against each strength make a decision whether you have something that people will buy. If you are not sure, think about it until you are. Ask friends, family and colleagues. Use any creative techniques that you know to find a way to turn your strengths into earning opportunities. Underline or highlight those for which you see market opportunities. From today everything which you have for which there is a market is your stock in trade. Don't sell yourself short. Work at it.

Having established your strengths, consider those which you can present as USPs (unique selling propositions). Anything for which there is a market and which is unique to you has an enormous value. And never forget: anything which is not necessarily unique to you, but which you promote when your competition simply takes it for granted, will look like a USP to the market.

Weaknesses

Look at your weaknesses from the perspective of the market. Only if a weakness affects your ability to attract and serve clients should it be included. Prioritize the weaknesses by using a scale of 1–5 in terms of:

Seriousness: Failure to address this weakness will have a severe adverse effect on your ability to attract and retain business.

Growth: Failure to do something to deal with this now will lead to it getting worse over time, therefore action is urgently needed.

Description of strength	Marketable?		USP?		Action
	Yes	No	Yes	No	

Description of weakness (and evidence that it will affect client service)	Priority		Action
	S	G	

Description of opportunities	Qualified?		Exploit?		
	Yes	No	Now	Future	No

What could go wrong	Avoidance plan	Contingency plan

On a clear understanding of the difference between importance and mere urgency, commit yourself right now to do something to overcome or ameliorate the one, two or perhaps three major problems. Never try to address more than a couple of problems at a time unless they are inter-related or easy to handle. Concentrate your attention on your strengths. Go back to them after looking at your weaknesses. Add to them and consider how much you have going for you. Commit yourself to reading the rest of the book as an exercise in how to apply your strengths to make money and provide value.

Opportunities

> *'When opportunity knocks you're always at home.'*   Victor Kyam

From today you are an entrepreneur, whatever your role has been in the past. Opportunities are your lifeblood. List everything that you can think of. Read with the intention of identifying further opportunities and add them as you see them. Watch television with the same goals. Carry a small notebook or a personal dictating machine so that opportunities are recorded and not forgotten.

To decide which to address first, highlight the opportunities that you are qualified to exploit and from them filter out the least profitable and most difficult to get to grips with, to leave yourself with those that you propose to address at once. Only answer with a 'no' in the final column where the opportunity conflicts with your intended image and reputation or with your strong values, beliefs or personal feelings.

Threats
Threats come into two major forms – those which are avoidable with prior planning, and those which are not. For those which can be avoided, decide what can be done, write it down and do it in good time. For those which cannot be avoided by proactivity on your part, identify the earliest indicator that things are going wrong and specify what you will do when you become aware of

the coming danger. That is the difference between contingency and avoidance planning and without both the best of plans are vulnerable.

When you have done all of the above

Define your mission

Now that you have completed the SWOT analysis – what Beckhardt calls the 'here and now' – I would like you to consider your future. Take the approach that nothing is impossible and answer for yourself the question:

'If I knew that I could not fail, what would I attempt?'

❑ **Precisely what ideal business am I in today?**
(Who will be my immediate clients? What services will I offer?)

❑ **Where do I want to be in five years' time?** (Who will be my clients? What will be my revenues and profits? What will I be doing? Where will I be doing it? With whom, if anyone? **What will be my personal reputation and status?**)

❑ **What will set me apart from the herd – now and in the future?** Why should people hire me rather than the others?

❑ **What are the key values and principles which will drive my business no matter what?**

'A man who has nothing that he would die for has little to live for.'
Martin Luther King

From what you have written, develop a mission statement for your new business. To help you a sample is provided opposite.

Last, write yourself some **objectives** which are **SMART**.

Specific: They express exactly what you intend to achieve.

Measurable: Put figures to things whenever you can, not just profits and revenues, but numbers of clients, standards of quality. Don't forget that 'all' or '100%' is appropriate to many objectives.

Achievable: Aim high, but don't saddle yourself with failure by going for the impossible dream. Identify the very best that you think you can do and then stretch yourself just enough to make the extra effort fun and worthwhile.

Realistic: Test your objectives against your resources, your vision of your future and your mission. Your objectives should ensure progress toward the attainment of your dream by moving in the right direction with what you have right now. Tomorrow you will get the other resources you need, and getting those resources is a proper objective.

Timely: Make it clear to yourself when you intend to achieve your key results, including critical subobjectives *en route*.

SAMPLE MISSION STATEMENT FOR TRAINING AND CONSULTANCY

Quality-driven Consultancy and Training

We provide superior consultancy and training because we believe in truly providing services designed to meet the client's researched needs, rather than standard packages.

We design interventions which reflect the best validated current research so we are constantly mindful of our own development needs.

Our fee structure reflects the need to be able to provide sufficient time and resources to ensure the achievement of predetermined measurable outcomes.

By ensuring that the client is made aware of government and other funding opportunities where they exist, we maximize client choice and minimize their investment.

We refuse any assignment for which we are not fully qualified, but will assist the client to find qualified and competent consultancy elsewhere, rather than leave them to the mercy of the less ethical members of the profession.

We believe in the need to build an ongoing client relationship through providing added value in the form of additional information and coaching. In this way we help the client to make accelerated progress towards self-reliance.

Uniquely, we carry no headquarters overheads and the client pays only for the services and results which are experienced.

We are global in operation and staffing and use only consultants and trainers with established international reputations.

Because we employ no junior staff clients have the services of a principal at every stage of every assignment.

Our focus is entirely on client delight at the end of every transaction and we are happy to relate our payment to our performance.

OBJECTIVES:

All checked for   Specificity   ☐
                   Measurability   ☐
                   Achievability   ☐
                   Realism   ☐
                   All Timed realistically?   ☐

Where now?

The following chapter will provide some brief notes on how to establish your practice. Subsequent chapters detail how to run your practice and a range of no-cost or low-cost approaches to marketing which have been shown to be the most effective by high earners on both sides of the Atlantic. Remember, they are offered for your consideration much as a menu would be. Pick out those which you will be comfortable and effective doing. Concentrate on doing the things that 'feel' right with commitment, energy, dedication and a sense of fun. And remember:

> *'If you are not doing it for money or fun, what the hell are you doing it for?'*
> *Bob Townsend*

SOAP BOX – IN-COMPANY NETWORKING

In the Knowledge Age it is essential that information held within a company is available to all when needed. The Nijenrode Business School (Netherlands) in some recent research identified the positive role which international management development can play in building relationship and knowledge networks within conglomerates.

It was found that corporations could usefully be surveyed under two headings: a high-complexity group of companies (HCG) in which strategy was largely dictated by headquarters, and a low-complexity group (LCG) which were decentralized and made a greater number of strategic decisions at or close to the market.

In general, HCG respondents put less emphasis on management development as a critical aspect of strategic planning. The effect of this downgrading of management development was reflected in other results. For example, in the LCG 68 per cent claimed that international management development helped to put in place and sustain a pool of managers committed to working together and using their network as a key factor in benefiting the whole business. In the HCG, only 40 per cent of respondents felt that such relationships existed. All in all, the members of the LCG felt that the reward systems of their firms were fair, while almost 25 per cent of the HCG believed that rewards were actually unfair; 100 per cent of the LCG believed that the company knew in detail where its best talent lay and exploited it effectively, whereas almost 40 per cent of the HCG believed this to be untrue in their firms. When communication was researched, 24 per cent of the LCG thought that informal channels were most useful, compared with 8 per cent of the HCG.

❑ What implications does this have for the massive conglomerate? The small company?

❑ If Prahalad and Hamel are right that the prime function of strategic thinking is to optimize present opportunity while redefining the future of your industry, how can you help your clients to develop market dominance through shared knowledge?

❑ Do people communicate most effectively through formal or informal channels? When you had a 'day job', did you put your trust in the formal communication system or the scuttlebutt?

2
Beginners Only

THIS SHORT CHAPTER IS WRITTEN TO HELP THOSE WHO ARE TOTALLY new to the concept of establishing and developing a business. It should only be skim read by the established practitioner. That way I may avoid the danger of teaching some wily old grandmas the art and practice of egg sucking. There is, however, a potential cost in this decision.

Strange things are happening in the legal jungle, and since this chapter is the appropriate place to discuss them, it may be that some who would benefit from a glimpse of even the most cloudy crystal ball may miss something of future significance.

I take some comfort from the assumption that if what I suspect may happen does happen, it will make sufficient noise for everyone to be aware of it – except its first victim. If you don't trust my assumption, or you feel that lightning would not strike without first picking you out as a victim, put your mind at rest. Scan quickly the material headed 'liability' and leave the rest of the chapter to those for whom it is intended.

For the real beginner I want to sketch in a few generalizations about starting a business. Please remember that they *are* generalizations. It is impossible for me to guess your precise circumstances and nothing in this chapter should be allowed to dissuade you from seeking professional advice from your accountant or lawyer. My situation is made more complex by the international success of the first edition. Clearly, I cannot hope to cover the law in every country or, worse, the law in each of the United States. All that I can do is to sketch in very broad brush some general ideas.

Forms of business

Limited liability

For the majority of those who are proposing to found a professional practice, there is little to be gained from establishing a limited liability company. The usual advantages of limiting your liabilities are unlikely to provide significant benefits to a management consultant. Consultancy is an activity which requires little or no investment beyond transport, a small computer and time for your personal development. Most of your stock in trade resides, as I have mentioned before, between your ears. In some countries, however, there is a growing climate of litigation. As a result more and more consultancies, including some of the big six, are seeking ways of limiting their liability. Check carefully with your attorney before you assume that for you, in the country in which you operate, incorporation has nothing to offer. You may be advised that the protection is worth the hassle where you operate.

Registering as a limited liability company requires you to submit your accounts properly audited and on time, and in a busy life it may be irksome to meet the time requirements. The penalties for failing to submit your accounts on time have recently been increased in some countries, and that alone is putting some people off the idea. The duties of a director have also been tightened in the last couple of years, although a cursory glance at the newspapers would do much on most days to confirm some in the belief that they ought to be tightened further.

There are almost certainly some potential clients who would feel more comfortable dealing with companies which are entitled to put 'Ltd', 'Pty' or 'Inc' after their name, but they are few. If you believe that a company which you can happily and profitably serve is one of that small number, and you want the business, take advice and take the appropriate action.

For those who prefer to take the limited liability path, it really isn't that difficult. For a few hundred dollars or less you will be able to buy a company 'off the shelf' and after registering a change of name and activity you can be in business relatively quickly. There are other costs, such as the company seal, but your accountant and lawyer will be happy to guide you through the details.

Partnership

Mr Punch offered unsolicited advice to those about to get married: 'Don't'. I feel the same way about partnerships. And since the world's great partnerships in the shape of the major consultancies and accountancy firms are having second thoughts, my view seems to be shared by those in the know.

Please think carefully about entering into a partnership, even with your spouse. Joint and several liability could land both of you in Carey St, and everything you jointly own would be at risk. There is a legal precedent in the UK which suggests that your spouse cannot be held responsible for your business debts if they have no role in the business, but I would not be prepared to bet on it always holding up in court.

If the house is in joint names you are advised to avoid having your spouse sign away their half to guarantee any bank loan which you may take out – if at all possible. As long as they give no such undertaking and play no role in the business, their half of the house remains that and it is not normally accessible to you, nor to your creditors. In practice, this means that the courts would probably, if the chips were down, protect their occupancy and ownership, which will keep a roof over your head – assuming that you are not thrown out into the street for putting the family fortune at risk.

Under no circumstances would I recommend that you form a partnership with anyone other than your spouse. Even if you meet an angel hot-foot from heaven (if they're from heaven, how come the hot feet?), don't even consider a partnership. Liability for your partner's debts is unlimited. And 'unlimited' means what it says. In different circumstances partners in a major consultancy practice are facing claims of more than $100 million as I write, so unlimited liability where others' debts are involved is not to be considered.

Sole proprietorship

The least glamorous-sounding approach to forming a business is by far the least complicated. You will be fully responsible for your debts, but only for those which you personally negotiate and you are free to trade without any major restrictions. To all intents you are free to start after about half an hour of friendly chat with your accountant. In some of the United States you are limited to trading under your own name if you choose to be a sole trader. That can be a major benefit in two ways. First, when you are not too well known it may give some clients added confidence in buying your services if they feel that you are putting your name, along with everything else, on the line. Later, when you are famous, your name is your brand image and it could be argued that you would be unwise to promote yourself using anything else.

Sources of capital

With assets limited to your skills and experience, don't look to venture capital companies; they are unlikely to find your venture worthy of their capital. A simple business plan, and a positive discussion with your bank manager backed by ongoing, timely communication, make absolute sense and are probably all the financial backing you will ever need.

In some countries governments provide limited but welcome financial support to new enterprises. Check it out and don't be concerned about what others may think. If there is government financial support available to your clients, most will willingly take it. Some will even expect you to get it for them, so don't be stiff necked. If you are entitled to it, take it. Talk to the appropriate agency, which will give you accurate and helpful advice.

Licences

In the UK management consulting is not a licensed profession. You may, however, need a licence to practise elsewhere.

The situation is a fluid one and although now anyone may call themselves a management consultant and practise the profession without restraint in most countries, this may change. Where licensing is, or is becoming, mandatory, it is probably because we consultants have not practised our professional skills as well as we should.

Liability

This is the brief section that I suggest every practitioner should glance at and consider. There are generally three types of public liability in law.

General liability

General liability requires of all citizens that they behave as 'prudent persons'. If I choose to allow my roof to get into a state of disrepair which leads to a tile falling on your head, I am liable. All you have to do is show that I have been negligent and you are entitled to compensation.

Professional liability

Specific to our business lives, we are required to work diligently in the interests of our clients. If we can be shown to have acted negligently or if we have committed an act of malpractice, the client has only to convince a court of our misdeeds and compensation is due. Some professionals take out considerable insurance cover against having to pay damages, and you would be well advised to investigate whether you ought to seek professional indemnity insurance. Membership of a recognized professional body is often an excellent way of obtaining discounted insurance cover, among the many other benefits. The problem for a newcomer to the profession is that newcomers are rarely accepted as members of an established professional body. Most expect new members to have been in business on their own account for a minimum period – usually at least two years. That notwithstanding, cheap insurance or otherwise, professional indemnity is an absolute must in a growing number of countries.

Product liability

For the best of reasons product liability is different in character from both of the above.

Imagine that you manufacture a car. Imagine further that you have designed that car in such a way that the fuel tank is dangerously close to the rear panel. In the event of a rear-end collision the tank is very likely to rupture. Any spark resulting from the coming together of metal bodies will almost certainly turn at least one of the cars into a fireball. Driver and passenger are likely to be incinerated. Your company is well into production of the mobile death trap when the worst happens. A minor rear-end shunt on your test track leads to a major fire and the burning to death of two employees. You are shocked and horrified. You order an internal enquiry. The report which you receive clearly indicates the danger. You ought to have the car redesigned and the fuel tank moved. Will you?

As it happens you have three additional pieces of information:

❑ The last redesign of a vehicle which had already entered production cost $20 million, and was just a change of door

handles, far less costly than resiting a fuel tank.
- ❏ Your actuarial experts tell you that the type of crash which would lead to the blaze happens to this class of car infrequently and would add to the number of fatalities just one additional death per thousand units sold.
- ❏ Less than 50 per cent of this year's customers will buy your products next time, so burning one in a thousand will have little direct effect on customer retention.

And you have the report. Lock it away and it will be almost impossible for anyone to prove negligence.

I am sure that if you were in that position you would withdraw the car from sale and redesign the positioning of the tank. Sadly, although your right-feeling attitude is one that you can be proud of, similar views and behaviours have not been shown by experience to be universal among business people. As a result, product liability laws were enacted to be different in two key ways:

- ❏ Negligence does not have to be proved: it is enough for the plaintiff to show that they have suffered harm, physical, financial or emotional, to win their case.
- ❏ The defendant (the business) is required to prove their innocence. In short, the company supplying the goods is guilty unless they can prove themselves to be innocent.

What has that to do with consultancy? Very little – until recently. In recent judgments it seems that judges have taken the view that services are covered as well as goods, and if services, why not professional services? If this is the proper interpretation of the law, the time may well come when a client who claims to have suffered harm as a result of a consultant's intervention may seek damages without the need to prove negligence or malpractice. If that day dawns in an increasingly litigious society, we will all need insurance cover and lots of it.

Business cards and letterheads

A worthwhile investment is buying a well-designed letterhead and having it printed on good quality paper. Your letterhead says much about you and can affect the chances of your letters being read.

Business cards should be plain and of good quality. There is an argument for the card to carry only your name and where and how you can be contacted, with no indication of what you do for a living. The argument goes thus:

> You hand me your card.
> I glance at it and ask, 'What do you do?'
> You reply, 'I'm a consultant, what do you do?'
> 'I'm in civil engineering. What do you consult about?'
> 'Civil engineering. Let's talk.'

Cheeky, but I am assured by those prepared to do it that it works.

Conversely, if my card says 'Marketing and Management Development', this, vague as it is, may be enough to enable some prospective clients to think, 'I don't want any of that!'

Working from home

It is becoming increasingly common for people to work from their homes, and as it becomes common it becomes acceptable. Gone are the days when no one would take you seriously unless you had a showy office in the right part of town. Unless you intend to offer some sort of therapy, or see your clients there, the spare bedroom or even the garage or garden shed can make a suitable office. If you don't want to use your home address for security reasons, or to stop salespeople cold calling, do not be tempted to use a PO box number: it makes potential clients nervy if they think they will not be able to find you should the need arise. If you must, use an accommodation address, but if you work from home you should be able to use your normal address without problems.

If you want to make your home address sound grand, just give your house a posh-sounding name. Poets' names sound good: 'Keats House' or 'Coleridge House'. I'm a little worried about 'Dunroamin'!

Try to have your telephone answered during business hours by a human being. I know it is difficult, but a lot of people still dislike talking to answering machines. That said, an answering machine is a must, since even the best-regulated households cannot guarantee always to be able to answer the phone all of the time. If nothing else happens, the occasional call of nature becomes more pressing than a telephone which may not ring at all.

I am of an age when I tend to regard mobile phones as new-fangled nonsense if you are working to a shoestring budget – and I'm fascinated by current research in Australia which suggests that the radio signals scramble the brain. Don't let my old-fashioned and Luddite attitudes cloud your judgement. When you recognize the need and have the means, buy as many mobile phones as you feel happy with. Add a computer with a decent integrated business software package and you will want for nothing else.

Getting your business off the ground

You need to ensure that as many people as possible who may either need your services, or may refer you to others, know that you are in business. The primary task in your first days is to spread that knowledge. It is infinitely preferable to have potential clients hammering on your door before you are totally ready to serve them than it is to have your 'store' superbly organized and beautifully laid out, but no potential buyers aware that you are open for business. The entrepreneur markets first and organizes afterwards. Since there is usually a delay between announcement and the arrival of clients, this is not a high-risk approach, even for the perfectionist. Put 'making people aware that I am in business' high on your 'to do' list. As a minimum:

Write a short press announcement that you are open for business and describing what you do. Make it as newsworthy as you can.

❑ Do you have an interesting or exciting background?
❑ Are you already well known in some local circles?
❑ Is the service which you offer aimed at something which is currently newsworthy? (For example, protecting the environment, helping the laid-off or the long-term unemployed, surviving in bad times or growing when business confidence is high.)

Read the press and tie in if you can to repeated stories.

Send your announcement to every local and regional newspaper, radio station, business magazine, professional body and trade association, chamber of commerce, careers counsellor, government office and to business colleagues and friends. Anyone, in short, who may refer others to you.

Make sure that your announcement makes it clear how you may be contacted for further information.

If you have some less than widely known facts which relate to your activity, include them. especially if you have conducted some form of market survey which throws a new light on the state of local industry and commerce.

Write a news release in addition to your announcement and send that to all newspapers and radio stations separately. Do the little which you can in the early days so that your name keeps being seen, everywhere people look.

Consider the possible use of posters. If you have a computer and a simple DTP package, posters are easy and cheap to produce. Place them in small business support group offices, enterprise agencies, employment offices and libraries.

Telephone or visit everyone you can think of who may send prospective clients your way.

Look proactively for ways to align what you do to the work of others to start networking from the earliest possible moment. The more like-minded individuals on the look-out for business opportunities the better. Don't expect others to cut you in on their hard-won existing business, but look for as many ways as possible to build future business together.

Offer yourself as a speaker to every local group you can find which attracts those who may become your clients. Most chambers of commerce are happy to invite new businesses to give a five-minute overview of what they offer at their regular lunchtime meetings, so you do not have to be prepared to give a substantial talk.

If you are invited to talk at one of these sessions, a concise rundown of the benefits of using your services is infinitely preferable to a detailed description of the features. Tell people convincingly and pleasantly that you can help them to achieve their goals and they will take the trouble to ask you how.

THE 21-DAY 'UP AND RUNNING' FORMULA

Days 1, 2, 3, 4 and 5

Step One: Find and talk to a good accountant
               Decide on the form of the business
               Register for VAT or other taxes

Step Two: Develop an outline business plan:
               Mission
               Objectives
               SWOT
               Strategic alternatives and strategies

                        Tactics
                        Budgets, revenues and **cash flows**
                        Financial and human resources
                        Potential problem planning

Step Three: Make friends with your bank manager
                        Open a business account

Days 6, 7, 8, 9 and 10

Step Four: Develop marketing/promotional strategy in detail

Step Five: Design and order stationery and business cards

Step Six: Order **essential** equipment:
                        Answerphone
                        Desk
                        Computer/typewriter/wordprocessor
                        Files and filing space

Step Seven: Draft press releases, advertisements and poster copy
                        as appropriate
                        Check media information in *Rates and Data* or
                        Willings Press Guide
                        (While in library get to know staff, resources and
                        layout of the reference section)
                        Prioritize sending of press releases in line with
                        editorial closing dates

Step Eight: Begin to list all possible prospective clients and
                        sources of referrals

Days 11, 12, 13, 14 and 15

Step Nine: Make preliminary contacts and appointments

Step Ten: Receive equipment and stationery
                        Print, or have printed, promotional materials
                        (carefully proofread all materials in draft)
                        Begin planned distribution

Days 16, 17, 18, 19, and 20

Step Eleven: Begin visits to best prospects

Step Twelve: Develop no-cost/low-cost marketing strategy
                (reread Chapter 8)

Day 21

Go for it. Good luck!

The above is by no means exhaustive, but it will give the absolute newcomer a starting point which will be fleshed out as you read this book. For the experienced professional whose business needs a quick fillip, there may well be the source of some quick and easy ideas even in so simple a guide.

SOAP BOX – ORGANIZATIONAL CHANGE

Almost all relevant surveys have shown that 'organizational change is the biggest challenge facing managers'. Too many one-size-fits-all, off-the-shelf solutions are being tried, leading to high costs, mistrust of the consultancy profession and the 'bus queue syndrome'. Given that few of us are capable of developing and implementing totally new ideas which work first time every time, how are you going to:

❑ Use established techniques more effectively than your competitors?
❑ Convince would-be clients that you can make it work where others have failed?
❑ Get your ideas into the public eye so that clients beat a path to your door?

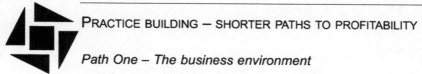

PRACTICE BUILDING – SHORTER PATHS TO PROFITABILITY

Path One – The business environment

What is the general economic, social and legal situation?
- ❑ What specifically has changed or is changing?
- ❑ Are there potential problems for the private or public sectors?
- ❑ Are there potential opportunities in the public or private sectors?
- ❑ Do opportunities exist to exploit my specialist skills or knowledge?
- ❑ Do opportunities exist to build my skills and knowledge?
- ❑ What can I do immediately to show that I can be of service?
- ❑ Which sectors or organizations should I target?

Path Two – Competition

What are competitors concentrating on?
- ❑ Should I climb aboard the same bandwagon?
- ❑ Do I have or can I gain the relevant knowledge?
- ❑ Can I offer unique added value?

What causes people to buy from competitors?
- ❑ What can I offer to gain an edge?
- ❑ Who specifically may be attracted by my unique offering?

What are competitors' key strengths?
- ❑ How can I combat them?
- ❑ Who specifically will prefer my offering?

What are competitors' key weaknesses?
- ❑ Do I have strengths in these areas?
- ❑ How can I exploit them?
- ❑ How will I make my offering appear credible?
- ❑ Is there the possibility of an exemplar project to make my name?
- ❑ What **unique** offering can I make?
- ❑ Who will buy?
- ❑ What is the best/most economical way to market to them?

Should I seek to work with, rather than against, competition?
- ❑ Is a strategic alliance a possibility?
- ❑ What do I have to offer?
- ❑ Who would buy?
- ❑ How do I reach them?
- ❑ Am I certain I would not rather 'go it alone'?

Path Three – Your unique offering

What makes me different?
- ❑ What is my unique experience?
- ❑ How do I make my skills and knowledge appear to be unique?
- ❑ What are my core values and beliefs?

What is the **image** I intend to create?
- ❑ Local company meeting local needs?
- ❑ Global knowledge – global activity?
- ❑ Rolls-Royce service at Ford prices?
- ❑ Big name one-man band?
- ❑ Price leader?
- ❑ Unusual personality?
- ❑ Highly specialized professional practice?

3

Consultancy at Work

THE PROCESS OF CONSULTANCY HAS 10 STEPS WHICH MAY TAKE A matter of hours, days, weeks or months to perform.

Research indicates that as a rule of thumb the lead time to win a contract correlates positively with the value of the contract. The bigger and better the assignment, the longer the lead time.

Consultants need to consider this when directing their attention to specific business opportunities. The lead time taken to land the contract tends to average about 12 per cent of the contract value. One day selling equals eight days sold.

If, as a matter of strategy, you set your sights on large contracts, you need to consider carefully how your activities will be financed up to the happy moment when the cheques start to roll in. Many who are new to consultancy find it politic to go for relatively small local contracts which will bring cash in quickly in the early stages, and having established themselves and their finances seek larger contracts at a later date.

The stages of consultancy

Marketing and public relations

Target your marketing efforts on the sectors and clients that you hope to exploit in the early days, but take some thought to building your reputation nationally and internationally if that is where your future lies.

Remember that if you choose to specialize in a limited market sector you will become vulnerable to any downturn in that sector. Try to broaden knowledge of your name and reputation in ever-widening circles like a stone dropped into water. That way your contacts with your primary area of experience and expertise will continue to support you as you expand your client base.

For example, work in the automotive sector can lead to vehicle leasing, which in turn can lead to financial services and from there to banking or insurance and so on.

Request for your services

As you become increasingly well known through your marketing activities, clients will approach you to provide support. The fact that they approach you facilitates, but does not obviate, the need to become a professional salesperson.

Face-to-face selling

Psychological advances increasingly provide compelling evidence of what people who are thinking of buying seek from their encounters with potential suppliers. Concentrate your attention on buyer behaviour and meeting well-validated needs and selling will hold absolutely no terrors. (Chapter 12 provides a brief, but hopefully useful, professional approach to selling. Those who want more detailed information might wish to refer to my book *The Power of Influence*.) Never forget that in addition to selling your services you frequently need to sell your solutions and ideas. Selling is therefore a vital skill to the consultant, even to those who, like myself, rely largely on others initially to sell my services.

Problem or needs analysis

In most consultancy situations the solution is relatively straight-

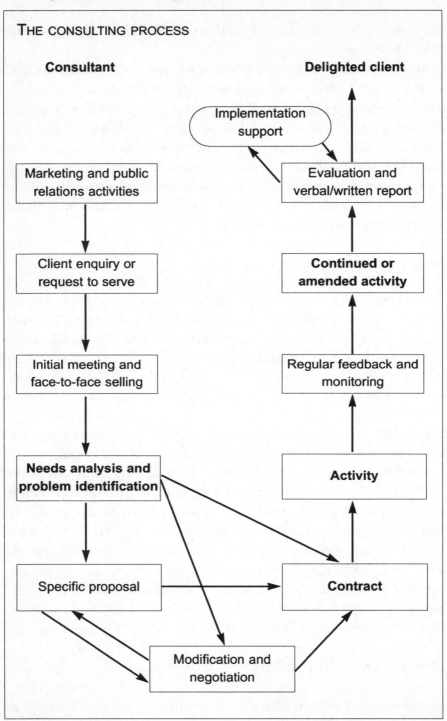

THE CONSULTING PROCESS

Consultant   **Delighted client**

Implementation
support

| Marketing and public relations activities | | Evaluation and verbal/written report |

| Client enquiry or request to serve | | **Continued or amended activity** |

| Initial meeting and face-to-face selling | | Regular feedback and monitoring |

| **Needs analysis and problem identification** | | **Activity** |

| Specific proposal | | **Contract** |

| Modification and negotiation |

forward once the problem has been fully diagnosed. If you are not already, become a master of rational and creative problem-solving approaches. And never forget, problem diagnosis is what you sell: avoid being tempted to do it for nothing to show what you can do.

By rational problem solving I mean that which is applicable to 'deviations from the norm', in short, where what usually happens now doesn't. For example, one morning your reliable car fails to start. Rational problem solving would enable you, step by step, to trace the fault. Creative problem solving would enable you to leave your car at home to be fixed by your local garage, but would get you to that vital morning meeting on time by other means.

A comprehensive rational problem-solving technique is that developed by Kepner and Tregoe. One of the most successful approaches to creative problem solving is Synectics. I believe that no consultant should be unaware of at least some of the 'problem-solving packages' which can save many hours of undirected labour. I assume that any marketing consultant is fully conversant with techniques such as morphological analysis, and I need say no more. Those in doubt about their abilities will find an excellent range of books in the library and both Synectics and Kepner-Tregoe offer proven seminars and workshops in many countries.

Development of a specific proposal

Too many very good consultants give their services away without charge. I shall have a great deal more to say about this in due course. For the present, let me suggest that the good consultant always produces a proposal, even if the client does not ask for one or want to see one. In doing so the planning and costing of the assignment are made much easier.

Modification and negotiation

The client may experience severe shock when the cost becomes clear. This is not an indication of the rapaciousness of consultants. It is simply the result of clients making inappropriate comparisons. By producing an effective proposal you will be well on the way to getting your client to increase their budget to hire you. (In Chapter 5 I will explain how a well-designed proposal gets you the outcome that you desire from the negotiation.)

Contract

A brief, specific contract is your best assurance that you will be paid, and paid on time. It is a means of communication second to none for the professional. You should be very wary of accepting even the most minimal job without an exchange of contracts having taken place. Far too many clients fail to pay for work for the very simple reason that they had a different view of what they would get for their money to that held by the consultant. Please commit yourself to using contracts, but make them relevant to the job and the client. Contracts need not be either time consuming or legalistic. In Chapter 7 I will tell you how to produce user-friendly contracts easily and economically.

Provision of service

When you do the job, remember that this is a profession of trust and total quality. Your responsibility is to delight your client, but to do so at a profit. That way you will still be around to delight them again and again.

Report and evaluation

I am not a fan of long and impressive reports. But I am a fanatic about predetermined meaningful outcomes. Whatever the appropriate style of report at the end of an assignment, it should always include three things:

❑ This is what we set out to do.
❑ This is what we achieved.
❑ This is what the client will do to exploit that achievement fully.

If that information can be conveyed on the back of an envelope or by word of mouth then that is fine by me, as long as it leads unfailingly to an empowered client taking the right action. If you need a weighty report for that outcome, then so be it – but beware the type who collects reports and loves them for their own sake. Such reports only increase the cost of serving the client and lead to very little by way of effective action. I write reports generally to be sold to businesses which either cannot afford my services or prefer to take on the job themselves. One thing my publisher and I both understand: in spite of my natural desire to give as much value as possible for the money, when it comes to using a report to get things done, shorter is very much better.

What consultants ought to do

Your primary responsibility is to end the assignment with a delighted client. That being so, let us look at what you do for your client, regardless of your specialism.

Do consultants, as Bob Townsend asserts, 'borrow the client's watch, tell him the time, and pocket the watch with the fee'? Apart from the final accusation of light-fingeredness, the answer is 'yes', but they do it in a way which gives added value immensely greater than any apparently inflated fee.

The only source of meaningful information about a client's business lies in and around that business. The consultant's contribution is to analyse the mass of information, bring a wider and less parochial perspective to bear, and leave the client with a richer range of useful choices than were previously apparent and greater power to exploit them. If that is what you mean by 'stealing his watch', Mr Townsend, you are right. What is more, I and my professional colleagues lift it with pride and return it more accurate than before and thoroughly cleaned.

In detail, borrowing the client's watch and telling them the time mean that you do the following.

Build rapport

Consultant and client have to work together creatively and pro-
ductively. They can work together a great deal better if they do
more than just rub along. When you or I go into an organization
we have a specific client who hires us and has our absolute loyalty
and support. The day we are unable to provide that loyalty is the
day we must back out of the assignment. That means that there
are no circumstances in which it is acceptable to go behind our
client's back, either to the board or to their secretary. In a position
of trust there is no such thing as 'wrong but acceptable'.

You must share your client's dreams. They may change under
your influence as the assignment matures, but at any time, making present dreams a reality is your goal.

Analyse information

Consultants thoroughly analyse the business situation, regardless
of their specialism or background. To provide off-the-shelf solutions without analysis is wrong, and so is developing departmental
solutions which damage the rest of the business. A business is a
complete entity: you either bring to bear sufficient knowledge to
analyse the whole or, if you lack the competence, you bring in others to help – or you walk.

Analysis must be dispassionate and objective, but it must be
underpinned by a mandatory and passionate commitment to the
interest of the client and the organization. Consultants must
enrich their depth of knowledge about the client organization
with the most current and effective best practice as well as the
best-validated research.

Develop alternatives

The creation of choice is often the consultant's most important
contribution. Choices are presented without prejudgement or bias
and with the weight of supporting evidence clearly explained.

Recommend options

Someone (do you remember who?) said, 'advisers advise, ministers decide'. Clients also decide, and unless that decision is unethical or illegal, consultants contribute to making it work. Effective consultants present their recommendations as forcibly as the evidence warrants, and then support the client in whatever they decide.

Motivate action

Recommendations which lie unimplemented are of no value to the client or to the reputation of the consultant. Recommendations which are badly implemented damage both. An essential part of the consultant's role is to ensure that the recommendations can be implemented with available resources and with the active commitment of all involved. Teambuilding in the broadest sense is a part of every assignment.

Ensure growth

The consultant should leave every assignment with a client who is more skilled, more knowledgeable, more independent and more self-reliant than when the contract began. If that sounds to you like the death knell of your future income, fear not. Skilful, confident, effective clients grow and as they grow they provide bigger and better contract opportunities for the consultants they have learned to trust. Conversely, 80 per cent of clients in a survey of client fears conducted by Howard Shenson indicated that they would have strong reservations about employing a consultant again because they feared that ongoing dependency would result. That says something about our profession, and I for one don't like the sound of it.

Ethics and values

To become a certified consultant you or I sign an ethical undertaking and a code of practice which has the same effect on me as the Hippocratic oath has on a medical practitioner. I have no wish to impose my values, my job is to offer practical advice, but I believe that there are practical benefits to be gained from working to a strict code, so I hope in your interest as well as that of the profession that you are prepared to bind yourself to a code of ethics. At the very least, your personal mission statement should incorporate your personal values and you should never deviate from these.

A practical approach which I stole from somewhere long ago might be a sound basis for those about to establish their own ethical and practice values. The consultant should recommend only that for which there is a sound business purpose, which will at least pay for itself in an acceptable time, and which can be explained in simple language to those who must make it work.

Teams within teams

Although consultants must be consistently loyal to a single client, they must also recognize their role as a part of the client organization's team. The central idea that the consultant's recommendation serves no purpose until it is successfully put to work means that all consultants, regardless of their discipline, need to have an operational understanding of teambuilding strategies.

One of the most practical and influential approaches of recent years is that developed by Dr R Meredith Belbin. There is a brief overview of the concept opposite, but I would strongly urge all professionals to study Belbin's book, *Management Teams: Why They Succeed or Fail*, with care. Belbin's research suggests that successful teams are a blend of people bringing together different personal styles to the effective completion of any task. No style has greater value than any other, although given a specific task one or more

BELBIN'S TEAM ROLES

Role description	Personal style	Key strengths	Key weaknesses
Chairman	Calm and confident Goal driven	Open minded Self-confident	Limited creativity Limited intellect
Company worker	Well organized Committed	Hard working Sees job through	Inflexible Limited imagination
Team worker	Socially oriented Promotes team needs	Self-effacing Sensitive to others	Indecisive under pressure
Shaper	Challenges and tests ideas	Dynamic Analytic	Often highly strung Irritable
Plant	Unorthodox thinker	Imaginative Individualistic	Sometimes impractical
Resource investigator	Makes contacts Drives progress	Extrovert Responds to challenge	Grasshopper mind Careless of detail
Monitor evaluator	Practical Hardheaded	Judgement Prudence	Lacks inspiration
Completer finisher	Capacity to follow though	Conscientious	Reluctant to let go

may make a uniquely important contribution because of the nature of the job in hand or the stage which it is at.

Given the wide range of activities which any team needs to address, it is probable that the key weakness in unsuccessful teams is the lack of someone with the appropriate team style allocated to the right task at the right time. Thus, a team of great creativity and intellectual brilliance may come up with an almost infinite range of superb ideas, any one of which would be a winner were it put into effect. But because the team lacks solid, dependable people prepared to beaver away to get the job done, no plan reaches fruition and the team fails because it is seduced by novelty and bedevilled by a low boredom threshhold. Worse, since an unsuccessful team eventually tends to seek the causes of failure in terms of the faulty contribution of its own members, even the flow of ideas may cease and the group may descend to pointless infighting.

As a consultant you enter your client's team when assigned. Although you must be careful to maintain your objectivity in analysing the situation and making recommendations, your role remains that of a team member throughout the assignment. You therefore need to consider carefully the appropriate team member behaviour at every stage of your work, and the effective consultant is prepared to find ways of plugging the gaps in the client's team. At the implementation stage this need becomes paramount to ensure economic progress. You will do much to ensure that your ideas are competently carried out by thinking constructively about the team which must implement them.

If consultants can do no more than identify the essential team roles, develop others in assuming those roles or take the responsibility themselves and help to manage the social and task effects of team operation, their contribution to the ongoing effectiveness of the client organization will be immense. Consultants should be, and often are, proactive role models.

The consultant should always be mindful that the organization is an integrated system. It is almost impossible to take an action in one part of the business which will have no effect, for good or ill, elsewhere. In my opinion, this makes it a prerequisite of professional practice that consultants take all opportunities to expand their knowledge of areas beyond the confines of their narrow specialism. I doubt the ability of any consultant to be fully effective without a working knowledge of:

❑ the way people behave in organizations
❑ the marketing concept
❑ finance and the role of profit
❑ management information systems.

This is not to say that every consultant should become a total polymath where business is concerned, but it does suggest that both self-development and working with fellow professionals are essential to us all.

Undertaking self-assessment

What follows is not a complex psychometric test. It is a simple self-assessment to enable professional management advisers to plan their ongoing self-development on the basis of current and validated research findings.

To use it, read through the statements and decide which are true of you:

❑ All of the time
❑ Most of the time
❑ Some of the time
❑ Rarely or never true of you.

Mark the applicable description with a cross.

Ideally, use the second copy of the inventory to have a trusted client or colleague complete a second assessment of your professional behaviour. Compare and discuss, if appropriate, the two results, focusing on any differences of perception.

Identify where you choose to change to more effective behaviour by drawing a circle around not more than four crosses. Transfer the key behaviours to the change planning sheets in the form of objectives and write a simple strategy statement for each to indicate the specific actions which you commit yourself to take – starting today.

Do not seek to change more than three or four behaviours at a time. Concentrate on those which you regard as most important and most easy for you to change right now.

Most importantly:

Commit yourself to rewarding every improvement which you achieve, no matter how small. In spite of the relative decline in academic support for behaviourist approaches, no more effective means of reinforcing desired behaviour has yet emerged than relating it directly to pleasure.

 SOAP BOX – IMPLEMENTING CHANGE

The biggest single challenge and opportunity for consultants, whatever their specialism, is, and will continue to be, the facilitation of change. For those who are not 'people people', here are some brief notes on how to help people accept change.

❑ Communicate with them.
❑ Listen to them.
❑ Train them to meet predetermined measurable objectives relevant to the new situation.
❑ Enable the immediate use of new skills and knowledge.
❑ Ensure that people are recruited and transferred in good time.
❑ Consider people's convenience, expectations and needs and make change as painless as possible.
❑ Elicit and handle concerns, remembering that feelings are important facts in any situation.
❑ Identify and sell the benefits of the change – honestly.

CONSULTANCY SKILLS INVENTORY 1 – GENERAL SKILLS

True of me	Always	Usually	Sometimes	Never
I think before I speak	☐	☒	☐	☐
I am comfortable with my education	☐	☒	☐	☐
I am comfortable with my experience	☒	☐	☐	☐
I understand my motives for wanting to work in a helping profession	☐	☒	☐	☐
I read group behaviour accurately	☐	☒	☐	☐
I can separate personal issues from work	☐	☒	☐	☐
I listen effectively	☐	☒	☐	☐
I appreciate the impact of my behaviour on others	☐	☒	☐	☐
I understand my need to compete with others	☐	☒	☐	☐
I can deal with conflict and anger	☐	☒	☐	☐
I can build an atmosphere of trust and openness	☐	☒	☐	☐
I work on the basis of a clear theory	☐	☒	☐	☐
I can use relevant theory as the basis of effective practice	☐	☒	☐	☐

CONSULTANCY SKILLS INVENTORY 2 – PROBLEM-SOLVING AND IMPLEMENTING SKILLS

True of me	Always	Usually	Sometimes	Never
I state problems and objectives clearly	☐	☒	☐	☐
I recognize the difference between rational and creative problems	☐	☒	☐	☐
I have skills in rational and creative techniques	☐	☒	☐	☐
I am skilled at summarizing	☐	☒	☐	☐
I sell my ideas effectively	☐	☒	☐	☐
I can keep people on track	☐	☐	☒	☐
I challenge ineffective approaches	☐	☒	☐	☐
I recognize key similarities	☐	☐	☒	☐
I recognize key differences	☐	☐	☒	☐
I am able to ask others for help	☐	☒	☐	☐
I can evaluate critically and effectively	☒	☐	☐	☐
I can contribute a range of proven techniques	☒	☐	☐	☐

CONSULTANCY SKILLS INVENTORY 3 – IMPLEMENTING AND EVALUATING SKILLS

True of me	Always	Usually	Sometimes	Never
I can intervene without threat to my clients	☐	☒	☐	☐
I can recognize my own defensiveness	☐	☒	☐	☐
I seek feedback on my performance	☒	☐	☐	☐
I can admit to errors and mistakes	☒	☒	☐	☐
I use my mistakes as a basis for learning	☒	☐	☐	☐
I learn from my strengths	☐	☒	☐	☐
I can accurately assess my own contribution	☐	☒	☐	☐
I can acknowledge both failure and success	☐	☒	☐	☐
I feel comfortable with clients reviewing my work	☐	☒	☐	☐
I can deal with unexpected changes	☐	☒	☐	☐
I can devise forms, inventories etc. to aid evaluation of my work	☐	☒	☐	☐
I can let go when the task is complete	☐	☒	☐	☐
I follow up effectively	☐	☐	☒	☐
I refuse to blame failure on 'client resistance'	☐	☒	☐	☐

CONSULTANCY SKILLS INVENTORY – INSTRUCTIONS FOR COMPLETION

By giving you these assessment forms, the person from whom they came is expressing great trust in your openness and ability to be constructive.

Please read each statement and assess on behalf of your colleague how true it is of him or her.

Is it:
❑ Always true
❑ Usually true (more often true than not)
❑ Sometimes true (less often true than not)
❑ Never true in your experience.

Please indicate your assessment for each item by placing a cross in the appropriate column.

Your colleague intends to make practical use of your input, so please approach the task seriously and be prepared to discuss your assessment constructively.

Please remember that the 'I' in this inventory is the colleague who asked you to complete this on his or her behalf, not you.

Thank you.

CONSULTANCY SKILLS INVENTORY 1 – GENERAL SKILLS

True of me	Always	Usually	Sometimes	Never
I think before I speak	☐	☐	☐	☐
I am comfortable with my education	☐	☐	☐	☐
I am comfortable with my experience	☐	☐	☐	☐
I understand my motives for wanting to work in a helping profession	☐	☐	☐	☐
I read group behaviour accurately	☐	☐	☐	☐
I can separate personal issues from work	☐	☐	☐	☐
I listen effectively	☐	☐	☐	☐
I appreciate the impact of my behaviour on others	☐	☐	☐	☐
I understand my need to compete with others	☐	☐	☐	☐
I can deal with conflict and anger	☐	☐	☐	☐
I can build an atmosphere of trust and openness	☐	☐	☐	☐
I work on the basis of a clear theory	☐	☐	☐	☐
I can use relevant theory as the basis of effective practice	☐	☐	☐	☐

CONSULTANCY SKILLS INVENTORY 2 — PROBLEM-SOLVING
AND IMPLEMENTING SKILLS

True of me	Always	Usually	Sometimes	Never
I state problems and objectives clearly	☐	☐	☐	☐
I recognize the difference between rational and creative problems	☐	☐	☐	☐
I have skills in rational and creative techniques	☐	☐	☐	☐
I am skilled at summarizing	☐	☐	☐	☐
I sell my ideas effectively	☐	☐	☐	☐
I can keep people on track	☐	☐	☐	☐
I challenge ineffective approaches	☐	☐	☐	☐
I recognize key similarities	☐	☐	☐	☐
I recognize key differences	☐	☐	☐	☐
I am able to ask others for help	☐	☐	☐	☐
I can evaluate critically and effectively	☐	☐	☐	☐
I can contribute a range of proven techniques	☐	☐	☐	☐

CONSULTANCY SKILLS INVENTORY 3 – IMPLEMENTING AND EVALUATING SKILLS

True of me	Always	Usually	Sometimes	Never
I can intervene without threat to my clients	☐	☐	☐	☐
I can recognize my own defensiveness	☐	☐	☐	☐
I seek feedback on my performance	☐	☐	☐	☐
I can admit to errors and mistakes	☐	☐	☐	☐
I use my mistakes as a basis for learning	☐	☐	☐	☐
I learn from my strengths	☐	☐	☐	☐
I can accurately assess my own contribution	☐	☐	☐	☐
I can acknowledge both failure and success	☐	☐	☐	☐
I feel comfortable with clients reviewing my work	☐	☐	☐	☐
I can deal with unexpected changes	☐	☐	☐	☐
I can devise forms, inventories etc. to aid evaluation of my work	☐	☐	☐	☐
I can let go when the task is complete	☐	☐	☐	☐
I follow up effectively	☐	☐	☐	☐
I refuse to blame failure on 'client resistance'	☐	☐	☐	☐

CHANGE PLANNING SHEET

The behaviour I choose to change is:

My objective with regard to this behaviour is:

My strategy for changing my behaviour is:

I see an ideal opportunity for changing my behaviour when (activity or situation):

My major reward when I am totally satisfied with the change will be:

Interim rewards for progress will be:

CHANGE PLANNING SHEET

The behaviour I choose to change is:

My objective with regard to this behaviour is:

My strategy for changing my behaviour is:

I see an ideal opportunity for changing my behaviour when (activity or situation):

My major reward when I am totally satisfied with the change will be:

Interim rewards for progress will be:

CHANGE PLANNING SHEET

The behaviour I choose to change is:

My objective with regard to this behaviour is:

My strategy for changing my behaviour is:

I see an ideal opportunity for changing my behaviour when (activity or situation):

My major reward when I am totally satisfied with the change will be:

Interim rewards for progress will be:

CHANGE PLANNING SHEET

The behaviour I choose to change is:

My objective with regard to this behaviour is:

My strategy for changing my behaviour is:

I see an ideal opportunity for changing my behaviour when (activity or situation):

My major reward when I am totally satisfied with the change will be:

Interim rewards for progress will be:

4

Networking for Synergy

THERE IS PROBABLY NO MORE IRRITATING A WASTE OF TIME TO THE dedicated consultant than networking as it is practised today. What happens is that a group of independents, usually with different specialisms, come together with the honest aim of developing mutual business. When I find a client whose needs are better aligned to your skills than mine, I introduce you.

You, it is to be hoped, contract to perform the assignment, and pay me a percentage of the total fee, usually about 10 per cent, for passing you the lead. In the fullness of time, it is expected that you will provide me with business leads on the same terms. We will both be busy, fat and happy.

It sounds great. So why doesn't it work? It does not work for a number of reasons, the first of which is human greed.

Most people who have attempted to establish networks have concluded, sooner or later, that the provision of hot leads is a one-way street. You introduce me to clients, but there is no reciprocal arrangement. Somehow I do not seem to come across others who need your skills. On the other hand, I do seem to seek your advice with some regularity about 'little problems that I have come across in a major assignment'. These 'little problems' are never enough to require your attendance at the client's premises; they are, however, significant enough to require you to spend long periods advising me in response to my frequent telephone enquiries.

The trouble is that I have realized something which has yet to register with you. The cost of marketing is substantially greater than the 10 per cent that you would pay me for handing the client to you. So it becomes a case of what is yours is mine, and what is mine is my own, regardless of the quality of service that my attempts to do work which I am ill qualified to do may provide for the client. What is more, although the client will get less than optimal service, they will probably never know, and I may be able to keep them. If I let you in to do a better job, whose client is it then?

In these circumstances I really am enjoying the best of all possible worlds. I keep my clients carefully to myself and I am kept busy while devoting myself exclusively to the development of my own practice. I benefit from my own marketing activities and yours. I have you as an unpaid provider of resources which in many cases will enable me to 'satisfice' my way out of potential trouble. If I can multiply you by half a dozen or so, and if each is as generous and ingenuous as you, my one-way street is a highway to riches – at least until you realize your problem.

And we have a number of problems:

❑ My greed.
❑ The client's ignorance of what could be achieved, and probable low expectation of result.
❑ Mistrust, in that I suspect, and judging by my own behaviour I am entitled to suspect, that you will 'elope' with 'my client'.
❑ My ability to ensure some degree of marketable professional development by taking advantage of your generosity (with free resources thrown in).

The potential value of networking is immense. In the early days of a practice when doors must be opened and the chances of hitting the opportunity window which relates ideally to your skills is minute, the ability to multiply your prospecting efforts could make a substantial difference to your capacity to feed your family until your growing reputation brings the clients to your door. So how do we resolve the problem?

Equitable networking

I suggest that networking arrangements would be better for a touch of formality. A simple letter of agreement which makes clear the reasonable expectations and the responsibilities of membership would reduce the possibility of misunderstanding. In the event of a member's specialist skills being required for less than a half day, remuneration on an agreed hourly rate should be paid. The circumstances under which such a special rate is payable should be included with the specified rate. Half days or more should be paid at the normal daily rate, and should be encouraged in the interests of quality.

On the subject of payment, the percentage paid to the 'finding consultant' should be considerably higher than 10 per cent. A minimum of 25 per cent allied to an understanding that the client remains that of the initiating consultant would enable you, having passed work to me, to visit your client at least one day in four of the contract, helping to ensure client satisfaction and keeping your eye open for work opportunities for other members in the team. Above all, it would obviate the untrue use of 'the client wouldn't like...' from the one member of the team who has client contact. (I pay 40 per cent of my, not inconsiderable, fee to my 'agents'.)

To be effective a network must be a team operation, providing, if not an equal amount of work for all, at least a fair opportunity for each member to use their skills and knowledge to provide the highest-quality service to the client. In a profession dependent for its survival on trust, client service ought to be our constant guiding principle.

It may be a sad reflection on our society that the most effective way to promote quality is through the distribution of cash. But that is the way the world goes. (I commend this thought to those consultants who specialize in ISO9000 or BS7750. Those who believe that the client will be best motivated to take action by an appeal to their concern for quality or for the environment will be disappointed. Try showing, factually, how the client will be more profitable by pursuing these valuable social and commercial goals and you will win more business.)

Networking is probably the only efficient way for the 'one-man band' to attempt to exploit the wider market. It can be made to work, as successful networks testify, but if you wish to build a network that is equitable, then get things agreed in detail from day one.

Networking agreement

The precise form and style of a network agreement will depend entirely on the way that the members wish their association to operate. It should, however, include as a minimum the following:

❑ An undertaking from each member not to carry out work for which another member would be better qualified.
❑ An agreement on the fee rate to be quoted by members when acting on behalf of the network.
❑ The level of the 'finder's' fee.
❑ Which consultant, 'finder' or 'doer', will be responsible for invoicing. (Personally I favour the 'finder' invoicing the client and assuming the role of 'project manager'.)
❑ Standard network terms and conditions of business to be binding on all members.
❑ The circumstances under which a third party **must** be introduced during an assignment.
❑ Rates at which third parties are reimbursed for interventions of less than a half day.
❑ The timing of payment to members of cash receipts. (This is vital.)
❑ Agreed quality-control arrangements.

❑ Whether the client will be seen by the network as being the customer of 'finder' or 'doer'.

❑ Any agreed period during which those who leave the network agree not to make a direct selling approach to any client of the network.

Unless the above are fully thrashed out, there will always be 'bones of contention' to fight over.

Networking is the key to effective solo or small firm consultancy, just as it is basic to the success of the largest practices. At least one major practice devotes 50 per cent of its total marketing budget to internal networking – that is how important it is. To be successful it must be done right. Try to ensure that you build rather than join a network if you believe that the rules under which the existing group operates are less than optimal. Take the lead in this as in all things. It is that important. Get it right first time. It will be in the long-term interests of yourself, your colleagues and your clients.

Rules for effective networking

❑ Ensure that the selling consultant has sufficient income from the job to ensure that they can afford to take a high-profile position with their client (at least one-quarter of the value of the contract).

❑ Work only with people who are fully agreed on the ethics and process of consultancy.

❑ Develop a written contract to avoid misunderstandings.

5

Business-Winning Proposals and Other Ways of Getting Paid

WHAT DO YOU DO IF THE CLIENT SAYS:

'I like the sound of what you are telling me. To hell with any proposal. When can you start?'

What I do is to look in my diary and agree a start date, shake hands and leave. Then I go home and write a proposal anyway. Let me counsel you always to write a proposal, whether the client wants one or not. It is an essential tool for planning your intervention. When you have completed your proposal it will be clear to you exactly what you will do, when you will do it, why you are doing it and how much it will cost.

As a planning tool a well-constructed proposal is useful. As a marketing tool it is indispensable. If something in your business is indispensable you had better have a labour-saving and effective approach to its production, but before we start down that track, let me tell you why it is so vital in marketing your business.

Forget for a moment any fancy definitions of marketing. Let's be both basic and selfish. What is your marketing effort for? It is to bring you profitable business. All the good stuff about 'creating, identifying and satisfying' only makes sense if it builds and maintains your business at a profit. The bible says something about 'What shall it profit a man if he gain the whole world and lose his immortal soul?' The consultant's version ought to be, 'What shall it profit me if I look a real smart ass, and give away my expertise for free?'

That is precisely what too many consultants do when they present a proposal. They make a present of their expertise in the form of a 'recipe' which tells the client, in ravishing detail, how to turn the assignment into a 'do-it-yourself job'. Or worse, where the client is completely without principle, the detailed and comprehensive proposal finds its way into the hands of a competitor who is either cheaper, or an old buddy of your hoped-for client.

So we have three basic requirements of any proposal:

❑ It should be easy to write with the minimum investment of time.
❑ It should avoid all danger of giving away your services for free.
❑ It should be an effective marketing tool which will win you business, and preferably win you business on your own terms.

Sounds easy enough to meet those little requirements, doesn't it? Let's have a look at how this can be done.

Writing the proposal

Put in your mind a simple thought, and cling to it through the process of proposal writing. Remember:

'The purpose of writing a proposal is to win business. It is not to explain my activities.'

Every time you find yourself tempted to explain, ask yourself: 'If I resist the temptation at this point, will it lose me the business?' Unless the answer to that question is an absolute 'yes', explanation will be at best merely incidental local colour, and at worst all that the client needs to do the work internally, or to pass it to a favoured but less qualified friend.

Have a formula for your proposal and stick to it. That is the way to make production of the document time efficient, and it will steer you clear of temptation.

A formula which has served me, and many thousands of others, is as follows.

Step One: Draw a flow chart of activities
Your flow chart will say:

- ❑ **What** you propose to do.
- ❑ The order in which things will be done.
- ❑ The time each activity is forecast to take.
- ❑ Any activities which are simultaneous or overlapping.
- ❑ Any optional activities which are desirable but not essential to the predetermined outcome.
- ❑ That the costs are justified because the activities are essential and the time carefully estimated.

Your flow chart will not say how you will do anything.

It is essential that you are clear on the difference between what is done and how it is done, so please bear with me while I ensure that I have made the key distinction plain. '**What**' might include:

- ❑ Complete feasibility study
- ❑ Identify training needs
- ❑ Conduct interviews
- ❑ Identify strategic alternatives
- ❑ Analyse statistics.

'**How**' you do these things is precisely what you are paid for knowing. It is your 'stock in trade' which you part with for cash. You should no more expect to tell your client how you will do things than your surgeon would expect to tell you in grim detail how and where to make the incision, how to deal with the problem of bleeding, the mixture of gases for optimal anaesthesia or whatever. He tells you, 'We'll remove your lump', and he expects you to like it. You must expect to build a similar relationship with your client.

Clients will, however, ask 'How?' Perhaps in spite of all our efforts to cast you in the mould of the surgeon, the situation is not the same. Surgeons enjoy a level of mystique to which few consultants aspire. Given that some clients will behave in this uncooperative way, how do you respond?

I suggest that there are two viable strategies.

If your relationship with the client is such that plain speaking is valued above all else, you may choose to reply, 'How I do it is what I am paid for. As soon as the contract is signed I will tell you that in detail.'

Or you may do what I do. I give them a more detailed level of 'what', but I never tell them 'how'.

The conversation may go like this:

Client: That's interesting, how do you do that?
Consultant: I interview your staff.
Client: How?
Consultant: I design a structured interview.
Client: How do you do that?
Consultant: I develop carefully designed questions which probe the areas I need to analyse.
Client: How do you know that you have the right questions?
Consultant: I test them on a small sample...

and so it goes on. Eventually the client is satisfied because they believe that they now understand how I work. I am happy because I have a satisfied client, and I have given nothing away.

Of course, if I am really in selling mode I might change to:

'Look, you're obviously very interested in this aspect of the work. Why don't you try to find a little time to sit with me while I'm doing it, and I can fill you in on exactly what I am doing and how it works. If we were to start on the first of next month, would you be free?' If they get their diary out I have an assignment.

Step Two: Develop a benefit statement for each activity
❏ Show how each box on your flow chart represents benefits to the client.
❏ Structure the list of benefits logically so that it is clear how each activity contributes to the achievement of the desired outcome.
❏ Avoid indicating through unnecessary justification of a benefit how it will be achieved.

Step Three: Detail the reporting and consultation timetable
❏ Explain when you will meet with your client management and what form the communication of progress will take.
❏ Show that management's ongoing input of ideas will be solicited throughout the assignment to ensure that your activities will be attuned to their possibly changing needs as the consultation progresses.
❏ Tell them that all necessary information and training will be built in to enable the client's staff to implement your recommendations.

Step Four: Prepare a time line
❏ Draw up a simple Gantt chart which shows the dates when key activities start and are forecast to be completed.

Step Five: Summarize costs

*Step Six: Add the **essential** extras*
These may include:

❏ Your terms and conditions of business.
❏ Your practice mission or value statement.

❑ CVs of the people involved, limited to what is relevant to this assignment.

Only add what is essential to help you to get the assignment. Remember that big is by no means always beautiful. Any extraneous information which you add to a proposal to make it look 'impressive' may contain something which for a reason unknown to you causes the client to react negatively. This is a case where brevity is the soul of discretion – if I can mix my proverbs.

If in doubt – leave it out.

What this form of proposal says about you

The flow chart shows that you understand the needs of the client in detail. Any fears which they may have about your competence are allayed. Together with the summary of benefits, the flow chart indicates the basis for your fees and shows through value that such fees are not excessive.

You have shown that there will be no lack of management control. Communication is central to your proposal, as is intelligent flexibility. Nor will continued dependency be a problem because you have stated that the implementation by the client team will be fully facilitated.

Finally, the Gantt chart demonstrates graphically that you plan to complete the work promptly and within the client's time frame.

Later you will read about research which shows that client fears concerning the use of consultants are:

❑ potential consultant incompetence
❑ lack of management control
❑ continued dependency
❑ high fees
❑ inadequate consultant time to do the job
❑ need for consultancy may be seen as an admission of failure
❑ fear of disclosure of sensitive information

❑ improper diagnosis of client need
❑ partiality of the consultant.

One simple document, kept to a practical minimum, does much to deal with them all. Only the consultant's possible dependence on a single product or style and the client's probable concerns over the communication of proprietary or sensitive data remain. Surely it can be argued that your proposal can and will demonstrate that you are flexible as well as capable. And since open and planned communication is central to your approach, a confident two-way flow of information can be readily demonstrated.

Have I missed something? What about 'fear that the need for consultancy may be seen as an admission of failure'? I contend that a professional, relevant proposal puts that to bed as well. Such a proposal provides your client with all the information they will ever need to refute such a criticism.

Writing proposals has never been easier. These days it is simple to store your chosen format and generalized content on computer and save time by inserting the specific and tailored parts of the proposal quickly and easily.

Don't miss opportunities to 'recycle'. When your proposal fails to get you the business – and that will happen even in the best regulated of worlds – don't throw it away. Take out any client-specific information. Write a letter which explains that you have been investigating the issues and problems facing the industry and have sketched a possible way to deal with some of the most pressing, and send letter and proposal to other key players in the same business sector. You may well find that your proposal wins you business after all.

How else can you win business and avoid giving your services away? Let us consider the tricks clients play.

Imagine (many readers will not have to!) the following situation. You have just completed an assignment. The work has gone well. Both you and your client are delighted with the outcome. Days or weeks elapse and you are busy with new work, or with finding it. One evening you get home to find a message from your satisfied client that they would appreciate a call. When you call it is not the half-anticipated referral. Apparently one member of your client's team is having minor difficulties implementing your recommendations. Could you just call by tomorrow and put them back on the right track? Of course you could, you are very pleased to have an opportunity to give exceptional service in spite of your slight surprise that there is a problem after the trouble taken to predict and prepare for all eventualities.

You travel somewhat out of your way, delaying the start of an important meeting and arrive to find that the problem has little or nothing to do with your work. It is just that they have a new idea which excites them, and they were keen to have a chance to 'bounce it off someone'.

You are still happy. It is good to know that your opinion is valued in other areas. A couple of weeks later, a similar call, a similar outcome. The new idea has some complex features, and 'What exactly was that planning technique you mentioned to Fred that time?'

Before long you find yourself conducting an impromptu workshop, and you feel really good. It's great to be appreciated, and you are being appreciated something like once a week. Of course, you are not getting paid for it and it does interfere with other work. But what the hell, you are laying up treasure in heaven! Or are you? Perhaps you have just signed up as an unpaid non-executive director, and if you continue to give such good service you may have a job for life. Unpaid, naturally.

Every professional worth their salt wants to give exceptional value. But there has to be a time when commercial pressures prevail. And there is worse to come. The more people enjoy your services for free, the less they value them. Your sterling efforts become just part of their ordinary day-to-day existence – nothing special. Just something that happens as routine. And if you believe that is the worst that can happen, think again. They may not greatly value what you are doing while you are doing it, but try to withdraw it, and see how ill and unfairly treated people can feel.

The answer? The answer is both very simple and very difficult.

It is very simple, because when it becomes obvious that the client has a continuing need for your services you can regularize the situation by drawing up a retainer agreement. It is difficult, because seeing the opportunity before you are enmeshed requires considerable powers of precognition. It is more difficult because raising the suggestion of the retainer at an early stage may look like rapaciousness.

Experience suggests that the only way to avoid problems is, as usual, through good communication. Do the first follow-up. Do it with good grace and do it well, whatever it may be. Then when asked to do the second, make it clear that, although you are happy to do the work, it is costing you the opportunity to sell your time and your time is all that you have to sell.

If the need for your services continues you will have to invoice. Do the second task at least as well as the first, and immediately suggest a retainer agreement for the future.

Do it quickly enough and on the back of exceptional service and you will have little difficulty in persuading your client that your continued availability is worth investing in. Do it late, or after being forced either to rush a job or to refuse to undertake it, and you will lose a client. What is worse, it is a sad reflection on human behaviour that through an excess of client care you can turn an ingrate into an enemy.

Retainer agreements

There are two basic styles of retainer. The first is where the client knows that your services will be required regularly for x days per month for the foreseeable future. This is sometimes called a time retainer. If you attract this type of retainer, regard yourself as shrewd, or lucky, or both. You will be able to prebook work. You will not have to wait around to discover if you really are wanted or not. You will have a regular source of income for which all marketing costs have ceased. It is even simple to decide what to charge. Start with your normal daily fee rate, and if you feel generous offer a small discount in recognition of the regularity of the income. If, however, you feel that a discount is appropriate, always use it to obtain a *quid quo pro*.

In this case it might be proper to suggest that payment be made on or before a given day each month. It would also be wise to establish that any discount which you are able to offer for regular work is not automatically transferable to other assignments, for which your standard daily rate applies. Put any such agreement in writing, and if any retainers are substantial, check with your accountant to ensure that nothing that you are contemplating is likely to prejudice your status as self-employed for tax purposes.

The second style of retainer is a little more complex. Perhaps your client is unsure whether there will be a need for you to do anything in any particular month, but would like you to pencil in a set number of days each month when you will undertake to be available if required. Now you have a slight problem. The client is unlikely to want to pay your full fee each month if you are not needed to do any work. On the other hand, if you have reserved time for your client you cannot sell it to anyone else. This means that for any day you are not used a valuable opportunity is lost. Worse, you may occasionally find yourself having to turn down work, because you are ethically bound to hold yourself available.

An appropriate fee structure for an availability agreement is as follows. For being available, and for nothing else, you should charge 50 per cent of your standard daily rate: if it turns out that in any given month you sit doing nothing for several days, waiting to be called, you have some, albeit limited, income. If you do work for the client you need to be compensated both for the loss of opportunity when not used and the outcome when you are. For days when you work you should therefore charge your full standard daily rate in addition to the 50 per cent levied for being available. In summary, available but not used, 50 per cent, available and used, 150 per cent. If your client finds that the need for your services is more frequent and regular than was anticipated, you can always return to a time retainer, where your full income, or something close to it, is guaranteed.

Needs analysis: a cautionary tale

When I was young, and more than a little green, I fell in, as luck would have it, with a client who would have described himself as 'shrewd', and whom others described as being anything between a cheap crook and an expensive one. Like all who are new to the business I was enthusiastic, anxious for work and trusting.

It was suggested that I should complete, without payment, a training needs analysis for the company which my client served. I should then develop a training plan, and having sold it to the board of the client company, I should design and conduct, for a modest fee, those programs for which I was qualified. It sounded like a promising start to my career which would bring in about half of my forecast income for the first year. It promised relatively early and regular income, and since I would be less than qualified to design and teach every program, it would bring me into early contact with fellow professionals in non-competing, complementary fields of expertise. I set about the task with vigour.

I completed the needs analysis, drew up the training plan, convinced the directors of the value of the program, provided a wide range of samples of materials which I felt would be useful, and even talked to manager and employee groups to encourage interest and attendance. I had no contract, but why should I care, I was dealing with nice people.

I woke up when I found that several of the programs which I was highly qualified to present were to be given by another consultant and I, having done all the prework and having no contract, had no redress. As it happened, I eventually found out why the contract had been placed with the other firm. You see I, and most of my competitors, charged $800 a day at the time, while the firm which had 'won' the contract charged $1200. An indication of higher quality? No, the programs were almost universally condemned by participants as useless or worse. An example of snobbishness gone mad? No, the answer was simpler and more venal. The company which had won the contract at the high price had a very practical approach to getting business. It was not greedy. Content with the norm for those days of $800 per day, the remaining $400 was paid to the manager who placed the contract in recognition of his placing it with the company.

I tell this cautionary tale for two reasons. First, it is true in every particular. Second, although an extreme example, it is typical of a favourite ploy to get you to provide your professional services for nothing.

The promise of a major assignment when the preliminaries have demonstrated 'what you can do' is almost never kept. Whether you complete a problem diagnosis or a professional needs analysis, you have done the most difficult part of most assignments. After your excellent groundwork almost anyone, within or outside the client company, can take over. They may be cheaper, or there may be other reasons for handing the work to them. Do not take the risk. Always charge for needs analysis, diagnosis or feasibility studies and charge at your full rate. You are providing professional services of a high order for work that is difficult and time consuming. If you must, and only if you must, do a deal along the following lines.

Charge for the initial work at your full daily rate. Agree in advance that if a substantial contract is placed with you for the completion of the assignment before payment of your first invoice is due, then you may waive all or part of your charges for the preliminary work.

The only circumstances which I can see as justifying such a step would be where competition had been foolish enough to offer to do what I so stupidly did when I knew no better, and you needed to find a way to protect yourself while being competitive.

A little diversionary tactic

You are working for Plant A on an assignment in a company with more than one plant. One day your client tells you how satisfied they are with your work, and asks if you would go over to Plant B and look at a 'little problem' there.

At such a request bells should sound a warning in your skull and distress rockets should be firing between your ears. This is truly a double trouble situation.

If you are a professional, you have agreed an outcome at Plant A which will be achieved within an agreed time.

That is what you will be measured against. Any distraction which takes you to Plant B chasing 'little problems' and their solutions puts your performance and your reputation at risk. Believe me, against that the fact that you will probably not be paid for the extra work is a minor irritant. Yet it seems a reasonable request from a valued client, so what do you do?

First, you take out your diary and, reminding the client of the agreed outcome and time frame and the progress which you have made to date, you indicate when you will be free to attend to Plant B's 'little problem' without adversely affecting your ability to complete the current job to standard and to time. Next, you politely ask whether the extra expenditure has been authorized or whether it would help if you drafted an amendment to the contract. Having established a time when you can properly attend to the needs of Plant B and that you expect to be paid for your efforts, you can concentrate on Plant A, or only address Plant B if your client is prepared to change their priorities. If such a change in priorities is insisted on, visit Plant B as requested and immediately put into writing your recommendation for completion of the now enlarged contract.

Dispensing advice

Once you become a professional adviser, people will seek your advice. That is reasonable and desirable. What is less reasonable, and far less desirable, is that many will seek to have that advice without payment.

You will find that you are approached on social occasions, at parties or in bars, by the kind of people who, were you the doctor, would remember as you took your pint the little pain that has been bothering them for weeks. What makes the matter worse, the fact that you feel that this is the profession for you is probably an indicator that you are a helpful person, at your happiest when passing on tips or information. Try not to do it. Steer enquirers gently and firmly toward business hours and your office or theirs. Help them to value your services, and remember that, in the eyes of most people, what you get for nothing is not even worth what you paid for it.

Of course there are, as always, exceptions. Consultants whom I train have the right to call me any time they need further advice at no extra charge. That's part of the deal and I stick to it with pleasure. The would-be client, however, who tries to pick my brain – such as it is – is told politely, but firmly, the circumstances under which the meter starts ticking.

In the chapter on selling your services I refer to an interesting recent study which suggests that there are occasions when from your perspective the client is trying to get something for nothing, while from theirs all they seek is value.

The study shows that around 15 per cent of clients expect to be billed for the initial 'marketing' meeting, and spend much of that meeting trying to get information which represents value. At the same time, the acute consultant, with no intention of charging for what is an exploratory meeting, fences skilfully to avoid giving anything away which might later earn fees.

The result of this miscommunication might be funny were it not that business can be lost and relationships can be mistrustful from the start. 'If in doubt communicate' is much better advice than 'if in doubt say nowt' in this case. If you have any indication that your client may expect to be billed for your initial meeting, explain that just as you always expect to be paid for work you do, you never expect to be paid for simply exploring the possibility of doing work. That way you can both relax and identify how you may most usefully serve.

That will lead to more business as surely as the use of a properly constructed proposal leads to more profitable and better business. And for the doubters – **it does**.

SOAP BOX

What people want from their jobs:

- ❑ Interesting work.
- ❑ Opportunities to use skills.
- ❑ A reasonable level of challenge.
- ❑ Some discretion.
- ❑ Personal and professional growth opportunities.
- ❑ Significant work which contributes to the success of the business.
- ❑ Some variety, but not a job-rotation, three-ring circus.
- ❑ A worthwhile role in a job valued by society.
- ❑ Recognition by peers and others.
- ❑ Self-satisfaction, self-reliance and support for a high self-image.
- ❑ Confidence in their own ability to handle the job.
- ❑ A secure job with a fair level of pay.

It is difficult to see how some current fads, for example 'Friday is jeans and sweatshirt day', contribute in any meaningful way to real-world job satisfaction.

- ❑ If you are in the business of introducing change into organizations, how will you ensure that people are not demotivated by having the perceived quality of their jobs downgraded?

6

Setting and Divulging Your Fees

IF YOU EVER FEEL SUICIDAL AND WANT TO DESTROY YOUR REPUTATION and career at a stroke, make it a habit to horsetrade over your fees.

Imagine the situation, if you will. You are completing the verbal presentation of the finest proposal that you have ever put together. You have seen buying signals from your potential client such as you have never seen before. You decide to end with a flourish and a trial close, after which you intend to sit silent for the few seconds which it will take for pens to be grabbed and contracts signed. You have everyone in the room on the edge of their seats with excitement as you summarize the key benefits, and you end with the words:

'And so you see, ladies and gentlemen, we will solve the problem and ensure that it will not return for only $45,000.'

You sit down, half expecting cheers of delight and tears of joy. What you get is:

'Well, we like your proposal, but there is a snag. The budget for this job is $37,000. We sweated blood to get that. There's no hope of getting it increased.'

What do you do? I will tell you what non-professionals do. They gulp, perspire a little, think about the mortgage and say:

'OK. I'll do it for $37,000.'

Now they have problems and we can afford to wish them joy.

❑ They probably don't know for certain whether there is profit in the assignment. (If they are bidding for a fixed-price job they could be in real trouble if any unforeseen snags arise.)
❑ More important, if anything can be more important, they now have a client who thinks they were 'flying a kite' with their first price. A client who no longer trusts them and is only delaying turning down the proposal in order to satisfy curiosity as to just how far the price could be driven down.

What does the professional do when faced with the problem of the diminishing budget? First, they congratulate themselves for their good sense in producing a professional proposal. Then they take their flow chart of activities, and say to their client:

'Let us see how we can reduce the cost. We are agreed that all of these activities are essential. So let us look at those which can be done either by your team on their own, or by your people with limited support from me.'

They then go box by box through the chart with their client, discussing the feasibility of having work done internally. If some jobs can be carried out by the client's team, that is fine: part of an assignment is better than either none at all, or a major job done for no profit.

What is more likely is that the client will want the consultant to do the work in its entirety just as proposed and will be willing to find the additional money. Try it, it seldom fails. But to be confident enough to make it work you have to be scientific about your fees.

Your fees must do four things:

❑ They must provide you with a personal income appropriate to your skills, knowledge and experience.
❑ They must meet **all** the costs of running your business.
❑ They must provide a surplus, or profit, which will enable you to invest in your business and allow it to grow in size, services and quality; and recompense you, the owner, for the risk which you are taking with your resources.
❑ They must enable you to compete effectively in your chosen market.

Let's start close to home with your personal income. Make a cool assessment of what your skills, knowledge and experience would bring you in the marketplace as an employee. Avoid any tendency to be modest. You are presumably good at what you do or you would not be offering yourself to clients. What is more, you have to build the client's confidence in using you and that means that you need to appear to be the kind of person who can command high earnings. Think for the moment only in terms of salary. Keep it simple.

Let me assume that you are worth $50,000 a year for the sake of example. You would expect to be paid, if you were in employment, for working days, high days and holidays. That is, you would expect to be paid for 261 days each year. (You do not usually get paid for weekends and 365 less 104 Saturdays and Sundays comes to 261.)

Divide $50,000 by 261 and you get $191.50 per day. That is your **labour rate**. Of course, you are probably worth a great deal more than $50,000 a year. I am just using simple figures for the sake of example.

With your daily labour rate established, we must turn our attention to your overheads, the cost of doing business. This is marginally more complicated, but not greatly so. Nonetheless, we will take it step by step.

Step One

Forecast the days you expect to be able to sell, on average, each month. Try not to be overly optimistic or you will fail to cover your costs fully. On the other hand, if you are unduly pessimistic you will make your forecast a self-fulfilling prophecy by establishing an unrealistically high daily rate.

My guesstimate of what you might reasonably aim for is 12 days each month. That is you will be billing clients for 12 days of the 20 that are available each month on average after fluctuations caused by holidays, variations in the business cycle and other activities which are not directly chargeable.

Step two

List and cost **all** your monthly overheads.

Step three

Multiply each monthly cost by 12 and add these up to get an annual cost of being in business.

Step four

Divide the annual overhead total cost by the number of days which you expect to invoice to customers. On the basis of my guess, 12 days a month for 12 months comes to 144.

At this point you have established a daily overhead rate which you can add to your daily labour rate to give you a complete cost of being in business and of employing yourself. Before we go the last step, let us develop an example which will both clarify what we are doing and raise some important points about what to include. My example will be reasonably comprehensive. That is, it will be, in the words of the insurance industry, 'of wide scope'. Your categories and the figures which you put to each must be as specific and accurate as forecasting allows.

As a total aside, my favourite definition of forecasting is one which I heard from David Myddleton:

'Forecasting is the art of stating what would have happened if what did happen didn't happen.'

Having got that off my chest, now for our example. Again, don't let the simple numbers sidetrack you – it's the principle which is important, and the principle is that the client pays for everything, but what they pay is fair and above board.

OVERHEADS

Item	Monthly cost $	Annual cost $
Secretary	1,000	12,000 [a]
Office rent	250	3000 [b]
Telephone	100	1200
Postage	65	780
Personnel benefits	40	480 [c]
Equipment	25	300
Stationery	12	144
Marketing		
Personnel (5 days)	958	11,496 [d]
Direct	500	6,000
Practice management (5 days)	958	11,496
Dues and subscriptions	12	144
Automotive	345	4,140
Insurance	26	312
Accounting and legal	225	2,700
Miscellaneous	200	2,400 [e]
Totals	4,716	56,592

Notes:

a If you charge any part of secretarial assistance directly to the client as an expense, you deduct that part from your overhead. The rule remains, 'The client always pays – but only once'.

b A proper, locally accurate office rent should be included even if you work from home. You may wish to compare your performance with others so you need to compare like with like, and you may need to rent an office one day. When you do, you do not want to have to put up your fees. Clients notice such things.

c You are entitled to whatever personnel benefits you would expect to enjoy if employed (health insurance and personal pension plans etc.).

d In case you have been wondering, this is where you cover the difference between billing clients for 144 days and paying your wages for 261 days. The shortfall is 117 days – in round figures 10 days a month. The other five are charged under 'Practice management'.

e I hate to see 'miscellaneous' in accounts, but it is useful for bringing together all the odds and ends and other things such as meals when travelling and travel costs which cannot be directly charged to the client as expenses.

On completion of this exercise we have an annual overhead of $56,592 which we divide by the days we expect to invoice, 144. This gives us:

Labour rate	$191.50
Overhead	$393.00
Total cost	$584.50

We are almost there. All that remains is to add our profit margin, but how much?

I can offer a rough guide based on experience. Most consultancies look to earn a profit of 15 to 25 per cent, and coincidentally or not, it seems to be closer to 15 per cent when interest rates are low, and nearer to 25 per cent when rates are high. (If you are borrowing in order to trade, you will not forget to add the monthly interest paid into your overheads, will you?)

So let us go for the upper limit:

Total cost of doing business	$584.50
Profit @ 25%	$146.125
Total	**$730.625**

But $730.625 is an awkward figure to use. So we are likely to round up a little and end up with:

Daily charge-out or fee rate of:	$735.00

And having worked it out properly we could, if we had to, justify it to the world as being the rate at which:

❑ We are properly paid for our labour.
❑ Our expenses are met.
❑ Our investment is rewarded with a fair level of profit.

You may be asked on very rare occasions (it has yet to happen to me) to break your fee down into its components. If you are, the above will satisfy most clients, with this proviso. Government employees tend to have a low regard for what they see as 'high salaries'. I would not wish to lead you into wrong-doing, but you would probably make a government employee happier by reducing your labour rate and profit and increasing overhead on paper – but, whatever expediency may dictate, keep to the daily fee rate you have established or you are the loser.

Unveiling your fee

Getting or failing to win the business can depend on how your fee is presented to the client. One of the questions which I suggest you must ask at the first client interview is:

> *'When you have used consultants before, what was the nature of the financial arrangement? Did they charge a simple daily rate? A fixed price? Or were they paid on results?'*

The answer can be an important piece of marketing intelligence. Let's analyse it.

Having established the type of financial arrangement, you need to know how the client felt about it. Did it seem fair? Was it perceived as professional? Please note, I am not suggesting that you ask the above questions, but I am indicating the information that you need to have for your proposal, verbal or written. More open questions, such as 'How did you like the arrangement?', intelligently probed, will give you the information you need to present your price in a form which is most likely to appeal to the client.

Fixed fee including expenses

If your client shows a strong preference for entering into a fixed-price contract and further wants it to include expenses, alarm bells ought to ring. A fixed-price contract means that the consultant carries all of the risk. If the job is more complex than it first appears, or if the client is more demanding of your time, you have a problem. No matter how long the job takes, you are only going to be paid the agreed amount. It is totally your responsibility to establish the precise nature and scope of the job and to make sure that the contract specifies in detail what the client may expect for their money. Clearly, the contract should also imply your willingness to take on additional work if the need arises, but it should state that such work will be charged at your normal daily rate. A fixed-fee arrangement which is exclusive of expenses is better from your point of view only to the degree that if you are suddenly asked to fly to Japan as a totally unexpected part of the job, you will at least be reimbursed for your travel and accommodation costs.

If you are forced to quote on a fixed-fee basis, estimate the cost of every foreseeable contingency and include this in your quotation. Remember that you are being invited to carry an unknown risk. This entitles you to:

❑ Minimize your risk as far as common sense will allow.
❑ Benefit from your own efficiency. If you succeed in completing the job in less time than was originally estimated, you, and not the client, are entitled to the additional profit which that implies.

A fixed fee for the job implies that the value of the outcome is seen by the client as exceeding the cost.

Share the attitude of the engineer who tapped the machine with his hammer to get it going after breakdown. Be prepared to charge a cent for the blow and $999.99 for knowing where to strike.

Don't be paranoid, but be aware that in a fixed-fee situation there is every inducement for the client to try to load the job and get your part of your services for free. Your main aim must be to protect your interests while winning business.

Daily fee rate

This is almost the reverse situation, and is the one preferred by most consultants. Here the client carries the risk. If the job is extended you simply keep on billing for time spent serving the client. A major reason for clients suspecting that the consultant is hell-bent on building dependence is that most are happy to go on billing from here to bankruptcy. If your client is happy with a standard *per diem* arrangement you are entitled to be happy too, but it is your responsibility to provide the client, through your proposal, with a realistic assessment of how long the job will take and the total likely cost.

You are not carrying the risk. If your efficiency is such that the job is completed early the client is entitled to benefit. Make sure, however, that if you are able to achieve the outcome in a shorter time than was initially estimated, the client knows what a bargain they have got and responds accordingly when asked for referrals.

A *per diem* rate is normally exclusive of expenses and so the client is carrying the risk there also. To minimize that risk, I offer the client the facility of making any hotel and travel bookings direct. This gives them control of the expenditure and enables them to take advantage of any discounts which their company normally enjoys. It also protects my cash flow, because when they book, they pay direct.

Performance contract

Recent research shows that approximately 12 per cent of assignments in the UK are now carried out on a performance basis. That is, the consultant is paid a share of the savings or additional profits which are made as a result of the intervention. Twelve per cent may not seem a lot, but only two years earlier the number would have been in low single figures and limited to specialist interventions such as energy conservation. The US level of assignments worked on this basis last year was estimated to have exceeded 70 per cent of all work. In matters of business much of the world tends to follow the US model, so it is important that all consultants and other professionals think carefully about how performance contracts work.

If you are invited to carry out work on a performance basis, the first thing you need to consider is your personal attitude to such an arrangement. Are you to be paid for results, or is it your 'best efforts' and your knowledge that justify your fees? This is not a silly question. When the patient dies under the knife, the surgeon expects to be paid for exercising their skill to the utmost. You are entitled to the reach the same conclusion if you see yourself as a 'business surgeon'. You may, however, take the view that in the world of business everyone should ultimately be paid against results. If this is your view you will welcome the performance contract.

Guidelines for assessing any performance contract

❑ Is such a contract consistent with your image and values?
❑ Is the desired outcome feasible?
❑ Can the outcome be attained with the specific resources that you can bring to bear? Can you control the outcome?
❑ Is the value of the outcome sufficient that your share of savings or profit will compensate you for the risk (and the cash-flow problems which may result from waiting for results)?
❑ Does a mutually acceptable and infallible process exist for measuring the outcome?
❑ Is the outcome clear and unambiguous?
❑ Will you enjoy sufficient income in the early stages of the assignment to enable you to resource it effectively?
❑ Do you have a clear and binding contract?

Unless the answer to all of the above is positive, it would be unwise to enter into a performance contract, but it is an area of the market which will grow and it has obvious attractions to the client. You may have little alternative at some point in the future other than to reduce substantially your market opportunities or seek performance-related payments. At least when that time comes you will not be taken by surprise. Take heart, the rewards can be enormous. A colleague of mine who works on a performance basis is currently involved in an assignment which, if it is successful, will pay him $3 million in a single and immediate payment. Of course, if he fails he gets nothing other than agreed expenses, but he has taken on the job not in a flush of careless optimism, but as a result of a detailed analysis based on the above guidelines.

If you undertake more 'normal' performance contracts, what can you expect to earn? Suppose that you are able to introduce into your client's business a process which will lead to substantial savings. You have thought it through and you are confident of the outcome. You may reasonably ask for:

❑ An upfront payment to meet your estimated expenses while working on the project.
❑ Reasonable payments 'on account' during the intervention.
❑ 30 per cent of savings made in the first year.
❑ 25 per cent of savings made in year two.
❑ 20 per cent of savings in year three.

That can be a great deal of money, which gives you the security of ongoing income for a period which is at least a fair part of the total during which the client is enjoying the benefits of your labour.

If the client complains about your fee

If during or at the end of an assignment the client complains about the level of your fee, the chances are that, somewhere along the line, you have done a poor job of communicating.

To be confident that you have communicated effectively, **always**:

❑ Agree specific and measurable outcomes for your work.
❑ Work to a contract.
❑ Explain precisely what your fees cover and what they do not.
❑ Produce detailed, accurate and signed invoices at agreed intervals.
❑ Keep your client informed of progress as it happens.
❑ Advise your client of extra expense before incurring it.
❑ Seek opportunities to boost the image of your client within their organization during the assignment.
❑ Create added value without giving your services for free by keeping your client informed of relevant external and internal information which you come across during the assignment.
❑ Build a trusting relationship with your client by never doing anything in their company without their knowledge.

Business terms and conditions

Fees for consultancy vary at least as widely as the value given and there is no necessary correlation. It is possible to establish your fee level by licking your finger, holding it in the breeze and trying to guess what the market will stand. It is possible, but it is unprofessional. A full assessment based on the interrelation between the value of what you have to offer, the cost to you of doing business and the volume of business which your best estimate indicates that you will enjoy is justified and necessary.

Few consultants are **always** able to do business in only one way. Most need to be flexible in line with the client's need and expectation and the job to be done.

It is highly desirable for you to establish your own terms and conditions with the intention of working to them on every contract where they are acceptable to the client. Where they are not, your negotiating skills come into play. Be careful, however, not to negotiate overgenerously when it comes to payment terms. Tardy cash flow is the principal cause of business failure.

Global research suggests that monthly invoicing appears to be the norm for more than two-thirds of consultants, while only 7 per cent invoice fortnightly, weekly or in advance. I shall have more to say about this. Never forget that monthly invoicing does not automatically lead to payment within the agreed terms. You owe it to yourself to ensure that payment of your fees is regular and reliable.

ESTABLISHING YOUR FEE LEVEL — SUMMARY AND WORKSHEET

1. Annual salary requirement/261 = daily labour rate
    Daily labour rate: $

2. Estimate number of days to be billed each month:
           x 12 = total billing days per year
    (Difference between this figure and 261 **must** be recouped as overhead)

3. Estimate overheads:

Item	Monthly cost	Yearly cost
Totals		

Annual overhead divided by estimated days billed = daily overhead recovery rate
DORR = $

4. Add DORR and daily labour rate $

5. Add **profit** requirement $

Soap Box – The mission thing

Mission statements are essential. They are useless, however, if they are vague collections of pretty words, full of business school speak and warm fuzzies which are framed, stuck on the wall and forgotten.

The mission statement is an important operational tool which ought to be in the mind of every employee, manager and director every day. To be used the mission must:

❑ Remind us and others of the business in which we operate in terms of customer or client benefits.

❑ Differentiate us from the herd and make it clear to the customer why they should come to us first and always.

❑ Make it clear to all stakeholders how they may be expected to be treated and how we treat each other.

❑ Enable us to make unsupervised decisions day by day in the absolute confidence that they are in line with the company strategy and its values.

❑ Provide the challenge which adds the spice to business life and leads to sustained peak performance.

If you are a strategic consultant, are you up to the implicit challenge of ensuring that, for your clients, the mission is lived?

7

The Contract

NO WORK OF ANY SIGNIFICANCE – AND AT OUR DAILY RATES ALL WORK is of significance – should be undertaken without a contract. Let me make myself clear from the start. A contract is not something on the basis of which you can successfully sue clients. To take your clients to court, whatever the provocation, is liable to damage you more than them. But a contract is more than useful, it is essential. It fulfils a key role in the process of communication which is vital to successful professional practice. Some of the uses of a contract may surprise you a little, so I shall tell you about those that I see as being the most important before I tell you how you can draw up a contract and what it should always contain.

Uses of the contract

The basic use of a contract is self-evident: it states what you are bound to do and what you are entitled to receive. It does a great deal more and what it does says much for your professional status.

The fact that you always insist on a contract immediately identifies you as a serious professional. It adds to your status, and your ability to attract and retain business is based firmly on your status.

When a client is dealing with you for the first time, the use of a contract helps to remove both anxiety and euphoria and gives you both a firm foundation on which to build a relationship.

Warren Bennis once said that business relationships are not founded on well-meaning exhortations to trust each other. They are based on doing things together and discovering that you can trust each other when there is a job to be done. By giving both parties to the agreement a sound indication of what is to be done together, the contract accelerates the process of building trust. The early period of uncertainty is clarified and that creates mutual confidence, while the sharing of information and knowledge develops rapport.

Imagine if you would a group of university students. Final examinations are approaching and for some the cold realization is beginning to dawn that the good times of the recent past may have to be paid for in the examination room. There is a sense of something greater than just urgency and expectation in the air, more quiet desperation. Now suppose that a kindly professor approaches the group and suggests that he can help. He is prepared to conduct additional tutorials which will help them to identify and correct any weaknesses before they face the exam papers. Will they be grateful? Will they vow to attend any such sessions? You can bet on it. They give their verbal assurances that they will be there whenever the tutorials are conducted. In due course our kindly professor announces that arrangements have been made. The tutorials will be held at his rooms at six in the morning each day for the three weeks prior to the examination. How many of those who so enthusiastically indicated their intention to take part will actually arrive? The experiment has been done and repeated. The turnout averages a little over 10 per cent. Very few of this small initial turnout will stay the course and attend at six each morning for the duration.

Now suppose that with another group the professor asks them to sign to say that they will attend and makes the time equally antisocial. How many will turn up? How many will stay? The answer to the first question is somewhere between 70 and 85 per cent and of those who start the course more than 90 per cent complete it in practice. The only changed variable is the requirement for a signature. That is why in US companies staff are often asked to sign the corporate mission. Even knowing that the 'document' has no power in law makes no discernable difference. Most of us place great store by our signature. When we sign on the line, we take our obligations seriously. That makes the contract of value even when we regard it as not being enforceable.

The contract also puts you, the professional, into a position of leadership. The fact that you are, from the beginning, dictating the conditions of business by insisting on and providing a contract creates the basis of influence on which you will have to build to ensure that your client receives optimal value from hiring you.

As a selling tool the contract has few equals. Most people who feel uncomfortable about selling manage to listen effectively, ask intelligent questions, present their solution and handle client objections without great difficulty. Why then do they not win the contract? Mainly because the aspect of selling which causes them most concern is closing the sale. The fact that you have a contract eases that problem considerably. At the end of a discussion with a prospective client, what could be more appropriate than to explain that you always work to a simple contract and that you would be happy to draw one up and have it ready for their checking and sig-nature the next day? If you have built the right relationship, there is an excellent chance that the client will take out their diary and arrange a time for the next meeting. In this case you know that it would be unwise to make any further selling effort. The sooner you can break off the meeting and leave the client to reinforce in their own mind their reasons for hiring you, the better. If, on the other hand, the client indicates that they are not ready to look at a contract yet, you know that you still have some selling to do.

That selling will be doubly easy for you because it is reasonable for you to explore where you have failed to satisfy the client of the need for your services. The end of the selling process is no longer the emotion-ridden act of reaching an agreement, but the less loaded situation of checking a contract.

Writing a contract

There are excellent books available on how to write contracts, some of the best of which include software, so I will not try to cover material which is readily available elsewhere. What I propose doing is to tell you:

❏ What constitutes a contract.
❏ How to put together a contract.
❏ How to get it checked economically.
❏ What you should include as the minimum.

What is a contract?

Let me warn you, I am not a lawyer and what I say is no more than a layperson's interpretation of what I have been told, what I have read and done without problems arising. Since I admonish you to regard the contract as a matter of clear communication rather than a legal document, a layperson's interpretation is appropriate and sufficient.

A contract is any agreement, verbal or written, explicit or implied, between individuals or legal entities such as businesses. Since a contract may be verbal and its terms may be implied, it is reasonable to deduce that it does not have to be signed. For our purposes, however, a contract must be written to fulfil its communication function and should be signed for the psychological reasons outlined above.

No contract needs to be complex for our needs. The simpler you make it, the better it will communicate. An ideal place to start is with a simple letter of agreement drawn up in duplicate which both parties sign.

Where possible, follow the guideline of 'keep it simple and straightforward' and construct a letter which includes the following:

❏ What you will do and provide.

❏ What your client has agreed to provide to enable you to do the work.

❏ How much, how and when you will be paid.

❏ Who owns the outcome(s) of your work.

❏ Circumstances under which the contract can be assigned by either of you to third parties.

Let me explain the above in case I have failed to make my meaning crystal clear.

What you will do

This will be a brief outline of the service which you undertake to supply. It may include specific agreed outputs and, where appropriate, dates for completion. It will not describe **how** the work is to be done any more than the proposal would. This is your undertaking to complete work. It is not a recipe.

What your client will provide

If your client has agreed to provide, say, secretarial assistance, or data, or the output of previous work, your contract should specify that input as clearly as possible. It should make clear that your ability to fulfil your responsibility under the contract is contingent on you receiving the promised support as you require it.

How much and when you will be paid

Do not rely on your standard terms and conditions of business as an assurance that you will be paid on time. Your client will have their own and those employees responsible for checking and passing your invoices will work to their normal routine unless your client instructs them otherwise. Only a contract is likely to have enough emotional force to ensure that the instruction is passed on. If any upfront payments are agreed, specify them and make it clear that failure to make a payment when due will delay the project.

Who owns the outcome of your work

If you write a training course, or design a psychometric test, or conduct a major market survey as part of the assignment, it is important to know whether you are free to use those outputs on some future occasion. With training programs in particular it is essential that you have worked out with your client whether their own staff can take over and conduct the training in your stead. If they can, the paragraph about payment above will show how you will continue to be compensated for your work.

Circumstances under which the contract can be assigned
As a general rule, I advise that all agreements include a statement that they cannot be assigned to any third party without the consent in writing of both parties. This means that your client cannot, without your permission, hand your assignment to any other consultant or to a member of their staff once they have sufficient information on the 'how'. It also means that you cannot subcontract to a colleague whom the client has not met and approved. That way you are both protected and the quality of the intervention is secured. If you want to be really legalistic, you may wish to include a release clause to cover the contingency of either of you dying during the assignment.

Drafting a 'proper' contract

There may be occasions when for the sake of appearances you need to produce a contract that has all the hallmarks of a 'proper' legal document, 'hereinafters', Latin phrases and all. If you do, resist the temptation to go running to your attorney. To do that prematurely may be ineffective and will certainly be expensive. I am not suggesting that lawyers overcharge, but it is unlikely that you will be able to explain exactly what you require and against vague instructions a lawyer can only do their expensive best. That will probably mean that several drafts are produced before you have the document you want and each draft must be paid for. Save some cash by producing the early drafts yourself.

Sit down with a pad and copies of old contracts. Write, cut and paste until you have something which seems to meet your needs.

When you are satisfied with the outcome, take the fruits of your endeavour to a solicitor, tell them why you need a more formal contract and ask them to answer two questions;

'Have I protected myself adequately with this document for the purpose which I have explained?'
'Is there anything else which in your opinion I should do?'

If your reasons for wanting a 'posh' contract are valid, the answers to the above will be well worth the solicitor's relatively modest fee and you will almost certainly end up with a better contract than many solicitors could produce from scratch with limited understanding of the need.

Much of what you will want in a contract will be in the form of a standard agreement. It is sensible, therefore, to have a master copy which you can amend ready in your computer.

When you cannot provide the contract

There are two main situations where you cannot provide the contract and it may be useful for me to comment briefly on both.

If your client is a major corporation there will be a rule that the employed legal officers always write any contract which executives sign. This is potentially a problem to you if the legal department has limited understanding of exactly what it is you are expected to do. Sometimes they write a paragraph which technically obliges you to perform something which is not in your power.

For example, you may have an assignment in which you are to assist your client to prepare for assessment for the quality standard ISO9000. Since this is a matter of third-party accreditation, you can at most only help to ensure that generally acceptable manuals and processes are in place – you cannot guarantee accreditation. If you are offered a contract which indicates that you will enable the client to achieve the standard, look carefully at the wording and get it changed to reflect what you are actually able to do or you may find yourself working for very much longer than you anticipated for no additional fee. You can also bet that any legal department will tend to underemphasize its own company's obligations and responsibilities. Make sure that these are completely defined before you sign.

Any variation in the corporation's standard terms and conditions which have been agreed may also be omitted, so check that the contract states fully what has been agreed about payments and ownership of outputs. Finally, make sure that your client is empowered to sign on behalf of the corporation or, if not, make sure that you at least touch base with the person who is. That person may have concerns which could lead to delays.

A second situation is the more simple one where an unsophisticated client tells you that they either do not need, or do not like, contracts. My response in such a case, assuming that I had no concerns about doing business with the client, would be to say:

'Fine, I will draw up simple terms of reference and let you have a copy.'

The 'terms of reference' will, of course, contain the same information as the contract. Terms of reference, for all its clumsiness as a phrase, is less threatening to some potential clients than the more legal-sounding 'contract'. Whether you have your client sign a copy to approve them is a matter of judgement in these circumstances. From a legal point of view I am told that the signature is irrelevant if the letter is accepted, but you still have the psychological pressure of a signature to consider.

Collecting your cash

Collecting money owing to you late is not as bad as not collecting it at all, but it is still bad and usually avoidable. Never forget that more companies are forced to stop trading because of cash-flow problems than for any other reason, and make a firm resolve that your practice is not going to go 'belly up' for want of timely cash.

If you are a 'one-man band' or a small practice it is easy for a client to believe that they could, at a pinch, do without your services more readily than you could do without their business. The market is unlikely to see what you do as being absolutely essential to their survival. Many will believe that you need them more than they need you and so if anyone is going to have to wait for their money, clients may see themselves as doing least damage to their own business by making you wait.

This means that you have to be doubly vigilant and doubly resourceful.

When you are considering working for a client for the first time, insist on a formal contract and ensure that the client fully understands and agrees to the terms of payment which are specified. This way you can avoid many collection problems. If you work to a signed contract you have the advantage that people tend to remember more clearly what they have agreed. If you are, for whatever reason, working to an unsigned, terms of reference style of document, go through it even more carefully with your client. Be as sure as you can be that it is understood.

Keep your client informed of every success as it happens during an assignment. A delighted client is more likely to want to ensure that you at least get paid on time. If you are working in a large organization, find out who has the responsibility for checking and approving invoices. If the arrangement to pay you varies in any way from the company's standard arrangement, make sure that all the relevant people know of your special arrangement. All major corporations have processes in place to 'walk an invoice through the system' and emerge at the other end with a signed cheque. Make an early opportunity as part of the process of getting to know the detail of how your client organization functions to find out about that system; but be discreet, you don't want a client to think that you are excessively concerned.

You may have to ask how they would ensure continuity of supply in the event of a non-payment to a key supplier. You may have to ask how they deal with a situation where a key supplier is

threatened by cash-flow problems and it is in the company's interest to accelerate payment to keep the supplier in business.
Whatever you have to do, do it. It is important.

Ensure that any progress payments which you are due to
receive are paid on a specific date rather than something vague
like 'the third week of the month', and ensure that every invoice
which you issue carries the date when payment is due. The
invoice should read 'payment due on 3 January 1998' and not
some vague and usually ignored message such as 'payment terms
14 days nett'.

The date is meaningful on its own to the most cursory of
glances. To make sense of '14 days' you need to look at the date
of the invoice. Most people just will not bother. While we are on
the subject of invoices, sign yours. The fact that your invoice bears
a signature differentiates it from the others from the moment it is
drawn from the envelope. It implies that the charges have been
checked and approved by someone in authority. That gives
authority to the invoice. You are, of course, wise to check thoroughly every invoice you issue. Any inaccuracy is grasped joyfully
as a reason to delay payment, as is any uncertainty about what is
being charged for. Make sure that your invoices specify the service
in sufficient detail.

Recent research suggests that a touch of colour helps invoices
to move more quickly through the system. If your capability is
limited, test what a highlighter passed over the due date can
achieve.

Limit your exposure where you can. Ask for advance payments
to fund the resourcing of the project. It is often true that the early
stages of an assignment involve the consultant in high expense.
Ask your client to bear that expense. Most will if asked. Few, if
any, will volunteer. Try to avoid making payments to third parties
on behalf of your client. Have the client book your hotel and have
your bill sent direct. It is no problem for the client. They probably will not pay the hotel any more quickly than they would have
paid you. The difference is that it is the hotel that waits.

If you have any serious doubt about the speed at which you are to be paid, withhold some vital information until the money you are owed is in your bank. Never continue providing a service to a client when payments are overdue. You don't have to be obnoxious about it. Just politely point out that your account has been overlooked and that you will be able to restart work as soon as your bank advises that payment has been received.

Any time that payment is slow, use it as an opportunity to evaluate the client and the quality of your service to them. They may be withholding payment because they are unsure that they are receiving value. Again, if in doubt, communicate.

Summary

Your work
- ❏ Are you achieving agreed goals to schedule?
- ❏ Are you maintaining good communication with your client?
- ❏ Is your work moving in a direction which is unexpected and potentially threatening to your client?
- ❏ Have you allowed yourself to be diverted into any activities which are not central to your client's needs?

Your client situation
- ❏ Is there any reason to believe that there may be a personality conflict growing between you and your client or within the client organization?
- ❏ Is the client developing unrealistic expectations?
- ❏ Is the client fully appreciating the value of your services?
- ❏ Are there signs of new and critical problems in the client organization?
- ❏ Have there been any signs of lack of interest in, or lack of commitment to, your project by influential client management team members?
- ❏ Is there a danger that the client suspects that time which you necessarily spend off their premises is time spent off the job?

If there is any problem – communicate.

Guidelines for collecting your cash
- ❑ Work to a contract – always.
- ❑ Keep your client informed and delighted.
- ❑ Understand the client's system of payment.
- ❑ Agree and insist on specific payment dates.
- ❑ Use actual payment dates on invoices.
- ❑ Check invoices carefully for accuracy.
- ❑ Detail services provided.
- ❑ Sign your invoices.
- ❑ Limit your exposure.
- ❑ Understand the client's system and people.
- ❑ If you still experience problems: **withhold key inputs when payment is due until the cash is in your bank. If payment is late – stop working.**

SOAP BOX – THE VISION AND VALUES THING

As with mission statements, so with the vision. The vision is nothing if it is no more than a fine-sounding peroration from the chairman captured for all time, and ignored by all except visiting consultants as it graces the wall of the reception area. The vision must be an ongoing inspiration to every employee which will get them to the barricades whenever the going gets tough. It must speak, therefore, about the things which people care about – and what people care about most is the values they hold.

Values should be taken as seriously as the marketing strategy and it is possible to use similar tools to 'identify, create and satisfy stakeholder values to create prosperity'. The next time your client seems to be hell bent on rewriting the same old tired clichés in the same old business school speak, consider completing a comparative/competitive analysis of employee values and get those which emerge as key aspirations written boldly into an inspirational vision statement. Have it communicated with honesty and impact and stand back to watch your reputation and your client's fortunes soar.

Part II

Marketing Your Practice

8

Tactical Marketing

HAVING SPENT MUCH OF MY WORKING LIFE AS AN INTERNATIONAL marketing strategist, I am completely committed to the concept of strategic planning. But this chapter is about tactics, not strategy, and my concern is with things for you to do, today or tomorrow, to build your business. We must balance the longer perspective with ways of putting some bread on the table today.

The strategic implications remain – they underpin everything, but as far as this book is concerned they can be expressed in a few words.

Your professional practice will grow as your personal reputation and status grow. The relationship will not be linear, but logarithmic: the time will come when your business growth opportunities increase at a rate far in excess of any accretion of fame. Some reading this page will reach that happy condition very quickly. For others, myself included, it takes a considerable amount of time and consistent effort.

You have an advantage over me. We can both learn from my mistakes, but I had to make them first.

Objectives

I always feel more comfortable in business situations if objectives are clearly stated and do not have to be deduced, so please bear with me for a few pages while I spell out where we are going.

On completion of this chapter you will have selected one or more low-cost tactics which have been proven to build profitable business in the real world and are consistent with your personal style. You will also have committed yourself to put your chosen tactics into immediate effect by making your name known so that clients come to you for your services and, in the early stages of your professional career, are exceptionally receptive when you go to them.

In short, the purpose of this chapter is to make you just a little bit famous.

Background

Some interesting and consistent data has emerged from careful research over the last 20 years concerning the marketing tactics of the low earners in the profession:

❑ They tend to do things which they hate, like cold canvassing by personal call or telephone.
❑ They spend considerable sums on mailings of expensive brochures.
❑ They do very little of what the high earners do almost all of the time.
❑ They say that what they do has very little effect on their business, other than to raise costs and personal stress.
❑ They continue to do what they have always done, because, they say, they know nothing else to do.

Consider high earners. Some, a very small number, do some of the things that the low earners do, but they do more. They are proactive in building their status and reputation and it is from these latter activities that the bulk of their earnings comes.

Image building and reputation

You are the product you sell and your product's brand image is entirely a function of how you are perceived. That is why your personal reputation and image are so important and why we need now to look at the tactical approach in detail.

The lecture circuit

How do you feel about a diet of rubber chicken?

That is how you are likely to be fed if you become a professional speaker. But it is still worth doing, because few things are so powerful in building your reputation at such little cost in money or in effort. In fact, when you are in demand as a speaker, you may find that you need no other source of income.

There are more than 4000 opportunities every week to give a talk somewhere in the UK. There are many more in the US. One estimate suggests between 9000 and 10,000. Secretaries are constantly on the lookout for people who have something to say. Those who can say it articulately with a little spice of humour are seen as being a gift from the gods.

With so many opportunities to perform you can and must be selective. When you decide that it would be useful to talk to a particular audience you need to know if they have an association. Two directories from your local library will be of immense value, both published by CBD Research:

❑ *The Directory of British Associations*
❑ *Councils, Committees and Boards.*

In North America:

❑ *Gales Encyclopaedia of Associations*
❑ *The National Trade and Professional Associations Directory of the United States and Canada.*

Other countries have similar publications. Each contains a gold-mine of information including the name of the appropriate contact, so you can write person to person and not have to worry about on whose desk your letter may finally arrive.

When you write offering yourself as a speaker, the information needed will be:

❏ Why you feel that what you have to say will be of interest to their members.
❏ The benefits to them of hearing your presentation.
❏ The unique things that you have to say. (More about this later, when I may appear to contradict myself.)
❏ The length of your speech.
❏ Where you are prepared to travel.
❏ Special considerations, including your fee and your expectations with regard to expenses.

Please be absolutely clear about the business of the fee. Professionals never speak for free and you need to promote a hard-nosed professional image at all times.

But suppose that you regard a certain group as being of such enormous potential value to you as a future source of business that you would be happy to speak to them if you had to pay! Am I saying that you would now pass up the opportunity for the sake of a few bucks?

The answer is 'no'. You speak – without payment if necessary – but you take the initiative. First, you make clear to them the enormous fees which your talk normally commands with ease. Second, you tell them how much you admire their organization and how you share their goals. (Make sure that you know what their goals are by telephoning to enquire about membership, asking what the association is seeking to achieve.) Third, make it clear that you are so enamoured of their aims that you would like to donate your fee to their funds, and so will not be issuing an invoice.

This harmless subterfuge will almost certainly ensure you a

warm and favourable reception. The secretary will find it impossible to resist telling the chairman how they persuaded a highly paid speaker to appear for nothing. The chairman will find it equally hard to avoid mentioning in their introduction how the association has engineered such a coup. It is highly possible that the announcement of the meeting also carried this important piece of information. You will have an eager and enthusiastic audience.

Your objective is simple. You want to talk entertainingly for the agreed length of time so that you appear to be intelligent, articulate and well informed about something that your audience finds interesting and useful enough to give up an evening's drinking or time with the family to hear. This is less difficult than it sounds.

The secret is to tell them what they want to hear and confirm them in their beliefs. If you can do so by bringing to their attention some new findings which support their views, they will love you for it. But be careful not to be too highbrow about new information. Although you are the fount of all wisdom in your chosen area, you want to appear approachable so that those who have the greatest interest in your subject feel relaxed about talking to you after the meeting. This way you have an excellent chance of meeting the one person in eleven that research suggests will be looking for an opportunity to become your client.

As for the speech, that part is easy. Although many famous speakers have maintained highly successful and lucrative careers on the back of one speech, I suggest you have two. For normal lunch or evening meetings one should be 25 and the other 40 minutes in length.

Without overemphasizing the point, each speech should make it clear that you have gained your expertise through working as a consultant. This simple and modest indication that you are prepared to accept fee-earning assignments can be backed up by weaving into your talk examples of your consulting experiences and the data that you and you alone have available. You do not, of course, offer any information which could be construed as being of a client confidential nature, but if you can indicate the sharing of prepublication information, so much the better. Here are three rules for the content of the speech:

❑ It should, in the interests of time management, be sufficiently general to be capable of being recycled to different audiences without onerous additional work.
❑ It must be sufficiently useful to be interesting, but it should not be so useful that it can have any worthwhile application without further recourse to you, the expert.
❑ It is wise that it should, to a major degree, reinforce the views and experience of your audience. This appears to fly in the face of offering them something unique.

But the research evidence is clear. Audiences like to believe that they are being offered information which is new, exciting and known to very few. What they like to hear, however, is something which will enable them to nod their heads approvingly and think:

'That's exactly what I've always thought. Nice to have it confirmed by an expert. I must get a word with him afterwards and tell him about my...'

That is how clients are born.

You may find that you are so well received that you are building a paid speaking practice. If so, target your marketing and content on those that pay. Some pay very well. Corporations pay handsomely for the right person. National and international conferences often pay well. National trade and professional associations usually pay something, but local branches seldom have a budget for anything more than that 'rubber chicken' dinner.

Trade nights for distributors can be a very useful source of income. Car dealerships, for example, have been known to pay $400 for an amusing, instructive 30 minutes which is supportive of what they are trying to achieve. It is not unknown for the speaker who is light-footed and able to resist the free booze to fit in more than one session in an evening.

Whenever you give a public talk, be sure that those who miss the opportunity to speak to you at the meeting know where to find you afterwards. This is not just a matter of handing out business cards. Create and distribute something of interest which they will keep, and to which they will refer. The more novel or useful the information, the longer life it will have.

My preference is for some useful data or formula, but an American colleague of mine hands out a little mathematical game which no one ever seems to throw away. Some have even been known, years later, to call to be reminded of just how it works. Those calls frequently turn into assignments.

Remember that at a meeting many will be without briefcases, so do not dish out copies of a glossy full-size brochure which they will clutch in increasingly moist hands as the evening progresses, waiting for an opportunity to dump it. Rather, have your handout produced on A4 folded to fit into a breast pocket or handbag. Not only will there be more inclination to keep it, but when it reemerges as pockets or handbags are cleared (immediately or days later according to the habits of the listener), it will serve as a potent reinforcer both of your message and of the skill with which you articulated it.

Be careful to ensure that your handout has your address and telephone number and an invitation to people to contact you for further information or to express their views. Always leave potential clients with a reason to want to contact you.

If you feel that the rubber chicken circuit is one that you would like to join, you can quickly be in business for the cost of a few stamps.

If you like the idea but doubt your skills, look in the telephone book and see if you have a local branch of Toastmasters. That way you could have fun and company while polishing your performance.

If you have real talent there is no need to do more than offer yourself as a paid speaker. The life is an exciting one which, at the higher levels, is often as replete with luxury as it is with rubber chicken. American readers who are really top-notch performers should try to get themselves on the books of someone like Dottie Waters, who has a life-time experience of placing top-class speakers. Everyone, anywhere in the world, who has a hankering to stand up and talk to business audiences should read her global bestseller, *Talk and Grow Rich*.

Professional meetings

The consultant must be prepared to get out and be seen in the business community. Your name must be the one that comes to mind when prospective clients are trying to identify a professional adviser. People are lazy. You will find that if your name is the one the client knows there is a better than even chance that when they invite you to visit and discuss their needs no other name will be in the frame.

Professional meetings are an excellent opportunity to be seen in a positive light if you approach them systematically. The important thing is to be noticed by those who can and will buy your services. This suggests to me that it is better in general to attend meetings of institutes and associations which are not those of your profession. When you attend a meeting of the Institute of Management Consultants, and I hope that you will, the purpose is quite different from that of participating in, say, a meeting of the Institute of Directors.

Among your professional peers you may expect an excellent social and educational opportunity in which you can share information and ideas without needing to feel that you have to outperform the opposition. Let's face it, they are all opposition and although their company may well be pleasant and even inspiring, the likelihood of any other consultant's hiring you is limited.

With potential clients the objective and therefore the role are quite different. Now you are marketing yourself, which means that you need to be noticed. What is more important, you need to attract members' favourable attention, which means that you need to be noticed for the right reasons. You require a tactical plan.

Get there early. A *prima donna* entrance after the speaker has started is a display of appalling manners which impresses no one, but there is a very practical reason to get there early. You need to select your seat.

Research indicates that people take most notice of those whom they can see as well as hear. They also are most inclined to look at those whom they can see with least effort. You need, therefore, to sit near to the front of the room where you will seen by the majority of the group without their having to turn and crane their necks. Research also indicates, though I am at a loss to say why, that the left-hand side of the room is better for the purpose of being seen than the right.

Discipline yourself to speak briefly and cogently no more than twice during the meeting. Resist the temptation to speak for longer than the guest, make your point clearly and briefly and sit down.

During the interval, or as the meeting breaks up and attendees socialize, take up a central position where people who would like to pursue the point you made will find you easily. If there is a bar, try to have a drink in your hand quickly – it does not help to be seen as trying to get someone to buy you a drink. Be single minded: you are there to attract potential buyers of your services. Identify and shrug off the professional citizens and fellow consultants who are always in evidence and attend to the potential clients.

I strongly recommend that you are selective in the meetings you choose to attend. Find organizations which, in addition to providing opportunities to meet potential clients, have purposes which you genuinely share. Once a member, be an active member and participate fully in the activities. Join committees and make a real contribution. I find that active membership of the appropriate organizations gives me an additional benefit which is worth a great deal in saving time and money.

I belong to a society where my personal development is facilitated by constantly hearing first-class speakers from disciplines different from, but related to, mine. At their meetings I am on a fast-track learning curve at almost no cost, while I market myself by seeking and expressing the tie-in between my major discipline and the proceedings of the society.

It is not difficult to do. Give it some thought.

Directory listings

No one other than a directory advertising space salesperson is likely to try to persuade you that many prospective clients seek professional help by sifting through a directory, but if only one does and you are not listed, your chances of that fee have just dropped from slim to zero.

Listing in telephone directories is straightforward. Many are free, although some will only list you if you have a business line. If you work from home and use your ordinary domestic telephone line, they do not want to know.

More important, because the potential for business opportunities is greater, is to ensure that you have an entry in directories published by trade, professional or business associations for the convenience of their members. If you think that it would be useful for you to be known to the Antediluvian Society of Bottom Knockers, it makes sense to try to be listed in their directory. Of the thousands which are published, approximately half are happy to list you without payment as a direct service to their members. For the cost of a postage stamp you can make yourself accessible. The other half either make a small charge or, more commonly, restrict entry to those who have taken full or associate membership.

You can jostle the big six by being listed in *Gales Directory of Consultants* or, by joining one of the growing number of professional bodies, you can be listed as a member.

Publish and be known

Publishing your own newsletter keeps your name in front of prospective clients. If a business regularly receives your newsletter it is perfectly possible that you are the only consultant they know by name. People like dealing with people they think they know. That is why 25,000 newsletters are currently published in the US.

In the UK the number is smaller, but so successful is the news-letter as a marketing tool that the total of publications is growing almost day by day. So if this is an area where you have something worthwhile to contribute, now is the time to get in on the act.

Although the majority of newsletters are used as promotional material and are distributed free, some 40 per cent are supplied on a subscription basis. If the content is right, prices can be high. Publishing a successful newsletter will promote your business at relatively low cost. Publishing a newsletter so valued that people will pay to read it will promote your business while it provides you with a source of income. So profitable has the market for news-letters become in the US that companies now exist which will write and distribute your publication for a fee. All that you have to do is to put your name to it and collect the excess income.

When you are tempted to mail a brochure to your prospects, it is worth your while to consider producing a newsletter instead. It may be a great deal less expensive. It will almost certainly be a great deal more effective.

An advantage of the newsletter as a form of promotion is that it insinuates a strong selling message without overt advertising. It says to the reader that here is someone who has valuable know-ledge. What is more, it implies that the knowledge you are imparting is not known to others. This raises you to the position of a guru. You may be well aware that the information you are pro-viding is freely available to many others, but the situation is precisely analogous to marketing. If you and your competition share a strength, but you are the only one to tell the world about it, then in the world's eyes you are uniquely qualified. If you pro-vide good, useful information in a newsletter, the world will see you as uniquely knowledgeable.

Newsletters are read. Let us imagine for a moment that you have invested in a glossy, beautifully produced, artistic brochure. Some $3000 to $4000 should produce something you can be proud of. You hire a mailing list and send out, say, three thousand. How many will be read?

If by 'read' we accept anything better than eight seconds of attention, the research suggests an encouraging 10 per cent, or 300. There is, however, a short window of opportunity during which the potential client is looking for consultancy support. If you hit it, fine – but what if you miss?

You cannot send out your brochure every month: the expense would be prohibitive and the potential clients' boredom threshold would quickly be breached. So you are dependent, when the need for your type of service arises, on the busy businessperson remembering your brochure and picking it out from the file.

Let us assess your chances. Research indicates that the average businessperson receives 90 to 110 pieces of junk mail a week. Let us assume that your beautiful brochure arrived one month ago. Let us further assume that it did its job and made an impression. One month and 400 mailing pieces later, what would you, on a common-sense basis, give for its chances of being remembered?

But did it even reach the decision maker? Half of the mail addressed to an executive is defined by somebody else as junk and is thrown out by them. Anyone who has telephoned to talk to a decision maker and has made the mistake of telling a secretary the reason for the call has experienced the response, 'Mr Brown would not be interested...'

How much easier is it for the decision to be made concerning Mr Brown's lack of interest when dealing not with an articulate and persuasive person, but with a piece of paper, be it never so glossy?

Of the 50 per cent that reach the executive to whom they are addressed, research indicates that a further 50 per cent are thrown away without a second glance. Of every 25 pieces left, 15 receive a quick glance and are then consigned to the wastepaper basket.

The remaining 10 per cent are treated with a little more respect: they get some attention. That is not to say that they are read. The average attention given is eight seconds. Given that by no means all executives are trained speed readers, that suggests that if some pieces are read in full others will get little more than the cursory attention necessary to establish that there is no cheque attached.

Compare this with the fate of a newsletter. The newsletter is not perceived as advertising but as information. It gets past the secretary. It then gets a brief glance from the executive and, depending on whether an item catches their attention, it may or may not be read. Assuming that it is not read there and then, what happens?

That depends on how easy you have made it for the recipient to treat it as a readily accessible resource.

If you have taken the minor trouble of having it drilled or punched so that it will fit into a standard two- or three-hole binder, there is every chance that it will be filed that way, kept on a shelf, readily available and read. If not, it will be consigned to the interior of a filing cabinet from which, since it is no longer visible, it may never emerge, even in time of need.

Thus far the advantages of the newsletter may be summarized as follows:

❑ A newsletter brings your name frequently under the eyes of your prospects, building your perceived image.
❑ It enables you to embed subtle selling messages in factual text, giving them enhanced credibility. 'In a recent consultancy assignment for a major global conglomerate...'
❑ It is far more likely to hit the executive's desk when that famous 'window of opportunity' is ajar.
❑ The newsletter is read.

If the content is of real interest and value, the recipient will actually look forward to its arrival, as I used to look forward to my comic papers a hundred years or so ago. If you are doubtful about whether or not you could charge a subscription, try this. Send out three issues *gratis* and make sure that they arrive on a specific day of the month. Write, but do not distribute, the next edition. If your telephone rings all day with hordes of angry readers demanding to know why their newsletter is late, send out the current number with a subscription form attached.

There are other advantages. The newsletter plays a major role in winning referrals. The regularity with which image-building information about your activities is brought to the notice of clients past and present reinforces their confidence in their decision to hire your services and reduces the perceived risk in recommending you to others.

If you want to start small, limit your newsletter to what the title implies. Send an occasional letter to contacts and clients with news of your recent achievements and the recognition which you have earned. People love to attach themselves to success. If you are good at what you do and achieve interesting and profitable results for your clients, find some means of telling the world.

Journalist for the day

Howard Shenson used to recommend another, rather subtle, use of your newsletter. You can use it as a means of getting to see people you would have difficulty meeting under normal circumstances. If you were to telephone the Chairman of Megaconglom Inc, the world's supreme widget makers, you may find that he does not talk to consultants because he employs people to do that for him. He does, however, talk to journalists. A call in which you introduce yourself as the editor of your publication, and in which you indicate that you are writing a piece on the widget industry and are seeking to interview the top three opinion leaders in the world of widgets, is likely to get a positive response. You may even be given lunch.

Ethics, good taste and common sense demand, however, that you act as a journalist and not as a consultant.

Conduct your interview. Draft your article and send a copy to the chairman for verification that he is happy that you quote him as indicated. After publication, send 20 copies and a brief thank-you note.

It is amazing that even people at the highest level still get a kick out of seeing their names in print. There is every chance that the chairman will mark a passage in each of the 20 copies that you have sent him and distribute your newsletter for you to 20 important people. If some of those people are widget manufacturers whom you somehow failed to interview, it is highly possible that they will contact you to enlighten you that they are among the industry's brightest and best, and that they have a point of view which has not been adequately represented. You will either know how to exploit this situation, or you should have serious doubts about your future as an entrepreneur.

Getting your newsletter into circulation

Decide on the style, content and budget. And, with budget as the determining factor, either send the first edition to the 200 to 500 people whom you already know in business, or rent a mailing list and widen your market.

To rent a mailing list you would be wise to use a broker. There are tens of thousands of mailing lists, some of them so precisely targeted that if you wish to mail to all newsagents, who formerly worked in the circus, have lost one or more limbs and now live or work in coastal towns, you almost certainly can. What you almost certainly cannot do unaided is to find the appropriate list. A broker not only can, but must – their future business depends on it. What is more, you do not pay the broker for their services. The list supplier does that and, since the owner of the list will not pass on to you any discount as a result of saving the broker's fee, you have everything to gain and nothing to lose by using the services of a professional. In the UK brokers are required to be registered under the Data Protection Act. The Act places responsibilities on the company which ensure that the registered firm is likely to use only reputable suppliers of lists.

It is wise to think twice if you are offered unusually cheap lists. List costs vary, but the range $115 to $150 per thousand named recipients is a reasonable guide. Highly specialized lists, such as the world's 10,000 richest widows, may cost considerably more and rental may be subject to very stringent conditions.

The rental of a list is for a single use. It is possible to buy lists, but it is wise to wait until you have tested their effect. If you cheat you will find that the list supplier is very nice about it. They will not complain, they will not threaten, they will simply send you an invoice for each use. How will they know? Every list contains a few dummy addresses which bring your mailing direct to the list owner. If you cheat they receive your mailing and respond accordingly.

Another reason for renting is that a list is only as good as it is up to date. Updating lists is difficult and expensive. I have a colleague who prefers to give others free use of his lists for life if they will undertake the cost and trouble of checking that no one has died or moved on. While they are at it, he usually has them carry out a survey for him. Surveys have a value all of their own (see press relations below). Once you have established your newsletter, use it to survey your readers on a range of business and consultancy topics.

Writing articles

Few things build the consultant's reputation and image more effectively or more quickly than having their name frequently in print. We have looked at the advantages of writing your own publication. Now let us rapidly assess the benefits of promoting yourself, and therefore your practice, through appearing in journals.

Let me make it clear that by journals I do not mean those solemn academic publications which are an essential outlet for the serious academic and of immense value as a source of information to the professional consultant. Any of us who take our trade seriously should budget time regularly to keep abreast of research and developments in our specialism, but as a means of developing business they are, literally, a dead loss. Write a brilliant paper for an academic journal and the most you can reasonably hope for by way of business is an invitation to present your findings at an obscure conference, at a distant location, at your own expense.

When I speak of journals, I mean trade and business magazines which are read by down-to-earth businesspeople. They are the people who will seek to secure your services if they find what you have to say interesting. What is equally important, having read your articles in the press they will be slightly in awe of you when you meet and, as we shall see later, you will be able to build on that situation to do business on your own terms. Nothing is more important to the long-term profitability of your endeavour.

It is not useful to fire off articles right, left and centre virtually at random. You will get the best results if you take a planned approach. For example, you may choose to write on a topic of interest to a specific industry or business sector, particularly one in which you have identified an opportunity which is not being exploited. Alternatively, you may prefer to concentrate your attention on a specialism, for example sales training, international trade or human resource development. Whatever your strategy is, you need the following information:

❑ The journals and magazines serving your target audience.
❑ The type of articles they normally print.
❑ Readership figures and demographics.
❑ The name of the editor.

For most of this information you have a reliable source in your local public library. *British Rates and Data*, or *BRAD*, is my preferred resource purely because I feel comfortable with its layout, but *Willings Press Guide* has the same information. Even the smallest of libraries tend to have one or the other of these invaluable publications in the reference section. American readers will find *Standard Rates and Data* and *Business Publications Rates and Data* on their library shelves.

For further information, including, almost certainly, a copy of the magazine from which you can get a clearer idea of what will be welcomed, you can telephone the advertising department of your potential publisher and ask for a media pack. If you are unfamiliar with the normal media pack of a quality daily or monthly, you are in for a treat. Most have valuable demographic and other information, beautifully presented. So rich a vein of information does a good media pack offer – and most are very good – that I am almost tempted to suggest that no professional consultant should be without a comprehensive library of them. However, their cost to the publications concerned urges restraint.

Once you have decided where to place your work, you will want to know what layout and form are acceptable. If you want to do it by the book, then suitable titles full of detailed advice exist in great numbers in your library. I have always found, however, that regardless of what the books advise in terms of everything from margin sizes to preferred punctuation, ordinary, error-free, double-spaced, typed or wordprocessed copy is all that editors require. I think it is wise to double space, because editors do edit. And that is no bad thing: some of my most wordy offerings have emerged with a lot more punch after professional editing.

If your work is accepted you may expect to have to wait about 8 to 12 weeks before seeing it in print.

If you are impatient and feel that faster acceptance of your opus is appropriate, just compare this to the two years or so which it can take to get your work into some academic journals.

Make sure that your article is accompanied by a brief biographical sketch of you, the author, and details of where you may be contacted. If you offer to send your readers some further information you can be sure that the magazine will print your contact address or telephone number. No magazine wants to deal with possibly thousands of requests.

Do not expect to earn a large income from your writing. Unless you specifically ask for a fee, the editor will assume that you are offering your work *gratis*. In any case, $150 for 1000 words is as much as you can reasonably hope for.

Those who feel that they would like to make a worthwhile income from writing articles need to consider syndication. This is a specialist area and you need a good agent who is an expert in the field. Until you have had a good deal of work published, it is not easy to find one prepared to take you on. You also need to write material which is in demand internationally so that your work can be placed simultaneously in publications all over the globe. Neither writing the material nor finding the right agent is easy, but the rewards can be great. You would be paid a small sum, perhaps $10 each time your work appears, but it may appear perhaps 200 times across the world and that is a lot of money for a thousand words.

A second, and perhaps more practical, way to make an income from your writing while you build your reputation is by becoming a columnist. If you could be the widget industry's agony aunt with a regular problem page in the *Widget Makers Gazette*, for example, you could rely on a small but regular income. You would rapidly build your reputation in the industry and best of all, through receiving a constant stream of problems and queries, you would have an unrivalled grasp of where the opportunities for consultancy lie.

Writing articles is of such value in developing your reputation that it is the one area where I suggest that you really ought to be happy to give your services for free. Not only will it help to get you known, but reprints from a recognized publication have much more credibility than brochures, sales letters or advertisements.

One last advantage. If you are perceived by the press as a fellow writer, albeit an amateur, there is a strong likelihood that when they come to write about the field in which they know you have expertise they will come to you for your views. To write articles confers credibility; to be quoted confers fame.

Writing books

For most of us in consultancy there comes a time when writing and publishing a book becomes a passionate necessity. We have a lot to give, and by God, they're going to get it – in spite of the fact that we know that 87 per cent of books lose money and only 10 per cent of books which are started by readers are read to the end.

But what is wrong with having a dream? If you can write a bestseller your name and your fortune are assured, but bestsellers are a minute sample of the vast number of books written. The time taken to write a book could be used to write dozens of articles, so are there any short cuts?

Four come to mind.

Always seek opportunities to **recycle**. If you have written something which was effective in shorter form – article, seminar handout or industry report – see whether it might be expanded to fill a chapter.

Write a **workbook** rather than a word book. You can save yourself a lot of toil by leaving much of the writing to be done by your reader and you can still describe yourself as an author.

Edit an **anthology**. Get a group of your friends together and invite each to contribute a chapter on TQM, leadership or whatever. Edit their efforts. Top and tail with an introduction and a summary and suddenly you are all authors. You will need an edition of about 12,500 to justify the first printing with a dozen of you sharing royalties, so why not be really cheeky. Choose a dozen contributors of means and not without vanity. Invite each to buy a thousand copies of their book for back-of-the-room sales at seminars, or to give to clients. Have 12 dust jackets produced so that on mine my photograph is central and bigger than those of my co-authors surrounding it to personalize things and bingo, you are an author with minimum labour and possibly a small profit.

Offer **practical workshops** on authorship. Sell places to those who are anxious to get their names in print.

'Ladies and gentlemen, the objectives of this seminar are simple. By the end of the week we will have produced a book ready for publication.'

You need to provide leadership, some knowledge, research materials and a colleague who is a dab hand on the word-processor, and you are an editor as well as a trainer with reasonable earning potential from what could be a popular seminar.

Letters to the editor

The most time-effective way to get into print is through writing letters to the editor. Avoid the 'I loved your article on motivation, please give us more' type. Find something you want to have a fight about.

Be truculent and aggressive. Spice what you have to say with irony and wit. Invite replies and a continuation of the fight.

Half the people who read what you have to say will write you off as an idiot, the other half will think that you are brilliant. Among both halves may be some who will hire your services – after further discussion. The time commitment is minimal and your name appears frequently in places where your potential clients seek information.

If you want readers to contact you direct rather than through the correspondence columns, ensure that your address is printed by offering some relevant information to those who ask for it. A journal may occasionally be willing to forward requests for further information that come from a major article; that gives them a measure of the market response. They are unlikely to accept the same inconvenience for a letter. So they will print your address, often with a reminder, 'write direct to Mr Green at... and not to us'.

Using the press

There is no promotion so effective or so satisfactory as 'free ink'. Any consultant should make it an absolute goal to become famous, even if only on a local basis.

To become famous you must become news. Most news is manufactured by someone with the necessary skills presenting it in such a way that it appeals to a news-hungry readership. (Can the presence or absence of cellulite on Princess Diana's thighs be news in anything other than a news-hungry world?) What you do can certainly be presented as news to the trade and technical press who serve the same markets as you do.

Your activities and triumphs can sometimes be news to the

national press, radio and television if you present them professionally.

Conduct surveys

Publications adore the results of surveys and it seems to matter very little if the findings surprise or simply restate the obvious in a way which adds fuel to a current controversy. If you conduct investigations of any kind, ascertain whether you can, without breach of any commercial confidentiality, release something to the press.

Analyse the social, economic, political (be careful), cultural and technological climates as they relate to your clients and the markets they serve. Become known as one who always has something to say, and before long you will not have to write so many press releases because the press will begin to approach you for comments.

To be published:

❑ Write your press release on a single sheet if possible.
❑ Leave adequate margins for editorial comment.
❑ Make sure it is clear where you may be contacted for further information (and be available when wanted).
❑ Include a specific release date after which your release may be used.
❑ Send it to the editor by name. (Check in *BRAD* or an equivalent publication.)
❑ Attach a press-quality photograph. (This alone increases your chances of publication by at least 28 per cent.)
❑ Having sent it, never badger the editor about publication.

If your release is published, show your gratitude by sending useful information to the editor when you can.

Giving seminars

The market for seminars is growing and will continue to grow.

What is more, seminars can create clients in good numbers as well as producing a source of income. Research indicates that an average of 8 per cent of seminar participants provide consultancy or internal training opportunities for the leader.

To enter the seminar market does not require you to spend months developing materials and program outlines.

Address the seminar business as a businessperson rather than as a trainer. Find out what the market wants. Decide what you could do, off the cuff, to satisfy a market need. Design simple handouts or a minimal workbook, promote your seminar and go. If you genuinely have something worth saying, people will get great benefit and your initiative will prosper. If by chance you have got it wrong, you have invested, and therefore lost, very little.

When you have a seminar that works you have a number of choices. If you have a real blockbuster of a success you may choose to franchise your materials and allow others to provide you with a steady living by the sweat of their brows. Alternatively, you may keep your program to yourself, refining and improving it to reach wider and wider markets.

A seminar which is an amazing success may be sold outright. To give you an idea of how profitable this route may be, a price for a real winner might be as much as five to ten years' gross receipts.

It is relatively difficult to get seminars which are aimed at the general public off the ground. Your problem lies in promotion. How do you reach that relatively small proportion of the total population that invest in seminars?

Usually it is necessary to advertise in the press, and press advertisements are costly. It may well be a worthwhile and cost-effective exercise to promote and conduct your seminar locally at first. Although receipts may not be exciting to your bank manager, neither are the costs a worry. You can go national or international when you are confident that you have a market.

To appeal to the general public your seminar needs to tell them:

❑ How to make more money.
❑ How to keep more of the money they make.
❑ How to develop their hobby or interest.
❑ How to enrich or empower their lives.

You can appeal to the corporate market where participants do not have to dip into their own reserves of cash with a much wider range of offerings. It is little exaggeration to say that as long as you conduct the program in a comfortable hotel, preferably near to the golf course, with good food and excellent wine, the content can be as uninteresting as you care to make it. You think you will not get consultancy assignments from a boring program? You are wrong. Give your participants a sufficiently good time and they will love you anyway. Some of the less reputable business schools rely almost exclusively on regurgitating tired and doubtful old materials in swish settings and they do pretty well for consultancy assignments as a break from the day job.

Please be assured that I am not advocating poor quality. In fact my passionate commitment is to high-quality outcomes from training and development. I only wish that others, including participants who regard any training as just a break from work, shared my views. I simply tell you what others are getting away with so that you may promote quality content with confidence.

Time management

In order to market consistently and do all of the other things necessary in practice management, as well as making a living, you will need to become an expert on time management.

This book would become of inordinate and unacceptable length if I tried to include a treatise on how to control your time, so let me do no more than draw to your attention to one point which you will not find in the standard texts. Whatever you do, ensure that you get the utmost mileage out of it. Make it a rule never to use anything only once and the gain in time and the increase in creativity can be dramatic. If you have written an inspiring talk, would it make an equally inspiring magazine article? Or could it be recycled as a seminar session? As Jay Abraham so often says, and demonstrates, you can find ways to leverage everything that you do in the interests of building business and delighting customers.

And whenever you have a huge and important thing to do and there seems no available time long enough to enable you to get really stuck into it, remember the old saw about eating an elephant a little at a time. Ten minutes here, twenty minutes there mean progress, and progress has a wonderful effect on motivation and confidence.

Finally, never confuse what is important with what is merely urgent. If you always do the important things you will find that the urgent wait comfortably until they become important, or they just fade blissfully away.

The tactics which we have discussed in this chapter are those which have been shown by Shenson's research in the US and mine in Europe to be those which the high earners in our profession have found most useful in building their image and reputation.

If you select and consistently use those which appeal to you, your practice will grow as more and more clients, knowing your name and assuming your reputation, invite you to do work for them. When you have to go out to market directly – and changing circumstances will ensure that from time to time you must go back to knocking on doors – the time that you have expended on building your reputation will be repaid as prospective clients are just a little more ready to meet you.

The most important factor in considering which of the above you will apply is personal comfort. Do only those things which you feel comfortable doing and do them consistently. I really do mean consistently. While writing this chapter I have also written and despatched five articles. That is what I mean by consistent:

you cannot afford to allow the major assignment, however important, to interfere with your marketing efforts.

Be sure to set aside some time every week to market yourself. It will pay dividends.

There's more… and some of it is work for you, right now.

INDIRECT MARKETING

The following are no-cost/low-cost marketing tactics which are consistent with my preferences and talents:

To get me started I will take the following steps tomorrow:

To maximize the opportunity I need the following personal development or information:

To resource the above I can:

Are you certain that your plans fully exploit:

❑ Your personal and professional strengths?
❑ The market opportunities?

If in doubt, please look back and check. Above all:

❑ Will you be comfortable and confident as you do what you have just committed to?
❑ Is it consistent with the professional image that you wish to project?

SOAP BOX – TEN REASONS FOR FAILURE TO TRANSFER LEARNING TO THE WORKPLACE

1. Training is routine, not carried out when needed.
2. The training method is inappropriate.
3. Training is not fully supported by management and application of new skills is not rewarded.
4. The objectives of training are unclear, and quantifiable behavioural outcomes are not specified.
5. Colleagues lack the new skills.
6. Trainees were not prepositioned to understand expectations of them after training. Often opportunities to apply what has been learned are denied.
7. Neither management nor colleagues are able to help when difficulties arise.
8. New skills require greater effort to apply, particularly at first.
9. New skills make the individual feel awkward – normal activities go less smoothly at first. The more important the area of work, the greater the discomfort as new skills displace valued, and previously rewarded, behaviours.
10. There is a psychological and emotional gulf between training and the real world.

For details of how to overcome these problems, dig out and study Gers and Seward's important research for the library service in Baltimore or, better yet, work out your own approach, test it, prove it and market it.

9

Making Your Brochure Work For You

IF YOU EVER FEEL THE NEED TO SPEND MONEY TO NO GOOD PURPOSE, an easy way to unburden yourself of unwanted cash is to follow the example of many of your fellow consultants when designing and using a brochure.

This is how to prove that you have more money than sense. Go out and hire a graphic studio to design something beautiful and exciting, then get yourself a copy writer to develop your dream message. Use a master printer to produce your masterpiece on an exquisite art paper and wrap it lovingly in the highest-quality folder that your inexhaustible supply of money can buy. Have 5000 printed and rush them to a direct mailing service with an order to mail them cold to a personally bought-in list that you have had no time to check.

After that you are in the ideal position to tell me, as so many of your fellow professionals do, that brochures serve no useful purpose other than to bankrupt the consultant. Produced like that, used like that, you and they are right. Fifteen years of talking to consultants who use their brochures that way indicates that the response to the mailing, in terms of business acquired, seldom pays for the stamps. Yet they go on doing it. Asked why, they respond that they 'don't know what else to do'.

I don't want to see you go bankrupt, so let me suggest what else you might do. First, consider whether you need a brochure at all. When your practice is small it is possible to write a tailored document for each client telling them precisely, and in sufficient detail, what they need to know.

You will not hammer on the wordprocessor keys until you fully understand your client's problem, but that is all to the good. Understanding your client's problem may lead you to concentrate on specifically how your unique skills and knowledge will help to provide the cure. Your client may then feel that their problem is more important to you than your own aggrandizement and may be more inclined to ask you to accept a contract.

There are some who try to avoid the brochure altogether and, working on the valid assumption that it is their skills, knowledge and experience that the client may buy, they market themselves with their CV. The assumption is valid, but in most cases the conclusion is not.

No matter how impressive your CV may be, it has certain disadvantages when used as a marketing tool.

There is a psychological response to a CV which is difficult to overcome. To most people the CV accompanies an application for a job. It automatically puts the sender into a subservient, almost supplicatory position.

Our image marketing approach has been aimed at raising the profile of the consultant to that of independent specialist who may be persuaded to accept an assignment. The sending of a CV can reverse the perceived relative status of consultant and client at a stroke.

What is worse, all business organizations have a well-defined procedure for dealing with CVs – they invariably pass them to the personnel department. I do not have to share Bob Townsend's view that the interests of the company would be best served if all members of the personnel operation were taken out and shot to suspect that their receipt of an unsolicited CV triggers a standard response. Many a consultant has received a letter which thanks them for their interest in the company and advises that no vacancy appropriate to their talents currently exists but their application will be retained and they will be contacted when such a vacancy occurs. I have to add that, although I know many who have elicited such a response, I am still waiting to meet that happy person who has been advised of a subsequent vacancy.

I suspect that in many personnel departments the knee-jerk response of such a letter is so ingrained that any written communication is likely to evoke it.

I know that when I was asked by the chairman of a blue-chip organization to send a copy of a letter I had sent to him offering my services to each of his 13 personnel directors, quoting his name, the first response I had was exactly of the type summarized above – and that was without a CV.

Do not use a resumé for marketing purposes for one further and compelling reason. Even if it is retained by the person you wish to influence and its purpose is fully understood, it is a poor tool for the job in hand. The CV contains a great deal of information which is irrelevant to your offer. Some of that information may detract from what is important. Some may give the potential client the opportunity to reject you because although extraneous, it indicates something that they are biased against.

I find it interesting that recruitment specialists, whose stock in trade is the CV, when asked what should be included often respond: 'As little as possible.'

There is one important exception to my strictures about marketing yourself using your resumé. Government agencies the world over tend to appoint consultants largely, or even entirely, on the strength of their CV. They believe that they are looking for a specific background that your resumé will identify with little or no thought on their part. If you plan to do largely government work you will need to develop and use a convincing resumé – indeed, you will need to develop more than one, each highlighting an achievement of particular relevance to the job not yet in hand.

Writing your brochure

When marketing with a CV is ineffective and writing individual information for each client becomes impractical, then it is time to write your brochure.

You may need two. The point of the brochure is that it will either open doors for you from 'cold', or it will reinforce a good impression which you have already made. These are by no means the same job, and it is by no means certain that the same tool will do for both.

If you publish a newsletter, or write articles, that will open doors, but if you choose speaking engagements or seminars as the main thrust of your marketing activities, a 'give away' which will be kept and referred to is a must. The less it looks like a standard brochure the better.

If you have a specific area of expertise, try producing a small leaflet which provides useful information – 'How to raise capital in a nervous market' or 'The environment and motivation' or whatever. Be careful not to answer all the questions and ensure that you invite and facilitate contact by those who need further advice or information. Some consultants go to the lengths of writing a small booklet and others have one of their practical articles reproduced in pocket-size format. I have used simple, self-administered 'psychological' tests with substantial, but less than comprehensive, interpretive data.

As long as people find what you provide useful, but not so useful that it obviates the need for your services, it will work for you. Some consultants offer such a piece free of charge to those who respond to an advertisement.

When you are composing the brochure proper, start by listing what my American colleagues sometimes call your 'stellar moments': those major achievements which demonstrate the range and depth of your abilities.

Don't worry if some of the principal attainments were accomplished as an employee, rather than as a consultant. As Howard Shenson used to say: 'No one gives a damn how you were paid as long as you did it and it worked.'

If the achievement was truly yours and it demonstrates the effective application of skill or knowledge which you would be happy to market today, get it down. Against each stellar moment write the objective which your work enabled the client or employer to achieve and the other benefits which were gained *en route*. Add a list of the special skills and knowledge that you brought to bear.

Write up each stellar moment, its objective, benefits and skills, as a short, 40–50-word 'case study' – and then spice it up a little. You add the spice by going to your CV and using those accreditations, skills or abilities which you cannot bear to have ignored and which make sense in the context of what you have written.

> *'My researches during my MBA program enabled me to be unusually effective in dealing with the essential culture changes.'*
> *'My fluent Hungarian ensured that I could advise the chairman on the nuances as well as the content of the President's statement.'*

Have your spiced case studies printed on quality, but not excessively expensive, A4 card or paper, folded to fit into the pocket. But not until you undertake the nine-year-old test.

Most who are drawn to consultancy number among their basic skills a better than average vocabulary. That would be fine if it were not for the fact that what we have, we use.

Most material written by consultants uses words and structures which are more abstruse than they need to be. (Including mine: how often do your intimate business acquaintances use the word 'abstruse'?) The result is ambiguity instead of clarity. If we pass our written work to a nine-year-old and test that what is understood is what we intended, we improve our style greatly. If I remember rightly one of the definitions in *Webster's* of the word 'communication' is 'the transfer of meaning'. If we are able to transfer meaning effectively and fully to a nine-year-old we have communicated.

We may have recourse to tools like the Fogg Readability Index or the Plain English Society's editing software Stylewriter, but in the short term at least nine-year-olds are cheaper.

A final test of your brochure can be made by taking your draft to a local college marketing faculty. Ask the head of department if they would have the students review your brochure as a case study in marketing communication and arrange to attend the session in which your work is discussed.

You may not enjoy what you hear, but it will be among the cheapest and most useful consultancy assignments that you will ever commission.

Using your brochure

Brochures mailed cold routinely attract less than eight seconds' attention, as the research quoted in the previous chapter indicates.

That is not to say that it is impossible to hit the jackpot with a cold mailing. It is not impossible to win the lottery. Achieving either, however, is less likely than being struck by lightning.

The purpose of the brochure is to build on the good impression which you have already made by feeding the prospective client with information which enables them to construct their own arguments in support of hiring you.

Its role is one of reinforcement. It reinforces the message that you are a competent, creative, successful consultant who will provide exceptional services to those lucky enough to be your clients and it endorses the client's feeling that they were right to talk to you. After reading your brochure they will feel that their risk in hiring you will be minute, if it exists at all.

Your brochure must offer something special to your client. By being heavy on fact and light on sales 'puff', it will win you business by letting the client become your salesperson.

Your brochure should be treated with respect by you and by those that receive it. It should be handed to the prospect after your discussion as evidence that they will experience the benefits which you have explained in detail and that those benefits will lead to the achievement of their most important current objective.

Draw the attention of the potential client to one of the 'cases' most closely related to their situation. Give them time and silence in which to read it and wait in silence for their reaction. If they comment positively, ask for the contract and, again, wait in silence for their response.

Silence is vital. If your brochure is properly designed and presented, it is the final and most potent selling tool. But it can only work by providing your client with information which they will relate to their needs in such a way that they develop stronger arguments than you ever can for why they should hire your services. For them to complete this act of self-influence requires that they have time:

❑ To relate what they read to their needs.
❑ To use the new information to reinforce the apparent desirability of what you have already offered.
❑ To remove any fears or concerns that they may have in hiring you.
❑ To project the benefits into their future to experience their enjoyment vicariously.

All of this takes considerable time and happens only in the absence of distractions. If you speak, tidy your papers or rise to leave, that will be sufficient distraction to enable the decision to be put to one side. The primary ability of the effective salesperson is to shut up and sit tight. I will have more to say about selling later, but for now commit yourself to the idea that silence can do much of your talking.

Brochure development

Take a yellow pad, think through and write the following:

Brochure development

❑ **Your personal and professional achievements (stellar moments).**
Including brief outline of *what* was done.

❑ **The client or company objective achieved or problem solved.**
Why it was done.

❑ **Specific benefits to the company or client of your intervention.**
Additional gains arising directly out of using your ideas and services.
Put numbers to the benefits where possible: 'Leading to a saving of $3 million in the first year'.

❑ **Appropriate CV spice for each triumph.**
Special skills, attainments, qualifications, experience, knowledge or attitudes relevant to this assignment.

❑ **Write a mini-case study of 40–50 words for each stellar moment.**
Avoid unnecessary hyperbole: tell it as it happened.
Highlight the objectives and the benefits.
Make your use of spice relevant and almost off-hand.

Five or six mini-case studies will be sufficient for a brochure and should enable you to indicate a representative range of abilities. Ensure that your brochure reads as factual and straightforward rather than as a sales piece. You might like to call it a 'Services factsheet' or 'Capability outline' rather than a brochure. When your client asks for a copy of your brochure, as they so often do, you may wish to reply:

'I don't have a brochure, they are too much of a heavy sell. I will give you a copy of my factsheet, which briefly outlines how we've been

able to help others. I'm sure that you will find a number of parallels with your situation which will give you some ideas.'

Lao Tse said of leadership that it was at its most effective when the led thought that they had done it all themselves. If your brochure proves to be an inexpensive but effective way to get the client to sell themselves on hiring you, that too is great leadership.

SOAP BOX – FADS, FALLACIES, FUTILITIES AND FOUL-UPS

Since the early 1970s major fads have emerged and disappeared at a rate of about three each year. This is a great pity, for two reasons. The 'bus queue syndrome' results from the perceived failure of so-called fads, but the greater pity is that the presumed fads are in many cases no such thing. They were excellent ideas which were either imperfectly or impatiently implemented.

Part of the fault here lies with academics, who sometimes can be accused with justice of having scant perception of the difficulties inherent in using their ivory tower concepts in the real, and often crisis-ridden, world of work. But the major part of the blame lies with consultants who board every passing bandwagon with gay abandon and almost total ignorance of what they are trying to do.

It is seldom a satisfactory qualification to have skimmed a book by Michael Hammer, Tom Peters or Faith Popcorn to be an expert on some new theory. At the very least, the professional should carefully study not just all the literature but also a wide range of related topics before peddling someone else's ideas. Ideally, they should be trained and certificated by the originator. Anything less is theft, and we are all, and I do mean we, guilty from time to time.

If you must seek to base your business on a fad of the moment, just where are you adding value beyond that which your clients could enjoy by investing in a good book?

10

Advertising for the Professions

FOR MANY YEARS THE PROFESSIONS VIEWED ADVERTISING WITH distaste. It was vulgar. It was unseemly. It was therefore perceived as unprofessional and for many it was banned.

Today things are different. Lawyers, veterinarians and accountants all vie for the best positions in publications – sometimes with the worst advertisements. Even doctors no longer stand aloof. Advertising professional services is in, and consultants have been quick to get involved.

Advertising is expensive and frequently ineffective, but sometimes it is the only way to reach your market. For example, before I wrote my first book I conducted seminars for consultants and other professionals. By profiling my participants I knew that most of my business came from independent professionals in a range of different professions or members of small but successful firms. Although some were new to their profession, most had been in the business for a number of years and were making good money – they were open-minded enough to be seeking practical ideas to make more. To reach such an audience direct mail would have been a non-starter or prohibitively expensive. This was a situation where it definitely paid to advertise.

I would not advertise my in-corporation consultancy or training services – the marketing methods discussed in Chapter 8 are more effective and cheaper – but in situations where your market is dispersed and difficult to locate there is no realistic alternative to paid advertising. I will spell out in this chapter some ways to minimize advertising costs, increase its effect and reduce the risks.

How not to waste your money

Most consultants, including marketing specialists who ought to know better, base their advertising strategy on two disastrous mistakes. They model their copy on advertisements which they have seen, enjoyed and admired, and they follow the advice of advertising professionals.

I have worked off and on for 30 years with advertising professionals and, with few exceptions (David Ogilvie, J Walter Thompson and Patrick Quinn come to mind), I have yet to find more than a heretical few who regard the real purpose of advertising to be that of selling anything.

The vast, and very expensive, majority are motivated by the following desires, not necessarily in the order given:

- ❑ To show how 'creative' they are.
- ❑ To sell the most expensive campaigns regardless of client need or means.
- ❑ To win the admiration of their peers.
- ❑ To win awards given by their peers.

Advertising is the one field in which do-it-yourself may be less risky than using professional services. Time and again I have seen 'ordinary' businesspeople totally outclass the advertising professional at less cost with just a little thoughtful advice. You can learn more from a little book of the quality and focus of Patrick Quinn's *Secrets of Successful Copywriting* than you can buy from an agency, whatever your budget. You *can* advertise successfully. All you need is a little imagination and a little guidance.

The philosophy

Small-budget advertisers need to understand that they are not in the same business as the corporation with megabucks to spend. The large company expects its advertising to build, over a lengthy period, its image, its brand awareness and the likelihood that at some unspecified time buyers with sufficient funds will add Product X to their list of possible buys. The beautiful advertisement for that sleek BMW is not necessarily aimed at getting you to grab $100,000 and head for the showroom. BMW will be happy if those who can lay their hands on a small fortune stand in line to buy, but for the rest of us all they want to do is to create a dream – and a burning ambition.

Alternatively, the massive spender in fields such as detergents seeks to so inundate purchasers with a constant stream of advertising that, once in the supermarket, they will grab and pay zombie-like for the brand which is currently being promoted with no more logical reason than that they thought they would give it a try. For Unilever, Procter & Gamble and the like, everything depends on repetition and shelf position, neither of which has much relevance to consultants.

I am being a little unfair, in the sense that both of the above strategies work. They will work if they are repeated sufficiently often, over a sufficiently long period. Were you to copy the style of, say, a Mercedes advertisement, it would eventually bring you business. The reason it would bring business is that people would eventually come to believe that you are good at what you do. They would know that you are good at what you do because you make so much money that you can afford to throw large amounts of it away on crazy advertising campaigns.

At worst, any advertisement which you place must bring you at least enough extra business to pay for the next advertisement. And that means you must forget about white space.

One day I may meet the individual who tells me that they bought Product X because of the tasteful and informative white space. Advertising salespeople, of course, love white space, but I continue to believe that it is what you *say* in an advertisement which will persuade people to buy.

What you write must include the following.

Heading

You are aiming to have your advertisement read by those few among the vast number in the marketplace who will be interested in buying your services now or in the future. It is competing with the other advertisements and editorial for their limited attention. Make sure that your header says 'read me' loud and clear to the right people.

To say 'read me' it needs to speak to people direct. You need to identify your readers by name, description, profession or shared problem. For example:

- ❏ 'Are you called Smith?'
- ❏ 'Young people'
- ❏ 'Consultants'
- ❏ 'Short of cash?'

Offer

Once the potential buyers have started to read, your prime requirement is to ensure that they keep right on reading until they take the desired action. They have to believe that there is something in it for them. So make it clear up front that their wishes will be granted, because if you fail to convince them early you quickly lose their attention.

- ❏ 'You will learn the secrets of the super rich in one fun-packed day.'
- ❏ 'Solve your money problems the new and exciting way.'

Evidence

Give your readers reason to believe that you can deliver what you promise.

❑ 'More than a million delighted users worldwide.'
❑ 'A unique, new, but proven approach.'
❑ 'Researched and validated by Cambridge University.'

Expand on your offer
If space and budget allow, develop the benefits which buyers of your services will gain. Create a logical linkage between benefits so that belief in the first guarantees belief in the second, which in turn ensures acceptance of the third and so to the end. The end should be the biggest benefit of all – your opening offer.

Facilitate action
Tell your readers what they must do to achieve the benefits you offer. Be sure to give them alternatives:

❑ A tear-out coupon to mail.
❑ Your telephone number for those in a hurry.
❑ Your fax number if you have one.

If you include a mailing coupon, make sure that some way of contacting you is printed elsewhere in the advertisement for those who see the advertisement after the coupon has been cut out.

The ninefold path to enlightened advertising

To determine what you may most effectively say about yourself and to get an idea of what it may cost you to say it, take the following seriously.

Step One: Understand the business environment

❑ What is the economic, social, legislative and business situation?
❑ Who are your competitors?

❑ What are their strengths and weaknesses?
❑ What are yours?
❑ What do you have to offer that is unique?
❑ Is there anything which is being underplayed by your competitors so that if you were to promote it the reader would assume that you have it uniquely?

Step Two: Opportunity analysis

❑ What are the opportunities right now? In the immediate future?
❑ Where could you make your biggest gains?

Step Three: Position your business
The least effective advertising is that which says: 'We do anything for anyone and do it cheaper.'

Position your business to ensure that those who seek to hire you understand that they are hiring specialist expertise from a company with a defined culture.

If you are the consultancy 'which cares and goes on caring', or if you 'do and charge for everything necessary, and nothing extra', or if you offer 'Rolls-Royce service at Ford prices', think how you will communicate the idea clearly in a few, inexpensive words.

Step Four: Write advertising objectives

❑ Establish the number of responses that you need.
❑ Calculate the incremental sales which you want the advertising to bring in.
❑ Clearly identify the market segments which you must reach.
❑ Determine the key points which readers of your advertisements need to recognize and respond to.

Step Five: Establish your budget
Obtain media packs from those publications which you are considering. Establish precisely what your advertisement will cost in terms of $ per 1000 target readers reached.

Step Six: Consider an agency

In spite of my views about advertising professionals, the reliable agency can save you much grief. If you are clear about what you want to achieve, who you want to reach and what you want to say, an agency can place your advertisements very advantageously. But be warned: approaching an agency as a means of avoiding having to think for yourself could lead to disaster.

Agencies are paid a commission when they place your advertisements by the media who benefit. If you have a large budget they may be willing to handle your account for free. In any case, their costs ought to take into account the 10 to 15 per cent commission which they are paid by the publication.

Step Seven: Measure the results

Compare the results from different publications, different positions and different days of the week.

Consider using a scrapbook to monitor your most and least successful advertisements. Never be afraid to repeat a successful advertisement – you are building your business, not soliciting prizes for novelty.

Used-vehicle dealers on both sides of the Atlantic tend not to advertise. They buy space in the paper and fill it with a stocklist. I was working with a dealership some years ago and we developed an advertising strategy and a range of copy which massively increased their sales. One week after I had moved on they were pushed for time. To meet the copy deadline they had no hope of producing anything new. They had many advertisements on file which had pulled like crazy. Did they repeat one of these? No chance. They had a stocklist typed and ran that. When traffic was barely better than zero that weekend they learned a valuable lesson.

Step Eight: Determine the risk

What could go wrong with an advertisement?

Incredible as it may seem, two quality national dailies in the same week forgot to print my advertisement for my pilot seminar, 'How to build and develop your professional practice'. From one

(the *Daily Telegraph*) I got an apology and a replacement advertisement, which it put in by taking out one of its own display
advertisements. From the other (*The Times*) I got the information
that it gives no guarantees of publication, and it is simply 'unfor-
tunate' if that ruins your business. It did manage to print my
advertisement the following week, but nine months and several
telephone calls later I am still waiting for its media pack, or a copy
of its terms and conditions. So do not assume that big necessarily
means efficient.

Step Nine: Don't get hung up on 'response rates'
Evaluate advertising by what it brings in terms of additional
profit, not enquiries. If you invest $1 and get $10 of additional
profit that's great. If you invest and get a load of enquiries but no
additional business, that's bad. If all you get is a report from an
agency that *x* per cent of people remembered your ad – that's a
disaster. It was a wise person who said: 'Whatever marketeers
claim about response rates – high or low – you know only one
thing. They're lying.'

Advance troubleshooting

Consider the following:

- ❑ What could go wrong?
- ❑ Can it be avoided?
- ❑ If so, what can I do to avoid or minimize the risk?
- ❑ If problems cannot be avoided, what is the earliest indication
  that things are going wrong?
- ❑ What contingent action can I take to minimize harm?

When to advertise

As I have said above, the most important reason to advertise is that
you know you cannot reach your target market any other way.

For example, part of my business is conducting seminars for those who are either running their own professional practices, or are thinking about doing so. Simple market research tells me that there are as many as 300,000 people out there at any time who could benefit from my training. My problem is that they are randomly distributed among a population of 60 million. To reach them all by mail I could follow a simple and obvious strategy: 20 million letters, one to each household in the land. The cost of stamps alone – nothing I mail ever goes with less than a first-class stamp; I want status for my letters as much as for myself – would cost around $7 million at current prices. But that is little more than incidental.

Twenty million envelopes, twenty million inserts. In time alone, stuffing and sealing an envelope every second, day and night without rest, it would take almost two years to get a mailing on its way.

What about the indirect methods I have recommended? Good press and public relations, articles and other seminars are all vital, but they do not make response easy or timely. When I need to be preparing the latest research material for the seminar is just when it would be most useful to appear on television, or give interviews to the press.

Advertising was, for me, a necessity until *High Income Consulting* changed things. Now people call, fax or write every day asking me to let them know when a seminar is scheduled. I no longer advertise: I mail to hot prospects at their request.

I suggest that you advertise only when there is no other way and stop advertising as soon as your no-cost marketing bears sufficient fruit.

All business is seasonal

Budget deadlines, high days and holidays, the subtleties of the business cycle, the harshness of the economic cycle: many factors great and small conspire to make every business to some degree seasonal. If you must advertise, you need to do so when the response is likely to be at its height. There is nothing to be gained by advertising my seminars at Christmas or during August, for the very simple reason that those who might attend at any other time have other priorities during holiday seasons.

Never advertise when business is slack for everyone. The hope of picking up more than your usual share is almost certain to prove unfounded. There are just not enough punters in the marketplace to justify the expenditure. The cost per enquiry is likely to rise to the point where even getting the business means working at a loss.

The point of advertising is to turn hot prospects into buyers. No hot prospects – no buyers.

If you are a low-budget advertiser you will be depriving yourself of the cash that would enable you to exploit a bonanza opportunity when it comes. Conserve your cash by concentrating on low-cost or no-cost marketing. Write and place some articles. Give a few well-targeted talks. If you must spend, spend on food for the family or keep up the mortgage payments and wait for the upturn.

You can bet your copy of the *Group Facilitator's Handbook* that others, ignorant of the realities of advertising, will be trying their luck and your advertisement would struggle to be seen among the other products of despair.

The time to advertise is when the market is about to hit a high point. Know your market, analyse the peaks and troughs and advertise to exploit the coming peak. Newspaper proprietors will continue to get rich on the back of advertising revenues from wise and foolish advertisers, but by the effective timing of your advertisement you will have a better than sporting chance of adding to your net worth without contributing unwisely to theirs.

The media

Because the majority of consultants who choose to advertise do so through that medium, I have concentrated on print until now. Some readers are likely to be more adventurous and will want to investigate other media. For them a brief overview is appropriate.

In order to make an informed choice it is necessary that you:

☐ Know the types of media.
☐ Consider the advantages and disadvantages of each.
☐ Buy space or air time to your best advantage.
☐ Understand some of the techniques which add an extra dimension to a medium's effect.

Understanding the media

An advertising medium is defined as being any vehicle which carries your promotional message to the targeted client. Professionals would normally list ten, of which by no means all are relevant to your needs. But for the sake of completeness I list them all.

Newspapers
Dailies (morning and evening editions), weeklies, Sundays and local free sheets.

Advantages	Disadvantages
Good market coverage	Circulation pattern may not efficiently cover all prospects
Readers are actively seeking information/ideas	Publication pattern may not meet your needs
Permanency: ads are torn out for future reference	Competition for reader attention
Credibility high	Mass medium, restricts ability to target prospects
Position of ad can select readers	
Illustration easy and relatively inexpensive	
Copy emphasis readily controlled by size and style of type, headlines, captions, subheads etc.	

Wide choice of size and therefore
cost

Geographically as well as
demographically selective

Magazines

Leisure, hobby, general interest, news, trade and academic journals, county or regional and business. If you would care to name
it, whatever 'it' may be, there is a magazine which caters for it.

Advantages	Disadvantages
Full-colour potential	Scheduling relatively inflexible – long lead time to publication
Prestige	Lacks immediacy, can imply lack of urgency for response
Effective targeting	Quality of artwork required may be difficult/expensive
Many more readers than circulation figures suggest, 'pass along' readership	
Can support and be supported by your articles, press releases and letters	
Frequently offer excellent deals to advertisers for copy close to deadline if space still unsold	
Some, such as *Management Today*, are the official organs of a professional body (Institute of Management)	

Outdoor advertising

Billboards and painted signs. This is unlikely to appeal to consultants, but it has been used to gain that massive and difficult account.

A major US consultancy practice was trying to land a multi-million-dollar account. After many unsuccessful attempts to make contact with the client, they bought space on a billboard which they knew that the MAN drove past every day to reach the office. When they called for the umpteenth time he saw them because 'I seem to see your name everywhere I go...' (Note: MAN is marketing jargon for the person who has the *money*, the *authority* and the *need* for your services. Man or woman, that's the MAN for you.)

Transport advertising

A mobile billboard sometimes used by software houses and IT consultancies, but more commonly the chosen medium, for obvious reasons, for the car trade. Unless you have a thing about getting your name known on a certain bus route, it is difficult to see how this kind of advertising could be applied to building your business. The fact that the advertisement is moving means that the message must be brief and catchy, and if you assume that your clients are apt to travel by car they can only see and read the lower rear panel.

Direct mail

A highly specialized area in spite of its apparent simplicity. The mailing list is the key to its use. If you are offering, say, a specialist seminar to a carefully targeted sector, direct mail can be very cost effective.

Advantages	Disadvantages
Messages can be directed to a highly selected target group	Total dependence on quality of list
Mailing personalized	Bought lists need constant updating

Messages can be any length – research says that long copy outsells short	Rented lists only usable once
Timing highly flexible	Built-in resistance to junk mail
Continues contact with existing clients, leading to potential referral and repeat business	Less than 8 seconds' attention on average
Can 'piggy back' with non-competing material	

Contrary to what the lovers of white space will tell you, all of the reliable evidence points to the fact that long copy sells. It is much more important when designing a direct mail piece to provide the detailed information that those who may be interested in your service will want than it is to create something slick and eye-catching that will have those who have no interest in what you have to sell saying 'Wow, that's clever' as they drop it in the bin. The same rules apply for content for direct mail as for advertising. The difference is that with a mailing piece you are not limited to *x* column centimetres. Make the most of it: tell the already interested what they need to know to become buyers.

It has been said that whatever response anyone says that they got to a mailing, they are lying. That notwithstanding, consultants often ask what response they might expect to a successful mailshot. Recent research by the Direct Mail Information Service investigated 38 mailings from consultants. The average response rate was 5.3 per cent. Never forget, however, that the response rate is a direct function of the quality of list used. The list alone can have a massive effect. The Drayton Bird Partnership found that the response can be multiplied by as many as 58 times if you get all of the following right:

❑ Mailing list (factor × 6)
❑ Offer (factor × 3)
❑ Timing (factor × 2)
❑ Creativity (factor × 1.35)

❏ Response mechanics (factor × 1.2)

$$6 \times 3 \times 2 \times 1.35 \times 1.2 = 58.32$$

Downsizing has noticeably improved the chances of getting your mail to the individual to whom it is addressed. Research comparing 1994 with 1990 showed that fewer executives now have their mail opened by others.

Radio
Radio and television stations are proliferating. Most of the new stations will be commercial. Some recent additions to the commercial network have proved to be far more successful than was anticipated. For example, in the UK Classic FM, which plays torn and bleeding chunks from the classics, attracts an audience of around 3 million.

Until the *British Business Survey 1995* was published I would have been highly sceptical about radio as a suitable advertising medium for professionals. The research indicated that in the UK 69 per cent of businesspeople listen to commercial radio. If more than two-thirds of the target population listen in conservative Britain, the numbers in other countries may well be higher. News, drive-in and drive-home programs are those indicated as most popular with business listeners.

Advantages	Disadvantages
High frequency at reasonable cost	You cannot use visuals to support your message
Flexibility: you can change copy right up to transmission	Lacks permanency
Cheap to produce	Very localized
Can be highly creative	Cannot put across detail effectively
Relatively low cost per listener	

Television

Cable television and information services are likely to offer more appropriate media choices for business-to-business communication. Specialist business channels are opening up and thriving.

Advantages	Disadvantages
High impact – sight, sound, movement	Production costs high
Memorable	Professional help essential to prepare commercials
Demonstrations convincing	High transmission costs
Scheduling flexibility	Desirable spots expensive and difficult to acquire
Closest approximation to face-to-face communication	
High credibility: 'saw it on television' and 'as seen on television' have inexplicable power to attract buyers	

Cinema

Unlikely to be of interest to consultants, but included for completeness and because professionals other than consultants who draw their clients from a local area have used the medium with considerable success.

Advantages	Disadvantages
Low overall cost	Limited exposure
Relatively low production costs	Need to check carefully types of advertiser you will be associated with
Large screen: colour, sight and sound	Cost per prospect highly dependent on film showing
Relatively attentive audience	Very difficult to measure results
	Very local coverage

Goodwill gifts

Pens, calendars and day planners inscribed with the donor's name are being seen with increasing frequency in the hands of seminar attendees and businesspeople in general. Specialist publications which feature only these gifts and the creativity which is devoted to their development testify to their success in some applications.

Advantages	Disadvantages
Keeps your name in front of client for as long as gift is useful and lasts	May be expensive
May last many years – e.g. leather or brass-edged document wallets, calculators	Much competition
	Message limited and static

Miscellaneous

Exhibition stands, audiovisual displays, newsletters and speculative cold (or even warm) brochure distributions come under this category.

Pulling it together

Advertising is always expensive. You cannot afford to let it become an expensive failure. Concentrate your attention as far as you can on the no-cost/low-cost tactics which build your status and reputation.

Use advertising tactically where no effective alternative exists and use it thoughtfully.

Buy advertising skilfully. Where you have the flexibility, place your advertisements just before press time at bargain prices. You can save 50 per cent or more on the cost of placing an advertisement by taking advantage of the offers which papers and journals are prepared to make when they are faced with the choice of either selling space cheaply, or of reducing the number of pages in the issue.

Measure the effect of each advertisement carefully. Do not rely on the ability of the client to remember where they saw your ad. If you want accurate information, provide some inducement for your client to clip and return the advertisement to you. By checking what is printed on the reverse you have a unique and accurate indication of when and where the advertisement appeared.

Do all that you can to predetermine the probable effect of any advertisement before it goes to press. You will still get surprises, but at least your chances decrease of missing an important error in style or copy.

Principles for evaluating your advertisements

1. Does the advertisement demand positive attention?
2. Is the headline powerful?
3. Does it offer meaningful benefits for my target audience?
4. Is the message clear?
5. Does it address predetermined needs?
6. Is the layout clear and easy to follow?
7. Is the overall image positive?
8. Is the stimulus for action now likely to be effective?
9. Is it clear how, when and where to respond?
10. Are address, telephone number and fax clear and accurate?
11. Does my advertisement indicate why **me**, rather than my competition?
12. Would I spend my money in response to this advertisement?
13. How do I rate the overall impression? What will be my readers' gut reaction?

If the answers to each of the first 12 questions is 'yes', and the predicted response in question 13 is positive, you are in with a chance.

If your advertising or mailing fails

Symptom
- ❑ Little response

Possible cause
- ❑ Message vague
- ❑ Insufficient frequency of repetition
- ❑ Advertisement too small
- ❑ Wrong medium or wrong publication
- ❑ Wrong placement of ad in publication or wrong timing of transmission
- ❑ Poor mailing list
- ❑ Buyers simply aren't there at present

Symptom
- ❑ Good response, poor subsequent sales

Possible cause
- ❑ Poor offer
- ❑ Inappropriate selling techniques
- ❑ Lack of sales skills
- ❑ Economic environment wrong
- ❑ Wrong stage in purchase cycle
- ❑ Insufficient promotional material
- ❑ Style of promotional material inappropriate to offer or potential purchasers

As you can see, there are many potential changes that can be made to improve the situation. Try to discipline yourself to making one change at a time. That way you can accurately identify and resolve problems.

ADVERTISING PLANNING

Header: What can I use to capture the attention of my prospective clients?

Offer: What promise can I make which will get them to go on reading and start wanting?

Evidence: How can I build confidence that I can deliver?

Action: How can I ensure that they take action **now**?

How to contact is clear?   Yes ☐   No ☐

Would I buy from this ad?   Yes ☐   No ☐

SOAP BOX – ECONOMICS FOR BEGINNERS

No consultant should be let loose on client premises without at least a smattering of knowledge of how the world of economics works, and you can take heart: the dismal science is fun until you get stuck in the quagmire of models that only work in an ideal world. Some basic principles can be acquired painlessly by reading Thurow, Galbraith, Krugman and the like. Indeed, the gentlemen mentioned tend to be a darned good read by any measure. (See the bibliography.) At least you'll know why anyone with a modicum of intelligence laughs at a Laffer curve.

You need to know a little of economics because:

❏ The businessperson is, or ought to be, in the business of wealth creation. Economics is about the creation and distribution of wealth.
❏ Economic theories, for better or worse, are espoused by governments and applied as ideologies. They are, therefore, the driving force behind the social, legislative and economic climate in which the business must operate.
❏ Business opportunities are either the result of economic decision making or lack of economic decisiveness – and so are many business problems.
❏ Strategic thinkers must take account of the national, transnational and global economic realities which underpin the key markets. Economics provides the nearest thing we have to an explanatory mechanism.
❏ Economic realities are an essential concomitant of identifying trends and comprehensive scenario planning.
❏ Strangely enough, economics, like business, is about people.

In short, any business professional who lacks a basic understanding of what does and does not work in economics is entering a gladiatorial arena naked and unarmed.

11
Referral Business Is Great Business

NO ONE DOUBTS THAT REFERRALS ARE OF VALUE. BUT FEW SEEM TO realize quite how valuable a referral is.

Research suggests that it costs eight to ten times as much to win an assignment as a result of your own marketing strategy as it does to gain referral business. If you could reduce 80 per cent of your costs to one-eighth of their present level, would you make money? You bet you would. And you ought to be aiming for 80 per cent referral and repeat business. Those who really take referrals seriously achieve that kind of level of success.

If you want referrals you need a strategy and you must have personal commitment. So let us look at those strategies which have been proven in the real world. The whole business of asking for referrals is one which is overlaid with strong emotion. Many suggested strategies are met with: 'I wouldn't feel comfortable doing that.'

The answer is simple. If you wouldn't be comfortable, don't do it. I will offer you all the ethical alternatives which I know work. Be selective and be consistent in your choice.

Sources

A good place to begin is to consider who could, if only they would, provide you with a constant source of referrals.

Current and past clients would head most people's list and a little additional thought would add former employers and colleagues, business acquaintances and possibly old college chums. If pushed, participants on my seminars sometimes include friends, neighbours and, if I insist, they might add, very doubtfully, relations.

If you are to be a big winner in the referral game you need to think wider and deeper than that. So who else has an interest in your success?

Four further possible sources of referrals come to mind.

Your friendly bank manager has, or ought to have, a deep and abiding interest in your financial success. What is more, they meet other customers every day who manage their own or other people's business. Many of these would benefit greatly from high-quality specialist business advice. So by recommending you the bank manager would serve the interests of at least two clients at the same time.

How close do you keep to your bank manager? Do they understand, in sufficient detail, what you do? Have you kept them advised of your successes and the recognition which they have brought? Have you ever told them how important referrals are to you? Do they receive a copy of your newsletter?

While you reflect on your future relationship with your bank manager, why not throw into your strategic mix two others with similar opportunities and responsibilities.

How much does your accountant or your lawyer know about the detail of what you do? That you are a consultant who enjoys a reasonable level of profitable business and has not yet been accused of malpractice is not enough to enable them to refer you to their other clients with confidence. Referrals always include an element of risk: others can never be sure that you are as good as you appear to be. From their point of view, it may be that you look pretty good because they lack the skill to identify your weaknesses. Why not develop a regular way of keeping them informed that clients, who have the necessary knowledge to judge, and your fellow professionals think very highly of you?

Take away the risk, and the barrier starts to crumble. Let them know how their practices might benefit from having access to you and there is a hole that they could drive a client through.

We have three further sources of referral, but I offered four. I am going to suggest that you ought to think seriously about using your competition to provide referral business. In a way that is what you do when you work as a network. Chapter 4 addressed the whole area of networking in detail, but I would like to draw your attention to something simpler.

Suppose you were to take one small area of your skills which you believe is of potential value, but is very rare. Suppose further that you practise and promote this skill until you build a reputation as a specialist. Would that be enough to persuade your competition to recommend you when their client has need of your skill? Probably not. There is every likelihood that they would not trust you not to steal their client. But suppose you became known, not through protestation but through experience, as being totally ethical in all your dealings. What then?

It may be that not only would your competition, who after all are constantly shaking the bushes for business, be promoting you, but if your specialism offered sufficient added value you might be able to charge fees that would enable you to live on that alone. It is a long-term strategy, but one that must be worth a few moments' thought.

Immediate tactics

If you and I do not get enough referral business it is probably because we do not actively seek it. Our clients, delighted as they are with our work, do not refer us for three reasons:

It takes effort to write a note, make a call or even respond positively to an enquiry in a conversation. You probably are aware of the times when your well-meant offer to 'dig out his address for you' has led to much frustration and a keen understanding of the shortcomings of your filing system.

They are never totally sure that the good work you did for them in the past is typical of a consistently high standard. Maybe your solution to their problem was good, but was it optimal? Are they sufficiently well informed to determine your merit? Unless you have taken proactive steps to keep them appraised of your triumphs on behalf of others, you can perhaps understand their doubts.

You have simply not asked them to refer you. If people are to be active in seeking out opportunities to refer you rather than just provide references when you have already unearthed the client, you must make it easy for them. You need to use your skills as a communicator to build their confidence in you.

Consider this case. Bill is an American with a practice which specializes in telesales training. He serves mainly large corporations and financial institutions. He has built his business by the twin strategy of practising what he preaches and encouraging referrals. And when he encourages referrals, he does it wholesale.

The prerequisite for obtaining referrals from a client is that the client is delighted and excited by the work that you have done for them. You must catch them at the peak of their delight, usually at the completion of an assignment when the good results of your labours are obvious. Your client is basking in the glory of success and all concerns which he might have had about retaining a consultant have evaporated in the warm glow of experience.

Then is the time to check that some tiny residual concern is not lurking under the general sense of well-being. Identify all the outcomes which were agreed and check off, one by one, that they have been achieved or exceeded. Ask your client if there is anything more that they feel ought to be done to ensure they are delighted with the outcome. If the answer is, as it should be, that they are more than happy right now, that is the time to get those referrals moving.

Explain how important referrals are to you and ask if they can think of anyone who might benefit from the quality of service that you have provided. If they work for a major company, ask specifically what other divisions could use your skills. If the client is below board level in the company, ask which directors ought to be given detailed and personalized information about their achievement and the way they have used your services.

Then make it really easy for them. Offer to write the letters, memoranda or reports. Make it clear that you will be happy to keep on amending anything you write until it represents precisely what they want to convey. Write what has been achieved, the benefits, their personal management and control of the project, your supportive role and their delight with the outcome. When they approve it, take responsibility for typing on their headed paper, producing all necessary envelopes and stamp and mail those items which have to be mailed yourself.

Leave them nothing to do but sign and smile.

When requests for your services, or appointments to discuss what you have to offer, begin to materialize, keep them informed of the results of 'their' labours. When contracts result, a brief note of thanks to your old client will keep them aware that you would appreciate their continued efforts on your behalf. Where interesting and useful new information results from work that you are doing, keep those clients who provide referrals informed whenever doing so does not breach client confidentiality.

In short, develop a reinforcement schedule which makes referring you almost a conditioned response.

It takes time, discipline and effort on your part, but that is small inconvenience when compared to the time and effort expended on making sales of your services from the ground up. Remember, when you have been referred to a client, it is only in the minority of cases that any other name is in the frame. You virtually wipe out competition and when you do business you do it on your own terms. That alone must be worth the work involved.

Opportunities to recommend you to others may be more frequent than you expect, but they will not happen every day. The importance of simply keeping in touch with your 'bird dogs' cannot be overstressed.

If you publish a newsletter, every old client should be on your mailing list. If you have no formal newsletter, write an informal note a couple of times a year which lets past clients know what and how you are doing and any good things that have come your way since your last contact.

Be alert for articles of particular interest to your clients which you could clip or photocopy and send.

If you write an article pertinent to a client's industry or specialism, send a prepublication draft and ask for any comments.

Divide your personal telephone book into 12 sections and make a few calls each month just to say 'hello'. Do not continually badger people for referrals. Once they know how important referrals are to you, the simple fact that they know you are still there and still doing good work will be enough to ensure that when the opportunity arises your name will spring to their mind and their lips.

Much of the marketing section of this book has been dedicated to building your reputation and status as an ethical and effective consultant. There is a way that you can use referrals to build your status in a unique way.

When your name has been passed to a third party, the expectation on all sides is that you will grab the telephone and make speedy contact. To raise your status in their eyes, have your potential client make the first contact instead.

An old client tells you that her good friend Bill Folds is considering putting into place a total quality management system. Your name has been enthusiastically recommended and you should get in touch with Bill post haste. For you to do so will make you appear efficient and concerned. You can appear efficlient, concerned and important while remaining accessible by not rushing to make a direct contact.

Find something which will be useful and interesting to Bill Folds. Some information. A 'model' or handout. An article about his problem or opportunity. Give it to your client and suggest that she pass it to Bill with your number, so that Bill can contact you when he is ready for a chat.

When you can do that, and it works, you really have the referral business sown up and you know that your personal reputation will stand any test.

REFERRAL ACTION PLANNING

Consider the following carefully:

❑ What information can I provide to my professional advisers which would make it easy for them to recommend my services to others?

❑ What legitimate concerns might they have about referring me, and how can I remove them?

❑ Which recent or current clients have expressed delight with my work?

❑ How might I most tactfully approach each of them?

❏ How will I ensure ongoing contact in the future?

Is the appropriate primary method by newsletter, letter or telephone?

Do I know enough about this client's interests to identify data or information which will interest them?

Make planning for maximizing your opportunities for referrals a basic part of your practice-building strategy. When the time comes that you can say to a prospective client, 'Who has recommended you to me? I only work for clients who are referred to me,' you can assume that you have made it. Until then, building your personal group of 'bird dogs' will more than repay the effort.

Find the approach which sits most comfortably with your personal style and start today – it really is that important.

12
Selling Your Skills

As Figure 12.1 suggests, very few good consultants are good salespeople. Equally, it is an interesting fact that few good salespeople easily become good consultants. There are very deep personality and value considerations which make it difficult for the salesperson, using standardized techniques, to place the client at the absolute centre of things. It is often at least as difficult for the good consultant to do something which they regard as 'pushy' or manipulative.

The status- and reputation-building tactics which we have described in previous chapters are intended to ease the problem by creating a relationship which reduces the 'pressure to pressure'. If you have worked on developing your reputation, your first meeting with the prospective client will be very different from what it would be under less propitious circumstances.

Your client will find themselves in the unusual situation of feeling just a little in awe of you. They will have heard of you in circumstances which give you exceptional credibility. You need to be prepared to capitalize on this.

It is important that everything you do, everything you say, is consistent with the image that your new client has of you.

KEY CHARACTERISTICS INDICATING SUCCESS

Consultant	Salesperson
Sense of **vocation**	Desire to **win**
Personal and organizational **development**	**Assertiveness**
Affiliation	**Influence**
Focus on the specific	**Affiliation**
Organizational **power**	**Discipline**

Figure 12.1: How different are salespeople and the people they sell to?

First impressions

Approach the meeting without any sense of inferiority.

No matter who your client is, your meeting must be a meeting of peers who expect to explore the potential benefits of working together. With the greatest of sincere respect to used-vehicle salespeople (some have literally been, over the years, among my best friends), you must be seen as the equivalent of a surgeon rather than a used-car salesperson, or any other kind. It is not a matter of snobbery, it is a matter of role, and different roles dictate different behaviours and different levels of sophistication.

You need to make it clear to your client from the beginning that in order to establish whether it would be appropriate to offer your services there are things that you must explore and understand. With that in mind, you will avoid wasting your host's valuable time if they could answer a few simple questions. Remember that it is the one who asks the questions, not the one who answers them, who controls the conversation.

If your client beats you to the punch by saying, 'Tell me what you can do for me,' resist the temptation to start talking about your wonderful services. You will almost certainly say something which gives your client the opportunity to think, 'I don't need that', after which their concentration will be less on what you say, and more on how politely to put off the decision, or reject your offer. Instead, say something like:

> *'We offer a wide range of services, and I will be pleased to tell you in detail those which may be appropriate to your needs. To avoid wasting your time with those which may be least relevant right now, could you tell me what is the major problem affecting your industry?'*

This should be followed by: 'How exactly is that affecting you?'

Once you have established the expectation that you will conduct the early interview, it is easy to continue. Most people enjoy an opportunity to talk about things which are important to them, and if you 'sell' them on talking to you, many will talk for hours.

Your questions must not be aimless, however: there are some things which you absolutely need to know before you can relate your services fully to client needs. We will identify the key questions soon.

When your potential client is talking, listen actively. By actively I mean think about what is said and use it to formulate other questions. Try to avoid jumping to conclusions. Only take notes if you must and after you have asked permission to do so. Keep notes brief – a mass of written screed is a distraction to the other person, who will find it difficult not to keep glancing at what you are writing. We remember by making connections and through repetition. Ask about key points and mentally connect them so that when you remember one the others come surging back. If a stage performer can remember the name of each of 200 or more members of an audience whom they have met briefly once only as they took their seats, you can remember the key points of a conversation.

A poor memory is a mixture of affectation, laziness and sheer bad manners, so learn to use yours.

Show by your body posture that what is being said really interests you. Nod to show understanding. Maintain eye contact, not with a fixed gaze but with occasional glances. If you find that you are looking at your client's face for a lengthy time, look at a central point on their forehead rather than directly into their eyes.

Ask intelligent questions to clarify your understanding or to direct the client's attention to an area you need to know more about. Avoid creating a sense of an interrogation by injecting your own occasional comments when you have something to contribute which shows that you have done your homework about the industry and the client company. Try to find a reason to sit side by side rather than face to face with the client. Sitting face to face accentuates a sense of being adversarial, while side by side suggests mutual problem solving which justifies in the other's mind almost any exploratory question.

When you have little which it is germane to add, punctuate the flow with expressions such as, 'Thank you, that is interesting.'

Reward the other person for answering your questions with smiles, nods and gestures of understanding or concern.

Recent psychological research confirms that women have a considerable natural or, more likely, cultural advantage in using these encouraging and relationship-building non-verbal techniques.

Lead the client gently to telling you what you need to know, which is as follows.

Vital questions to be asked at every first visit

What is the client's previous experience of consultants?
- ❑ Have they used consultants before?
- ❑ What good results came from the experience?
- ❑ Were there any problems?
- ❑ What would they seek to do differently this time?
- ❑ Do they have any fears or concerns about having consultants in the company now?

❑ Is there anything that they would wish a consultant to be particularly sensitive to at present?

Research shows that any company which has used consultants once is likely to use them again. But they may want things to be very different this time.

What was the nature of the financial arrangement?
Not how much did they pay, but were the consultants paid a fixed fee for the job? A daily rate? Or was the work done on the basis of a performance contract? (If a client goes on to tell you exactly how much they paid, great. You can realistically take that as a buying signal.)

What specific outcomes does the client seek from your intervention?
'If I take on an assignment for your company, how will we measure my contribution? How will you and I know that I have done a good job?'

What is the client's ideal outcome?
In a year from today, how will the company be different if the client's wishes are fulfilled?

Regardless of any work that you might carry out for this client, what is their most important goal right now?

With many clients you will find that they only have vague answers to the last two questions. My experience is that asking them and helping the client to clarify their thinking enables me to define measurable outcomes for my intervention, and establish important client goals that I can help to achieve. More importantly, at a time when I am trying to build a relationship, it causes the client to place a very high value on our discussion and creates a proper foundation for the future relationship.

Talking of placing a value on the initial discussion, may I remind you that research suggests that as many as 15 per cent of clients expect to be billed for it. This can lead to an interesting source of conflict.

The potential client, believing that consultants charge for everything, expects to receive an invoice for the marketing call and works hard to get some information or work done by the consultant which will represent value for money. The consultant, sensitive to the fact that clients try sometimes to get something for nothing, is determined to give nothing away. They talk in frustrating and ever-decreasing circles until the assignment disappears in a game of 'catch as catch can'. If you have the slightest reason to believe that the client misreads the situation, clarify it:

'I have found that some clients expect to be billed for the first exploratory meeting. I like to make it clear that I never raise an invoice unless I have carried out client work, or have given specific business advice or information.'

Professional selling

Professional services must be sold. We can do a great deal to predispose the client towards hiring you, but in the end everything comes down to your ability to demonstrate why your services should be retained today.

The contract must be signed. With that in mind I am going to try to explain within the constraints of a short chapter exactly how, step by step, you can use well-validated techniques to ensure a very high success rate.

First, a little background. Our approach to marketing has been one of building your status and anything which we do to make the sale must be congruent with that status. We must never be seen to be using obvious and doubtful sales methods. Our approach must flow naturally from what has gone before and must create a state of maximum comfort both for us and our client.

People love to buy, but they hate to be sold to.

If we keep that maxim in mind, we will find that we are kept easily and comfortably on track.

A great deal of dedicated research has gone into analysing what works in enabling people to buy without feeling that they have been sold to. The research has shown that it is possible to develop a simple and accurate cognitive model of exactly how people think as they go through the buying process.

The salesperson must relate to that process successfully. More than 60 years' in-depth analysis of what works in practice enables us to lay out a step-by-step approach. Professionals facilitate that process.

The thought process is presented graphically in Figure 12.2. Each box represents an exact thought pattern for the potential buyer of goods, services or ideas. For each the sequence is precisely the same, the questions and the feelings do not vary, only the words with which an individual might express them are liable to variation. Each thought expresses or implies a question. If that question is answered to the satisfaction of the client, their mind moves comfortably to the next. If all questions are answered satisfactorily the decision to 'buy' is only constrained by the ability to proceed.

Selling your services

An approach which will reduce the chances of rejection, demonstrate your professionalism and gain you more assignments is as follows:

Step One: Plan your presentation from the listener's point of view

❑ Make your listener feel important by basing your discussion firmly on their objective.

❑ Test your understanding of the most important issues or problems your listener faces – from their viewpoint, **not yours**.

❑ Remember that their present point of view is based on their past success and makes absolute sense to them. To change it

you require compelling reasons.
❑ Match your mood and manner to that of your listener.

*Step Two: Create for the listener an awareness of the need to act – **now***

❑ Demonstrate that conditions beyond the control of either of you are changing.
❑ Show how the changes taking place **could** cause your listener problems in the future.
❑ Indicate that you have the means to change potential threats into opportunities.

Step Three: Maintain and build your listener's interest

❑ Mention one or two benefits which the listener will gain from using your services before indicating what you will do.
❑ Make sure the listener regards them as benefits **and appreciates their worth**.

*Step Four: Tell your listener **all** that they need to know about your services*
Explain in sufficient detail:

❑ What you will do.
❑ When you will do it.
❑ Who else will be involved.
❑ What special skills and knowledge you uniquely offer.
❑ How the client will retain control.
❑ How they will remain fully informed.
❑ Who else, whom they respect, has already successfully used your services.
❑ What they say about the experience (if you have their permission to quote them).

Never be tempted to say **how** you will do it.

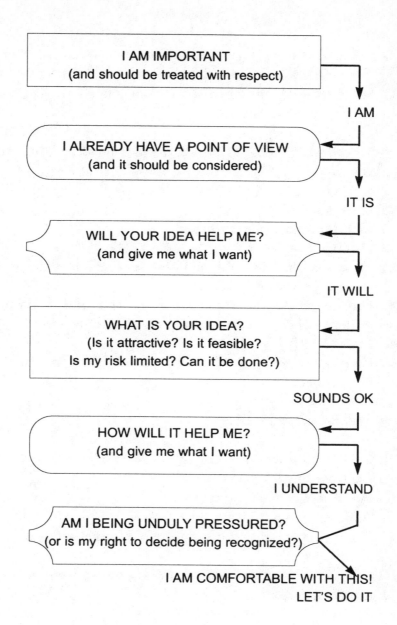

Figure 12.2: The path to assent

Step Five: Explain the benefits of your services

❑ Link the benefits logically to prove that if one is achieved the others follow as a consequence.
❑ Show that the final benefit in your chain of logic is the listener's key objective.

Step Six: If you lose your listener's favourable attention during the discussion

❑ Stop talking.
❑ Wait for your listener to speak.
❑ Listen actively.
❑ Show that you have listened by repeating a key idea or feeling in your own words.
❑ Diffuse the emotion by showing that you understand the right of the listener to react **in any way they choose**.
❑ Deal with their problem.
❑ Continue when you are convinced that they are satisfied and not before.

Step Seven: Ask for the assignment

❑ No tricks or 'closing techniques' – **just ask**.
❑ Look for 'buying signals':
   Nods of agreement or approval
   Building on your ideas
   Willingness to give you supportive information or data.

Having asked – stop talking and stay absolutely silent until you have a reply.

Figure 12.3 shows how this ties in precisely with the client's thought process when facing a decision of whether to buy.

Always start, as indicated at the beginning of this chapter, by asking essential questions. As soon as you have the information

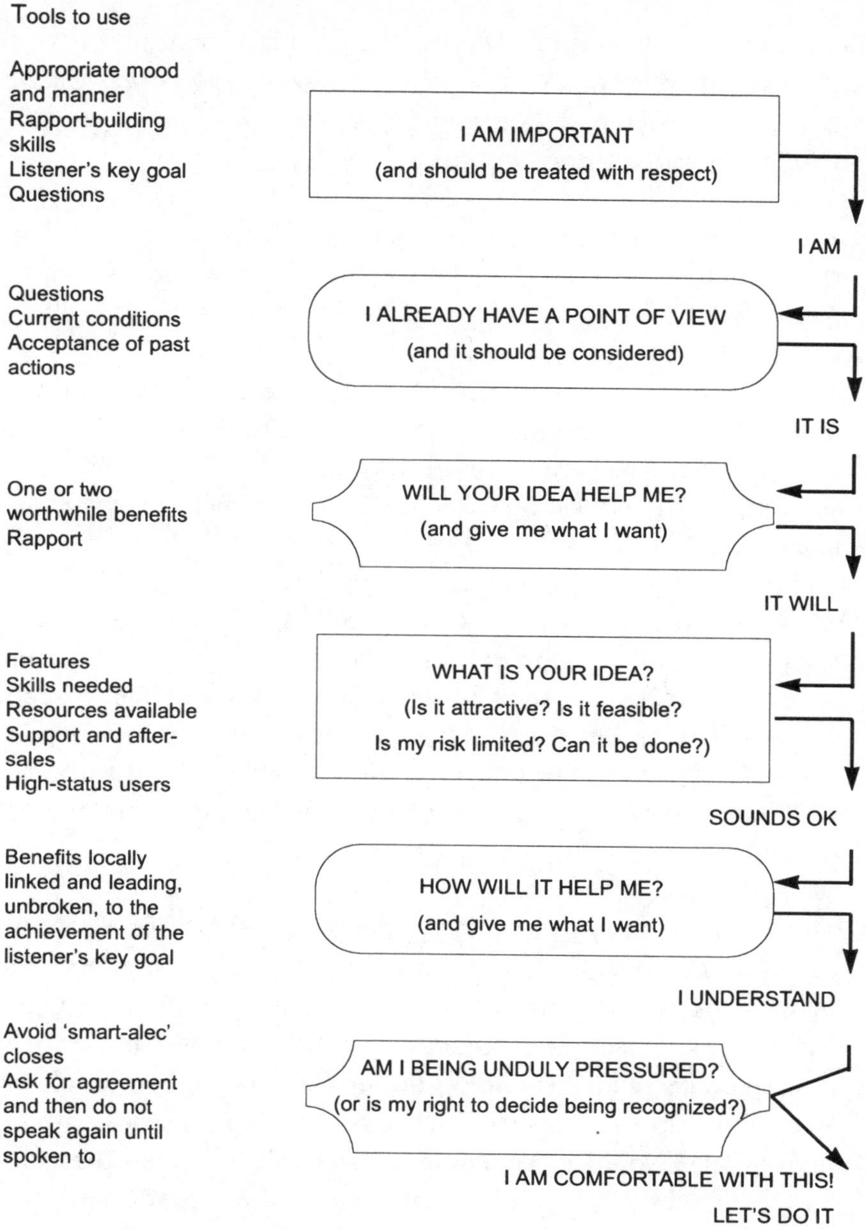

Tools to use

Appropriate mood
and manner
Rapport-building
skills
Listener's key goal
Questions

I AM IMPORTANT

(and should be treated with respect)

I AM

Questions
Current conditions
Acceptance of past
actions

I ALREADY HAVE A POINT OF VIEW

(and it should be considered)

IT IS

One or two
worthwhile benefits
Rapport

WILL YOUR IDEA HELP ME?

(and give me what I want)

IT WILL

Features
Skills needed
Resources available
Support and after-
sales
High-status users

WHAT IS YOUR IDEA?

(Is it attractive? Is it feasible?

Is my risk limited? Can it be done?)

SOUNDS OK

Benefits locally
linked and leading,
unbroken, to the
achievement of the
listener's key goal

HOW WILL IT HELP ME?

(and give me what I want)

I UNDERSTAND

Avoid 'smart-alec'
closes
Ask for agreement
and then do not
speak again until
spoken to

AM I BEING UNDULY PRESSURED?

(or is my right to decide being recognized?)

I AM COMFORTABLE WITH THIS!

LET'S DO IT

Figure 12.3: Tools to use on the path to assent

which enables you to do it, suggest that it might be useful if you were to summarize the key points as you have understood them. This summary is your sales presentation.

It might go something like this:

'As I understand it your primary concern at the moment is that the reduction of headcount be totally voluntary. Am I right?' *(client objective)*

'Yes, that's essential.'

'Am I also right in believing that the mess the economy is in has affected managers' confidence and you are finding that there is deep concern over even asking for the facts about voluntary separation?' *(conditions the client faces and losses they cause the client to experience)*

'There certainly is, and it's getting worse.'

'Then I think I have an idea of how I might help you. Your people would be more inclined to consider accepting your generous separation package if they believed that they were able to keep a number of options open. *(throwaway benefit used to maintain favourable attention)* Those who would happily accept the idea of retirement would have no problem, so if I could focus on the others?'

'That makes sense.'

'Good. I think that you could give people an increased sense of security and confidence in their future if you initiated a series of workshops which would enable qualified people to prepare themselves for self-employment as management consultants. *(benefits leading into expression of the key idea)* These would follow the application of a psychometric test which is very comprehensive and would help people to make an informed decision about whether self-employment would be appropriate for them. The workshop I have in mind provides participants with strategies for building a professional practice. Research shows these strategies to be highly effective in all cultures. We would also prepare them for the administrative side of running their own business with precise and detailed information on how to write proposals, develop contracts and set their fees. Much of the material is transferable to any kind of high-quality business, so those for whom consultancy does not seem to be the answer would still gain a great deal from the workshop.' *(features)*

'What about those who would be looking for another job?'

'Our team includes experts with a proven track record in the field of recruitment. I suggest that through the use of practical job-hunting workshops we could offer a service to those who prefer to look for new jobs which would compare very favourably with 'outplacement' at considerably lower cost. By backing this service with one-on-one counselling under the supervision of a qualified psychologist, we could make a major contribution to alleviating stress at this difficult time. Your company could make this service available to families, whose needs are often overlooked, showing that you are prepared to do everything possible to continue to support your people through difficult times. This would have a positive effect on the morale of those who remain.' *(more features)*

'It does sound interesting.' *(Buying signal? Maybe, but not strong enough to lead to intelligent trial close, benefits have only been implied.)*

'By approaching the problem this way, you would ensure that your people have the best opportunity to establish themselves quickly in new careers even in these difficult times. That is certain to build their confidence, and by initiating a program that gives continued support to everyone whatever their career plans, you would be offering a level of service which may well lead to your separation program being oversubscribed. What do you think?' *(logical flow of benefits, leading to achievement of the client's objective and followed by a very gentle trial close which will not make the client feel pressured)*

'I think it sounds interesting, but I need to think about it.'

'I understand that, it's a major decision. Why don't I let you have a detailed proposal which will give you all the information you need?' *(trial close)*

'When could you get it to me?'

'If we can make an appointment now for early next week, I will ensure that it is ready. I could answer any questions that you might have and you would be in the best position to make your decision. As you know, we always work to a formal contract so that you have details of exactly what we undertake to provide, I'll have that drawn up for the same meeting. Is that OK with you?' *(trial close)*

'As long as you don't expect me to sign it first and read the proposal afterwards. How about Wednesday? If you could be here for about ten, we could arrange for you to meet the chairman at noon. I'd like her to know what we're doing. She's very keen on PR and I think I see some spin-off here.' (I think they've bought it!)

Leaving aside the inescapably stilted feel of written English in lengthy passages of speech, it is easy to write sales pitches. In real life, however, it seldom goes from start to finish according to plan.

Clients take you off at tangents by raising new ideas as they think of them. Sometimes you inadvertently say something which triggers an unexpected negative response and you may have no idea why. I would like to give you a little help with both of those problems.

Your client suddenly thinks of something which is of great interest to them, but which does not fit snugly into your flow of argument. For example, in real life the client in my little vignette above was suddenly struck by the PR potential of providing stress counselling for the families of early retirees and started talking at great length and with considerable enthusiasm. What did I do?

I listened with keen interest and encouraged him to go on talking. My interest was keen because:

❑ The client was selling himself on the idea and sales arguments which he develops for himself have more power than the best I could devise. (People love to buy, they hate to be sold to.)

❑ If, in spite of the signs to the contrary, I met some sales resistance later, I should be able to build a convincing case around satisfying the chairman's desire for PR.

❑ If I needed to convince the chairman, I could not assume her enthusiasm for PR, but it gave me a foundation for some sensitive probing when we met.

❑ And in terms of my relationship with my client, I knew that if I could help him to come up with good PR ideas it would enhance his status in the eyes of the chairman. Building up my client is an important aspect of the business I am in.

So in spite of my carefully thought-out approach I was happy to let him talk on. I lie, it was *because* of my structured approach that I could encourage the client to interrupt me and chat away to his heart's content. I have a structure so it is easy for me to remember exactly where I am. I do not have to remember detail, only one key word. My structure is:

❑ Client's **objective**.
❑ **Conditions** they are up against and problems they may face.
❑ Indication that I can **help**.
❑   **enefits** from listening to me.
❑ Detail of my **idea**.
❑ **Logical** benefit flow to attainment of client's objective.
❑ Ask for **action**.

I have a road map, and by mentally registering a single word as my client takes off, I can return to my route at any time. It does not matter if I repeat a benefit or part of my idea, the flow will make it seem natural and easy. I can relax and listen and learn. Listening is the key to the next little technique.

The SARAH technique

No matter how careful you are, regardless of the sensitivity which you show towards others' needs and feelings, there will be times when suddenly and for no obvious reason your client shows clear signs of being upset. By word or gesture they will indicate that you have done or said something which has triggered a negative response.

Many salespeople, seeing the signs, break simultaneously into a sweat and a gallop. They feel that if only they can finish what they are saying all will be well. After all, they have an unanswerable, logical case.

Unfortunately, using logic to deal with emotions does not work. Think about those times when you get upset with little reason. If someone tries to change your mood with logic, do you listen to them? If you are anything like me you don't. What I do is to ignore what is being said while I think of all the convincing reasons for being right to feel as I do. If necessary, I will dredge up wrongs of such distant history that I can remember them only in times of intense determination to feel ill used. And it works. The more others try to make me feel better with their appeals to logic the worse I feel, and the worse I feel the more aggressive I become.

So what do I do when my client shows signs of anger or distress? Do I panic? No. I relax and enjoy another opportunity to win a brownie point because years ago I was introduced to SARAH. She will help my situation. If I use her skills with sensitivity I will have a grateful and more compliant client.

So when things start to go off the rails think SARAH. The full technique is explained below.

Before reading the details of the technique bear with me, if you will, while I indicate briefly why you have much to gain from practising this technique, and not just in the sales situation. The SARAH approach is a well-validated way to bring into the open and begin to deal with client complaints at any stage. Research shows that even if clients have serious complaints about the way a consultancy assignment is being completed, they are unlikely to raise them unless encouraged. They do, however, often tell their friends – and therefore your prospective customers.

If, on the other hand, you are able to get clients to express their thoughts and feelings immediately, and if you resolve problems, even serious problems, quickly, three things happen:

❑ Between 56 and 83 per cent use your services again in spite of problems initially experienced.

❑ The number of others to whom they speak about their problems is at least halved.

❑ They are happier about referring you to others because they know that even if problems arise you handle them, not merely effectively, but sensitively.

SARAH can help to make you seriously rich.

SARAH's gameplan

Stop talking

Do not talk faster, in fact do not talk at all. Give your listener the opportunity to express their feelings. No matter how painful the silence seems to you, there is absolutely nothing you can usefully say. If there was your client would not listen to it anyway.

Hold your tongue and within seconds (it will feel like minutes) your listener will break the silence.

Adopt active listening

Listen as if your life depends on understanding how your client feels and what they think. Make no attempts to second guess, always accept what is said as if it were true. Most of all, do not listen as smart-ass salespeople listen to customer objections with the intention of hearing something which enables them to think 'Gotcha!', followed by an attempt to devastate the listener with their lucidity and grasp of facts.

Feelings are facts, and in this situation it is your client's feelings which are the most salient facts of all. So when you are sure that they have said all they are going to say for the moment:

Reflect content or feeling

Paraphrase a key statement your client has made to demonstrate that you really have been listening. Say it musingly to show that you are carefully considering what is being said and not doing parrot-like imitations. If nothing coherent enough has been said then reflect what is clear to you about what the client is feeling:

- ❏ 'You are very upset.'
- ❏ 'You feel that it is unfair?'

If you reflect feeling, wait for a response. The listener will almost certainly now expand on what the problem is and, if you have remained concerned but calm, you will find that they become a little calmer too as they realize that there is no need to try to convince you of the validity of the arguments they have been rehearsing internally to justify the mood swing.

Act with empathy
Show your acceptance that others have an absolute right to feel any way they please. They may be wrong. They may have completely misunderstood. You may have inadvertently triggered a prejudice of which any right-minded person would be ashamed. Nonetheless, they have an absolute right as individuals to deal with their own problems their own way. But be sure you can tell the difference between 'empathy' and 'sympathy' and take care that you never express sympathy – 'You are absolutely right to feel as you do' – when you intend to convey empathy – 'You have an absolute right to feel as you do'.

The difference allows you, after expressing empathy, to correct their thinking and consequently change their feeling. Once you have shown sympathy you are locked in to their feeling no matter how injurious it is to your case. 'Yes, you're right' is not a particularly useful answer to 'all consultants are liars and thieves'. It will not help you to win a sale, or respect. Neither will 'That's nonsense, and I can prove it.'

Empathy is shown in expressions like:

- ❏ 'I can understand you feeling that way, many people do.'
- ❏ You have every right to be concerned until I have proved what I can do.

❏ That's a perfectly reasonable point of view.
❏ It can seem like a lot of money until we've fully worked out the savings.
❏ Others have expressed very similar worries.

Empathy allows you to accept the reasonableness of others' feelings and still correct their understanding.

Handle objections

When your calm, sensitive handling of the situation has made it easy for your client to listen to reason again, deal with any objections raised. Always deal with what your client says. Never try to second guess 'what they really mean' – you will almost certainly get it wrong. Even if you get it right, you will destroy the belief that you have been listening carefully and with empathy and understanding.

Research over the last 60 years shows that objections can be classified and the most appropriate tactics for handling each type suggested.

Price

Something appears to cost too much when it seems to offer insufficient benefit for the price to be paid in money or effort. Your service will deliver many benefits which will not fit into the logical flow towards the achievement of your client's key goals. Use these additional benefits to convince your listener that you are providing exceptional value.

Habit

'We've always done it this way, and it works' is not an invitation for you to focus on why the old way is stupid and your idea is infinitely better. It does give you the opportunity, however, to recognize that you have not shown sufficiently clearly how the changes in the environment in which your client operates are such that major problems may result in the future if steps are not taken now. You will, of course, need to convince them that the steps you are advocating are going to be effective in the new or emerging conditions.

Competition
'We have always been happy with Ernest & Elderly' is asking you to expand on what is unique about your offer.

Your client is asking you to give more detail about your idea. But be careful. Be aware at all times that you stick to **what** you will do, not **how** you will do it.

If your potential client has a pal at E & E, you may find that they will soon be offering their clients what was once your unique service if you have proudly given away the recipe.

We have covered in this chapter how you approach the initial meeting with the prospective client:

❑ Essential questions to be asked before you start selling.
❑ How to structure your sales presentation and how to deal with outbursts and objections.

Before we leave this important area there is one more piece of research which I would like to share with you.

Howard Shenson, who did more to put fact into the places formerly occupied by mystique than most, conducted some research in 1990 into what it is that clients fear – and fear is not too strong a word – about hiring consultants. You will be well repaid if you take a little time to think about how you will most comfortably ensure that these fears do not get between you and a profitable assignment.

Remember, fears are not something that we openly talk about in our society. We expect people to portray themselves as confident at all times. The manager who honestly admits to doubts about anything gets short shrift from peers and bosses, so do not expect anyone to admit to these concerns when face to face, or to welcome any clumsy attempt to bring them into the open. What is needed is for you to present your service in a way which resolves the concern without embarassment to the client.

The Shenson survey

The survey covered 600 companies which used, or were actively planning to use, consultants. The fears are presented in order of importance, with the first being regarded as most important by most respondents.

Consultant incompetence
Clients consider hiring a consultant because they doubt their own ability in a certain area, or because they lack the time or internal resources to do the job.

It is not surprising if they wonder whether they have enough knowledge to judge the competence of a specialist. By marketing yourself using the methods I have described, you will build client confidence in your ability. By approaching the initial discussion as a surgeon considering whether to operate and by avoiding 'pile 'em high, sell 'em cheap' sales techniques, you will reinforce the client's belief that with you at least they need have no concern about consultant competence.

If they feel good about working with you, why should they look elsewhere?

Lack of management control
Consultants are often perceived as scuttling about the business, clipboard in hand, answerable to no one and finally presenting a hitherto secret report which embarrasses the client who is paying them. I have even known, to the profession's shame, of consultants who, without any reference to their client, have recommended that the client is at the base of the problem and should be removed forthwith and without option.

The person who hires you is your client and has an absolute right to your loyalty. When you describe what you will do if assigned, explain precisely how you will keep your client informed of progress and how you will, if appropriate, provide them with information which they can present to their bosses. Your job is to support your client in managing their company and to enhance their standing. It is not to usurp or undermine their position in any way. If your client is doing it all wrong, you find a way to help them to get it right or you withdraw from the assignment.

Honesty and honour rule in the profession which you have chosen.

Continued dependency

Respondents reported that this problem was of the same importance as lack of control. It is not unknown for consultants to put in systems far beyond the capacity of the client company to operate, with the result that the company is faced with the choice of buying in specialist knowledge on a permanent or periodic basis. Clients believe that this is a conscious strategy on the part of consultants to ensure a job for life. Conscious malpractice or sheer incompetence, it is unacceptable.

Tell your client what steps you propose to take to ensure growth in the self-reliance and autonomy of their team as part of the work you are doing.

Excessive fees

This book explains in detail how to establish fees which will give you high earning capacity while offering exceptional value for money.

Be proud of the benefits which your intervention will create and do not assume that the client will value them unless you explain them fully. By showing logically that important and valued objectives will be achieved, you will put a significance on your services which will make it unlikely that price will ever be questioned. If it is, follow John Fenton's excellent advice and 'take pride in your price' as an indicator of exceptional value.

Lack of time

Recently there has been an influx into the profession of cut-price consultants who are unable or unwilling to establish sensible fees. Many have tried to make up for the low fees charged by cutting corners, including charging two or more clients for the same rushed work. The result has been unspecific and slipshod. Explain to your client that your fees are set at a level which enables you to resource the job properly and devote adequate time to their needs.

Need for a consultant seen as an admission of management failure
Stupidly macho organizations are found in industry and commerce on both sides of the Atlantic.

Put this concern to rest by emphasizing that although the client could probably do what you will do themselves if they had time, your position as an outside specialist enables you to concentrate totally on this one small aspect, and use techniques which ensure a positive outcome in the least time with minimum expense.

Fear of disclosing sensitive data
You may need to convince the client of the absolute confidentiality of *all* information they may give you.

Consider the possibility of even refusing to disclose to anyone who your clients are without their specific permission. When faced with the rare, but occasional, request for client references, I say that I never disclose even the names of my clients without their permission, but I will be happy to ask people for whom I have done similar work to provide any information required.

That is usually enough to put the client's fears about confidentiality to rest and it almost invariably obviates the need for references. When Howard Shenson was asked for a reference he would make a joke of it, pointing out that he would never give the name of anyone who might speak less than ecstatically of his work and that all clients knew that they would be off his Christmas card list if they failed to perform as required. More seriously, he believed that the request for references was a clear indicator that he had failed to sell effectively. He would carefully probe for where he had gone wrong and put it right.

Improper diagnosis or needs analysis

It is always easier to market a product than a service, and in the past consultants peddling off-the-shelf nostrums for all complaints have had more success than they deserve. Because they have only one solution which they cannot amend, they force-fit the client problem to their cure, with often disastrous results.

Explain to your client that you develop processes appropriate to the problem, and never use inappropriate methods just because they are easy or popular at the moment. Be warned, however: never be tempted to show how good you are at diagnosis by attempting something off the cuff at the first meeting.

You get paid for identifying and solving problems: diagnosis is often the hard part of the assignment.

The Chartered Institute of Marketing recommends that the service provider can overcome the problem of not being in a position to demonstrate a tangible in which the bells can be sounded and whistles blown by presenting your service as a surrogate product. Try to think of a name for what you do which will give the sense of a product without limiting you to off-the-shelf nostrums. After all, few clients have any real understanding of, say, business process reengineering until it is explained in terms of their perceived business needs.

Pushing a product

There is a well-founded concern that some consultants are salespeople in disguise whose main aim is to push a product. Where possible avoid recommending specific products. Your independence is something you should value and promote.

Summary

The approach to sales outlined in this chapter is one which is congruent with the role and status of a professional, and which research has consistently shown to be highly successful in many cultures. If you study and practise it you may expect a high percentage of positive outcomes and you should expect no rejections.

Although you may not make every sale every time, sensitive use of this material will build respect for your professionalism even when you lose out for some reason. That respect will keep doors open to you.

If you want to make every sale, every time, there is a mass of psychological information to help you. My *The Power of Influence* brings the current research together in a 'how to' format.

Clients can be Janus-like when, as I explained above, they simultaneously want tailored unique solutions and the concrete appearance of a product. Consultancy is, or should be, a service rather than a product. As such, it is always intangible to a degree. What is worse, it is often by its exploratory nature a particularly ill-defined service. This makes some research completed in the early 1980s by the sociologists George and Myers particularly relevant to the seller of consultancy services.

As you end this chapter and prepare to put down the book, I ask you to consider the following in the light of what you have just read.

Differences in (client) perceptions, attitudes and behaviours when buying services

Consumers' purchase perceptions

- ❑ Services are less consistent in quality than goods.
- ❑ Any service purchase is a high-risk purchase.
- ❑ Service purchasing is a less enjoyable activity than buying products (you cannot 'twiddle the knobs' of a consultant).
- ❑ Services need to be bought with greater consideration of the seller's reputation.

Consumers' purchase behaviour

- ❑ Consumers make fewer price comparisons when buying services.
- ❑ They place heavy reliance on the supplier's reputation and

their own and others' experience.
❑ They are less influenced by advertising and more by personal recommendations.

Personal selling of services

❑ Clients seek greater personal involvement in the service activity.
❑ Long-term satisfaction is greatly influenced by the salesperson's attitude and personality.
❑ Salespeople may need to spend more time reducing anxiety about the purchase.

Does the above help to convince you, if you needed convincing, that marketing your services on the basis of building your reputation, status and image makes total sense? Does it further help to explain why an approach to selling which makes the client central to the process is essential rather than optional?

Finally, a brief outline of some recent research into what clients are looking for when a consultant is selling their services.

What clients say they want at the selling stage

❑ Willingness to apply original thinking to our problem – not suggesting the solution to someone else's problem that was supposedly 'the same'.
❑ Solid agreement on goals, outcomes and scope of work.
❑ A detailed and realistic commitment of time to undertake the assignment.
❑ Structured methods but not inflexible packages.
❑ Expertise that really relates to our problem.
❑ Interest in bottom-line improvements or cost reduction.
❑ Admission of the need to learn first about my business.
❑ Desire to get going with the project for the project's sake and not the consultant's immediate income needs.
❑ Looking for a positive win–win relationship.
❑ Presentation of a range of feasible options.

- ❑ A fresh approach, but not one that is excessively risky.
- ❑ An impression of competence and energy.
- ❑ Doing their homework before and during the visit.
- ❑ Spending adequate time defining the problem.
- ❑ Knowledge of new developments in our industry, our company, our market and management in general.
- ❑ Indication of partnership mentality with in-house brainpower.
- ❑ Complete confidentiality.
- ❑ **Reasonable** prices.

What clients say are the major turn-offs at the selling stage

- ❑ The 'all singing, all dancing' approach, where the 'stars' do the selling, but the 'donkeys' do the assignment.
- ❑ Dishonesty or evasiveness about credentials of project team.
- ❑ Making promises that cannot be met.
- ❑ Talking too much – listening too little to learn what is really different about our situation.
- ❑ Name dropping and breaching confidentiality.
- ❑ Canned rather than customized approaches.
- ❑ Trying to 'play it by ear' without any attempt at preparation.
- ❑ Asking the same question again after it has been answered.
- ❑ Tying savings in to cost of fees merely to justify the *per diem* rate.
- ❑ Talking about other clients and their irrelevant problems.
- ❑ Pushing canned solutions.
- ❑ Selling as opposed to marketing.
- ❑ Trying to sell the package rather than join us in solving problems.
- ❑ Seeing all problems as their strong suit.
- ❑ Overemphasis on only one solution to our problem.
- ❑ Hard sell.
- ❑ Promising savings before they know enough about our organization to be confident that they can deliver.
- ❑ Telling us that our problem is the same as someone else's problem.
- ❑ Too much 'packaging' – too little content.

Selling is a *bête noire* which many professionals fear. There is no need to be unduly concerned. At its best selling is exploring client opportunities or problems and identifying solutions. As long as the professional avoids 'pile 'em high, sell 'em cheap' quackery, they will find that this essential capability can be developed to the level where it is as estimable and enjoyable as any other professional skill.

SOAP BOX – NON-ACCELERATING INFLATIONARY RATE OF UNEMPLOYMENT (NAIRU)

Economic well-being for corporation or country depends on productivity per unit of labour and productivity per unit of capital. That means that we must constantly and consistently build and develop human resourcefulness. So what do economists do? They invent a concept which claims that, if you want to keep inflation from taking off like a rocket, you need to build a substantial measure of unemployment into the system. Are they able to tell us what an appropriate level of human wastage is? No, they simply warn us not to go below what we have whenever inflation is low. Ironically it was Milton Friedman himself who first proved that the apparent relationship between inflation and employment levels was an 'optical illusion', but it appears that you only listen to your guru when he says what you want to hear.

As I write Taiwan has GDP growing at a rate of 5.3 per cent, inflation well under 3 per cent and an unemployment rate of 1.6 per cent, all that and a relatively steady currency – has nobody told them it just cannot be done?

According to current research by the McKinsey Global Institute, the US is so effective in its use of investment that it is able to produce 1.5 times as much output from a unit of investment as either Germany or Japan while getting twice as much out of a unit of labour as Japan. That is productivity and much of it is down to management.

Global consultants might be well advised to study less what US gurus say and more what US managers do. Maybe some at least have learned Tom Peters' key lesson of the 1990s and are managing the human imagination.

Part III

Advanced Skills

13
Consultancy Roles

THE ROLE WHICH THE CONSULTANT ASSUMES IN ANY WORK UNDERtaken must be consistent with the client's needs, the situation, and the skills, knowledge and experience of the consultant. In any one intervention it is possible, indeed likely, that the consultant will assume different roles as the work matures. Effective flexibility is one of the hallmarks of good consultancy.

One can be effective either unconsciously as a result of some fortunate and God-given talent, or consciously as a result of planning, thought and sensitivity to changing need. An actress was once quoted as saying, 'I have been very poor, and I have been rich. Rich is better.' Conscious effectiveness is like 'rich'. It is better. Conscious application of knowledge makes the talented more skilled and gives the less gifted a better than even chance. So when you engage in the practice of consultancy you will be more effective in direct proportion to your understanding of your role.

Let me see if I can help by clarifying the range of roles which a consultant may be required to perform. They move from being highly prescriptive to very non-directive. Try to avoid thinking of 'directive' and 'influential' as having the same meaning. The effective consultant is often non-directive, but successful consultants are always influential. It is the form the influence takes which varies.

More directive roles

Advocate

It is possible that, given sufficient consultant expertise, the proper role is that of an advocate in its simplest sense. The action which needs to be taken may be clear and unambiguous and the consultant may become the advocate of that action. For example, a skilled engineer may be in a position to identify one and only one solution to the client problem: 'Move that machine to there and the production bottleneck will be eased and one employee can watch both machines.'

In such a case the consultant's role as advocate is clear and appropriate. There are always, however, points to be borne most carefully in mind.

Problems are usually solved more effectively and stay solved longer if the client plays an active role in reaching the solution. Passive acceptance of someone else's ideas tends to be seen as a form of release from the responsibility for making solutions work. (Consultants who study behaviour may be interested to know that recent psychological research hints that the need to be in control is a more basic and powerful need than that for food or sex. If this finding is borne out by further studies, it will be clear that enabling the client to see themselves as retaining full control moves from being very important to essential to effective implementation.)

Consultants sometimes assume on too little evidence that their first solution is the optimal solution. Too often a situation is seen as being 'just like' a previous experience when in reality it is only 'somewhat like'. The growing tendency to peddle fads and fallacies tempts me to say 'barely like'.

If a consultant chooses to say 'do this', they had better be sure they are right. (See my brief thoughts on 'liability' in Chapter 2.)

The advocate role is more frequently assumed by consultants in the sense of influencing the client to become involved in the problem-solving process, allowing and encouraging others to become involved and recognizing that in general, the more people are engaged in finding the solution, the better the solution and implementation are likely to be. This is not a plea that should be listened to when oversimplistic trainers coo seductively that consensus cures all ills.

Research shows clearly that consensus is most effective in situations where the problem is one in which not only is the solution not clear, but the situation is so novel that it is not even clear what information will prove to be relevant. In more common situations where it is known what information is needed and where that information lies, the decision is best made by the expert after consultation limited to establishing what, if anything, has changed and what feelings need to be taken into account.

An alternative and widely used form of advocacy is when the consultant seeks to persuade the client that certain changes of value are germane to an effective solution – for example the removal of fear from an organization which is moving towards a total quality management philosophy, or where the consultant seeks to persuade the organization to use a particular process in its search for a solution. An interesting example of this must occur from time to time when Charles Hampden-Turner identifies to his clients 'laughter' as a powerful tool for analysing the organization. When using advocacy in the sense described, it is important that the consultant does not become enmeshed in the coils of advocating a solution rather than a process.

Expert

The traditional role of the consultant is that of a specialist who, through the application of unusual skills and knowledge, can lead the client to the solution of the problem. It is unlikely that any assignment exists that totally lacks the need for the consultant to act in this role. The danger is that the consultant may be dragged into imposing a preferred solution rather than developing the client's ability to solve their own problems. The perception of the consultant as expert can also tend to create the belief that 'there is more to this than appears on the surface'. This can undermine rather than build client confidence and can lead to ongoing and undesirable client dependency.

I am reminded of my father, who used to run a public house. He spent many hours in the cellar and it was generally believed that this time was spent in doing arcane and wondrous things to improve the beer. Great was my father's reputation locally as a seer of the beer. While casks were of wood it was possible to do a certain limited amount to care for the ale. Careful attention to temperature, filtering from one barrel to another and so on. But the advent of aluminium barrels should have put a stop to that. They could not be broached and the only thing to be done with a less than perfect barrel was to return it to the brewery. My dad, however, continued his long vigils in the cellar, much to the satisfaction of his regulars who believed totally in the effectiveness of his interventions. Of course, he now descended the cellar steps carrying a newspaper, some tea and a half-pint glass. His chair was already in place.

Trainer and educator

The best consultancy is innovative and developmental. All consultants will find themselves from time to time adopting the role of trainer. The need is, as always, to separate the role of educator from that of propagandist. The top-flight consultant is careful to avoid indoctrination and seeks instead to build a critical and creative approach to new information in the client organization. Effective consultants demonstrate skills both as designers of learning experiences and as direct teachers, but always with the aim of leaving the client and the organization with increased autonomy and self-reliance as a result of the experience.

Less directive roles

Collaborator in problem solving

Notwithstanding my frequent warnings about seeing one situation as being too much like another, consultants are employed in part at least because they bring to the situation knowledge and experience of what has worked for others in similar situations. By providing information, stimulating thinking and maintaining objectivity, consultants are able to develop a truly synergistic role in which the client is influenced towards finding for themselves a more effective solution than would otherwise be available. The information will, of course, frequently include processes relevant to different problems which will not respond to a single problem-solving approach.

Identifier of alternatives

The key to effective decision making is the future attainment of clear and worthwhile objectives. A key role for the consultant in the decision-making process is the identification with the client of a richer set of options than would otherwise be apparent. By establishing a range of possible strategies and their attendant risks, each of which would enable the achievement of the objective, the consultant is performing an important service to the immediate needs of the client organization and to its future growth.

Fact finder

Fact finding within and outside the client business is an integral part of the consulting process. Internally it is the vital 'borrowing of the client's watch' in order to tell them the time. Externally it is the objective assessment of information from the market, the customer, the competitor and the supplier about how the company is perceived and experienced. George Feiger, a partner in

McKinsey, is often surprised to find that his clients are astounded at the level of understanding he demonstrates of the business in what they see as an amazingly short time. He tells them that his approach is simple. He is an unrepentant watch borrower who asks those most likely to know, their employees, their customers, their suppliers and their competitors. He goes on to suggest that in future they may care to do the same. Fact finding is often as simple as that, but the added value that you bring is that it is easier for you to be objective: you are less likely to hear only what you want to hear. You will be more probing. You will always follow the receipt of information by asking for the evidence which supports it. Professor Don Thain taught me years ago always to probe by asking, 'Could you give an example please?', or, more simply, 'What's your evidence for that?'

It is a lesson I have never forgotten and one I commend most heartily to all fact finders who need to be sure that the facts they elicit are real and relevant. I also recommend consultants to avoid a temptation to ignore 'feelings' when searching for the facts. In most human situations the way people feel are facts, and possibly the most important ones.

Internal manager and external consultant

The role which the consultant takes is in part dictated by the sometimes complex interplay between themselves and the client management. The expectations of individual members of the client management team can influence the appropriateness of the consultant role at any time, but so do the realities of the situation. Tensions can be created by the differing perspectives of consultant and manager. It is always the consultant's responsibility to be aware of and respond appropriately to the changing needs of the situation. The sources of tension may include:

> The client manager has a greater investment in the client system as it has developed than has the external consultant.

Frequently outmoded behaviours will be valued for reasons which are historic and far from obvious to an outsider. Change may be resisted because the manager, not unnaturally, values the experiences and achievements which have been part of their personal development. This is in spite of their irrelevance, or worse, in today's situation.

The internal manager as part of the system may be part of the problem and may find the situation threatening.

Although the consultant is seen as free to remove themselves from the client system, the manager may feel trapped within it and may seek security in unrealistic levels of certainty of outcomes and reduction of risk.

Additional work or responsibility placed on the manager as a result of the intervention will often fail to attract immediate compensation. Managers who are under an increased work burden may be intensely aware of what they see as the excessive earnings differential of the external consultant.

In the very short term the internal manager is less costly to the organization than the external consultant and this may reinforce any feelings of 'unfairness'.

Internal managers may have made many attempts to promote a solution without success and may see themselves in the position of a prophet lacking honour in their own country. They may try to undermine the consultant activity by constant reference to 'That's nothing new, I suggested that years ago...'

The internal manager is unlikely to have the breadth of experience of the consultant and may believe absolutely that the business is so specialized that all knowledge gained elsewhere is meaningless.

An internal manager may have been able to 'get by' with less than optimal performance within the system and may see changes to the system as both threatening and unfair.

Internal managers may compare their opportunities to exert influence within the business with that of the consultant and may either attempt to play politics to reduce the consultant's influence, or try to use the consultant's power to influence to promote 'hidden agendas'.

Internal managers will understand the informal hierarchies within the organization better than the consultant and may seek to mislead the consultant in terms of where power lies in order to enhance their perceived position or to block change.

Whatever the problem, it is the consultant's responsibility to identify it, address it and resolve it.

It is an unrealistic expectation that the client will have the breadth of knowledge, the sensitivity or the detailed knowledge of a professional adviser. That is why, directive or not, the consultant is always influential. Without influence, the consultant is an expensive waste of space. The only ethical alternative to solving the problem is to withdraw from the assignment, having first introduced and gained client approval of a qualified replacement.

 ## SOAP BOX – MOTIVATION MYTHS

- ❑ Motivation, long hours of work and productivity necessarily go together. In many situations productivity is increased by shortening the hours worked.
- ❑ Motivation is dependent on high earnings. Although there should be no doubt that very low earnings can destroy motivation, there is little, if any, evidence that high earnings increase it.
- ❑ Fringe benefits motivate. The perks of the job, when new, bring a

small frisson of pleasure, but in the longer (not much longer) term what started as a reward becomes simply a right. The psychological evidence is that the withdrawal of an established perk has a powerful demotivating effect.

❑ Being nice to people motivates them. Human relations training has its undoubted uses, but motivation has nothing to do with how you treat people. As Herzberg pointed out, when it comes down to basics, how you use people has more to do with motivation than how you treat people.

❑ Sensitivity training: the attempt to build trust, openness and honesty in employees is great fun and can be useful, but it does not motivate. If you build winning teams, however, and know how to stop them from falling into the rut of believing that they now have the cure-all formula for every situation – then you have motivation which grows and grows.

❑ Empowerment: there's the buzzword for the early 1990s. A wild cry of 'let my people go' does little for motivation and a great deal for anarchy.

❑ Communications: the vogue of the 1970s does little for motivation unless the communication concerns accurate and timely information related directly to what is important to the receiver, and what is normally important to the receiver is their own job. Tom Peters has said, 'Communication is everyone's panacea for everything.' Communicating the right thing in the right way to the right people at the right time can work wonders. Get any of the above wrong and communication is little more than yet another way to expel wind.

❑ Satisfying needs motivates. Motivation comes from seeking, not getting, satisfaction. A satisfied need does not motivate. You ain't inclined to scratch where it don't itch.

❑ If behaviour is initially rewarded with tangible benefits, it will continue to be motivated long after the reward is withdrawn. This is one of those complex ideas which has been driven by animal and badly designed human research. It tends to be untrue of people in general.

❑ You can motivate others. When you come right down to it, external rewards, whether solid or intangible, move rather than motivate. Motivation is something that people find for themselves. It comes from the internal need which is encapsulated in Maslow's aphorism: 'Man is a wanting animal – what he wants is more!'

14

Outline Strategies for Each Stage of the Assignment

THE CONSULTANT WILL HAVE ESTABLISHED A CLEAR OVERALL STRATEGY for completion of the entire assignment. As new information emerges at each stage, it will be useful to assess the strategy in the light of experience and refine the tactical approach for each defined stage of the intervention.

The appropriateness and thus the effectiveness of the strategy are subject to the answers to the following questions for each stage in the activity.

Pre-entry

❑ Who is the client? What are the client's important products and services? What is the organization's projected image? Who is the primary contact and what are they like as a person? How was the consultant invited to work with the client?

❑ What are the consultant's ideas or theories about the client organization's needs at present? What are the issues and problems facing the client's sector at present? What relevant knowledge or experience has the consultant which may enable them speedily and accurately to analyse the needs of this client?

❑ What expectations does the consultant have about the probable behaviours of the client? How would the consultant prefer the initial contact to go?

❑ What behaviours on the part of the consultant would facilitate the initial meeting? What additional information should the consultant have at their disposal before the first meeting?

❑ What could go wrong? Are any problems which have been foreseen avoidable? What should the consultant do to avoid them?

❑ What contingency plans should the consultant consider to deal with those problems which are possible and unavoidable?

Initial contact

❑ What are the objectives of the intervention, and how will the results be measured?

❑ Is the client clear on their needs and/or problems?

❑ Why is external help being sought?

❑ Is the consultant's style appropriate to this client and this organization? Does it appear that necessary information is, or will be, forthcoming?

❑ What are the important moving and restraining forces in the organization or department? Are there any recognized 'champions for change'?

❑ Can the consultant work with this client? (On a personal as well as business basis?) Will taking this assignment affect the consultant's professional image?

❑ How can the consultant best advance the client/consultant relationship to the next stage?

Data collection and problem analysis

❑ What is to be accomplished? What is the likely timeframe? Has the client indicated any constraints which may affect the consultant's ability to perform? Have any 'no go areas' been indicated?

❑ How is the client business organized? Are there signs of an informal hierarchy? Who is likely to hold critical information? Has the consultant immediate access to the key people?

❑ What are the key issues and problems? How aware is the client of the issues? Are any issues potentially threatening to the client? What is the actual or likely attitude of employees to having an external consultant on the premises? What are the values and beliefs of the organization? How ready is the organization for change, if change is indicated?

Intervention design

❑ What are the key variables which will determine the success of the intervention?

❑ What ideas, processes or concepts will the consultant use to ensure a successful intervention? How sophisticated is the client group? How likely is the client to be able to understand and use the process?

❑ Who within the client organization will be involved?

❑ What education or training of the client organization will be necessary?

Intervention

❑ What progress towards agreed objectives has been made?

❑ Are agreed measurement criteria being applied?

❑ Is an agreed feedback system being maintained?

❑ Are hidden agendas or other unexpected developments emerging?

❑ Are beliefs, values, behaviours or norms changing? Is the change in the desired direction?

❑ Is communication accurate, timely and appropriate? Are members of the client team involved, informed and committed?

❑ Are new and different needs and/or priorities emerging?

❑ Are the techniques, processes and ideas introduced by the consultant proving to be appropriate to the client organization in practice?

❑ Is the client **delighted** with the results to date?

Separation

❑ Have expected outcomes been achieved? What specific outcomes have not been achieved? Are they important to the client in the light of present knowledge and goals?

❑ Is the client organization capable of managing the changes from now? Has every affected employee had the benefit of any necessary training or development?

❑ What does the client expect of the consultant in terms of future commitments and follow-up activity? Are those expectations realistic and in line with the real needs of the client organization?

❑ Is the client **delighted** with the outcome?

Exit

❑ What can the client organization teach the consultant about the way the relationship was handled?

❑ How does the client assess the consultant's impact on the organization?

❑ Is the client completely delighted?

❑ Has the client been able to express that delight by confidently providing referrals?

Consultancy planning guide

A professional adviser or change agent succeeds in direct proportion to their personal reputation and image. Each is ultimately dependent on the level of success which their interventions achieve. This planning guide is designed to assist the professional by drawing attention to key issues which frequently emerge at specific stages in the assignment.

It is a platform for thought and creativity by the practitioner. It is not designed to offer facile and superficial answers, but rather aims at ensuring that the right questions are asked and answered at each stage of the intervention.

The instrument is comprehensive rather than exhaustive and it is hoped and expected that users will ask themselves other questions specific to the assignment, sometimes triggered by the questions in the guide. Use this as a framework rather than a straitjacket and it will provide useful support in that most vital of tasks – economically and consistently bringing TQM to the field of client service.

CONSULTANCY PLANNING GUIDE

STAGE ONE: PRE-ENTRY

Questions to be considered:

Who is the client?
> Individual
> Department
> Organization

What are the client's important products and services?

What is the organization's projected image?

What is the primary contact like as a person?

What adjustments, if any, to their own behaviour will the consultant need to make to work successfully with the client?

What are the consultant's ideas, theories or assumptions about the client organization's needs at present?

What are the issues and problems facing the client's sector at present?

What relevant knowledge or experience does the consultant have which may enable them quickly and accurately to analyse needs and diagnose problems?

What expectations does the consultant have about the probable behaviours of the client?

What is the evidence which supports these expectations?

What behaviour on the part of the consultant will facilitate the initial meeting?

What outcome(s) does the consultant seek from the initial meeting?

What additional information does the consultant need before the initial meeting?

Where can that information be sourced?

What could go wrong at the initial meeting?

Which anticipated problems are avoidable?

What action should the consultant take to avoid them?

What contingency plans should the consultant consider to deal with those potential problems which are possible and unavoidable?

Stage Two: Initial contact

What are the objectives of the intervention?

How will the consultant's performance/results be measured?

Is the client sufficiently aware of their needs/problems?

Yes ☐ No ☐

Why is external help being sought?

Does the consultant suspect or recognize any political power-play within the client organization?

Yes ☐ No ☐

Is the consultant's preferred style appropriate to this organization?

Yes ☐ No ☐

What alternative approaches might usefully be considered?

Is it agreed that all necessary client information and resources will be forthcoming?

Yes ☐ No ☐

What action needs to be taken to ensure availability when required?

What are the important forces for change within the department/ organization/client?

What are the important constraints/restraints?

Are there any identified 'champions for change'? Yes ☐ No ☐

Will the consultant have ready access to them? Yes ☐ No ☐

Who are they?

Can the consultant work with this client?
Professionally? Yes ☐ No ☐
Socially? Yes ☐ No ☐

Will taking this assignment affect the consultant's professional image and opportunities?

      Constructively?   Yes ☐ No ☐

      Adversely?   Yes ☐ No ☐

      Neutral?   Yes ☐

All things considered, does the consultant want this assignment?

                                               Yes ☐ No ☐

If 'yes', how can the consultant advance the client/consultant relationship to the next stage?

Stage Three: Data collection and problem diagnosis

What is to be accomplished?

What is the likely timeframe?

Have any constraints been placed on the consultant's ability to gather information?

Have any specific 'no go' areas been indicated?   Yes ☐ No ☐

Can the consultant perform adequately in the face of any constraints?

                                               Yes ☐ No ☐

What needs to be done?

How is the client business organized?

    Highly structured/bureaucratic?   ☐

    Organismic?   ☐

    Flexible/matrix?   ☐

    Boundaryless?   ☐

    Is there an informal hierarchy?   Yes ☐ No ☐

Where does **power** reside in the structure?

Who is likely to hold critical information?

Do you have immediate access to them?   Yes ☐ No ☐

Action to be taken to gain access?

What are the key issues and problems?

How aware is the client of the issues?

Are any issues potentially or actually threatening to the client?

    Yes ☐ No ☐

What is the likely or actual attitude of employees and management to having a consultant on the premises?

What are the key values of the organization?

Is change indicated?   Yes ☐ No ☐

Is the organization ready for change?   Yes ☐ No ☐

It is strongly recommended that, should the consultant consider that change is indicated, an appropriate instrument be used to assess readiness for change and to build an outline strategy of how change might most economically and effectively be carried out. A traditional and satisfactory inventory is 'Harrison'.

For those who might wish to have a more extensive set of instruments at their disposal, Dr J Jonker has recently completed a research project identifying the most effective change instruments for every phase of the change process. He has published the global 'winners' in his *Toolbox for Organizational Change*, which is available direct from The Katholic University of Nijmegen, the Netherlands.

Stage Four: Intervention design

What are the key variables determining the success of the intervention?

What ideas, concepts or processes will the consultant use to ensure a successful intervention?

How sophisticated is the client group?
  Highly?   ☐
  Adequately?   ☐
  Less than desirable?   ☐

What steps need to be taken to ensure the ability of the client to use/understand the process?

Who within the client's organization will be involved?

What education/training is necessary?

What is the likely sequence of events?

Are amendments to proposal/timeline indicated?   Yes ☐ No ☐

Client informed: Date:_____

Stage Five: Intervention

                                                          Date:_____

Key points of progress to date:

Client informed and approved: Date:_____

Essential notes to file should be completed.

Are agreed measurement criteria being applied?   Yes ☐ No ☐

Is non-compliance acceptable?   Yes ☐ No ☐

Agreed action(s) should be confirmed to the client.

Are 'hidden agendas' or other unexpected developments emerging?

Yes ☐ No ☐

Is any action by the consultant or client required?

Are beliefs, norms, values and behaviours changing?

Beliefs	Yes ☐ No ☐
Norms	Yes ☐ No ☐
Values	Yes ☐ No ☐
Behaviours	Yes ☐ No ☐

Is change in the desired direction?   Yes ☐ No ☐

Is any action by the consultant or client required?

Is communication accurate, complete, timely and relevant?

Yes ☐ No ☐

Are members of the client team involved, informed and committed?

Yes ☐ No ☐

Is any action by the consultant or client required?

Are new or different needs emerging?   Yes ☐ No ☐

Is any action by the consultant or client required?

Is the process proving to be appropriate to the client needs in practice?   Yes ☐ No ☐

Is any action by the consultant or client required?

Is the client delighted with the progress to date?

Yes ☐ No ☐

What priority action would ensure client delight?

Measuring the results

It is essential to hold a specific post-intervention discussion to ensure that all parties have gained the maximum from the work that they have done together. The following questions are offered as the basis for a final assessment of the value of the consultant's work to the client, the consultant and their ongoing relationship. I strongly urge that such a discussion takes place.

MEASURING THE RESULTS

Does the client feel that the desired outcome was achieved?

Is the client **delighted** with the results?

Is there a general feeling in the organization that it was helped?

Has the consultant learned anything of value about their own skills or style?

Has the consultant been totally successful in avoiding causing other problems while solving the first?

Does the client feel that the consultant could help in the future in other ways?

Is the consultant likely to be invited back into the organization?

Does the client organization have a new look, a new approach or a new confidence about addressing and solving future problems?

Are the members of the client team better able to deal with problems in the future?

Do they apply the new skills and knowledge they have in current day-to-day activities? (If they do not, what steps are being taken to ensure that they retain the ability to use learned skills and behaviours until needed?)

Does the client organization now know something about itself that it did not know before?

Is the organization comfortable with the new knowledge?

Has the client provided referrals?

How will the consultant remain in contact with the client?

What further personal development on the part of the consultant has this assignment indicated?

SOAP BOX – GLOBALIZATION

The ability to transfer resources, production, cash or technology virtually anywhere in the world at little less than the speed of light is leading some concerned citizens to cry 'foul' and talk about 'exporting jobs' and 'the end of civilization as we know it'.

Certainly by the end of the twentieth century there will be approximately 1.2 billion jobs which used to be performed in the G7 countries which have been transferred to emerging economies, economies in which, at present, wages are less than $3 an hour – but is this the tragedy it is made out to be?

The answer, as is so often the case, is a matter of perception and action. If it is seen as a tragedy and leads only to weeping and wailing and gnashing of teeth, that is precisely what it will turn out to be.

If, however, it is seen as an opportunity, that too will turn out to be the truth. If we see the change as resulting in 1.2 billion new consumers in the medium term for more sophisticated goods and services; if we recognize a potential for massive growth in world trade; if we are prepared to rethink our industries as the US has, in part, done and create millions of new, more technical, more satisfying jobs; if we can perceive this as the opportunity to work with labour unions to help them to find a new role in a rapidly changing world rather than insisting on maintaining the old conflicts because macho morons believe that, for the present, they have the upper hand; if we can combine all our capacities to fight inflation, increase productivity and competitiveness with what the Taiwanese call innovalue – then and only then will we turn threat into opportunity.

And who are the heroes best placed to do these wonderful things, or at the very least influence the thinking of businesspeople and politicians? They are my fellow professionals, and I believe that we are up to the challenge.

15
Avoiding Problems

NO BOOK WILL BE PERCEIVED AS A COMPREHENSIVE GUIDE WITHOUT some indication of the problems which may be encountered and some hints on how to avoid or deal with them. Some problems and their solutions have been addressed where relevant in the body of the book. This chapter is intended to provide an outline quick-fix guide to many of the remaining problems that professionals meet from time to time.

Apparently overwhelming competition

Occasionally, you will be invited to present a proposal to a new client 'out of the blue'. On arrival you find yourself awaiting your turn in the company of half a dozen representatives each of McKinsey, Coopers and Lybrand and PA Consulting. They are laden down with fancy audiovisual equipment and suddenly the hand-drawn overhead foils that you were so proud of yesterday seem to shriek of amateurism. You know that the opposition's presentation will be slick and plausible at the least and possibly exciting and inspirational as well. So what do you do?

The first thing to remember is to play to your strengths. You weren't invited just to make the numbers up, so:

❑ Consider what it is that you have that caused the client to invite you and centre your thoughts and your presentation on that. (Do you have recent experience of the client's problems? The industry? A high reputation in a specialist field?)

❑ Competition will almost certainly try for a wham bam dog and pony show. Be different. Try to make your approach an informal two-way discussion.

❑ Involve the client from the start and use questions to get guidance about what it is that they want to hear.

❑ Make it subtly clear, without directly knocking the 'big boys', that unlike your competition with you it's a case of WYSI-WYG (what you see is what you get).

❑ Look for the motive behind the client's invitation to the major practices and try to deal with any implied but unspoken concerns. Could they be concerned about continuity? (What will happen if you go under the proverbial bus?) Resources? State-of-the-art knowledge? Are they seeking the sometimes spurious internal reputation that is perceived to come from hiring the big firm? (The consultancy variation on: 'No one ever got fired for buying IBM'. Is there conflict within the organization with half the board championing the large organization while others are committed to the small?

❑ Offer personal added value which is unique to you and stress its uniqueness. (Be careful not to give your profit away.)

Do not be tempted to cut your price in order to get the business. If the assignment were price sensitive the major firms would not be there.

Insolvent clients

While working on a contract you uncover reason to believe that the client may not be able to pay for your services.

❑ Breathe a few happy sighs that you are working to a contract and that you have the payment schedule tied up tight. (You have, haven't you?)

❑ Hold back vital input until you are satisfied that your account is settled.

❑ Where you can, work on those aspects of the assignment which will be useful to you later and possibly elsewhere.

❑ If payment is not made on time, stop working immediately and tell the client why. Make it clear that you will restart work as soon as their cheque is paid into your account.

❑ Have your bank process the cheque preferentially and let you know when it clears.

❑ Start to look for, or bring forward, a replacement assignment and if two payments are late ask for payment up front or bow out.

Consultants are often wary of walking away even when payment is not being made as agreed. Too often they think that they cannot afford to lose the assignment. What they cannot afford is to work without being paid. Like any successful salesperson, a consultant only has the power to influence outcomes if they have the ability to walk away from the deal if they must.

Conflict of interest

You are deeply involved in work for a client when you are approached by another prestigious company in the same industry which asks you to undertake an identical job.

Politely turn them down, indicating if you can do so without breaching the confidentiality of your first client that there might be a conflict of interest and you cannot ethically involve yourself. Do not mention the second approach to your original client. That too would be a breach of confidence.

No matter how prestigious or profitable the second assignment might be, do not seek to duck out of the first job in order to take the second. Your loyalty remains to your existing client. Handle this situation professionally and you will almost certainly be able to add the second client to your list soon. There are still people around who recognize and admire ethical behaviour. Word will get round and what is said will be entirely to your credit.

Your marketing is not working

You have identified what you see as a major market, but you are unable to access it.

❑ Ask yourself whether you have sectored the market effectively. Do you know in sufficient detail who your prospective clients are and how they may be contacted?

❑ Identify a specific key player and opinion leader in the sector and target them rather than blast away at the whole sector.

❑ Try to get some articles printed in the relevant trade magazine, or write letters to the editor.

❑ Write to the national quality press expressing your views on issues which the industry faces.

❑ Check your promotional material for appeal and communication.

❑ Establish a clear and specific goal for yourself. Put a time limit on it and go for it.

❑ Look for a niche market through which you can enter.

If all else fails raise your fees, and make a point of why you are worth more.

Bad business

You are invited to serve a client but you recognize one or more of the signs of bad business. The signs of bad business are:

Unrealistic client expectations
If the client expects more of you than you can possibly deliver there is only loss for you in taking the assignment.

❑ Either: teach your client the facts of life and emphasize them in your contract or terms of reference.

❑ Or: explain to the client politely that you only work to pre-determined outcomes for which you have the time and the resources. Since you cannot expect to complete the job within the time required with the budget and resources at your disposal, you must regretfully decline the assignment. If asked to recommend another consultant, politely decline, explaining that since you know that the job cannot be done within these constraints, to give the name of another consultant would be to encourage the client to waste money.

You lack qualifications to perform to your quality standards
If you are unqualified, as a professional you are disqualified from even considering the job. If possible, introduce a qualified member of your network, ensuring that you continue to maintain a high profile with your client by working as project manager. This enables you to take a part of the assignment, receive a finder's fee from your colleague and remain in touch with the client, so that there is an excellent chance that you will continue to get 'first refusal' on contracts.

Where no member of your network is qualified to meet the client's needs, withdraw from the assignment, but only say 'I don't do that' if you really don't and have no intention of doing it in the future. Used as an excuse to get out of the clutches of an undesirable client it sometimes misfires, as the client appears to be hell bent on telling the world, 'No good going to him with that kind of work, he doesn't do it'.

The client fails to appreciate the value of your services
If the client cannot see the value in hiring you it is unlikely that even a heroic level of performance will have them change their mind. Evoke your constant working to determined outcomes. Set a fair value on what you can achieve and if the client tries to beat you down, withdraw.

Insufficient time available to do the job

❑ Have a member of your network assist, but only with the agreement of the client.

❑ Or: check your diary and tell the client when you could start and give sufficient time to the job.

❑ Or: seek to transfer the job in its entirety to a member of your network, with you acting as project manager if time permits.

❑ Or: turn the job down. (If you do this, do not be surprised if the client offers you more money to handle the job at once. If that happens, establish whether you can get help with the other work, and whether that would be acceptable to existing clients. If so, use part of the extra income to ensure exemplary service to **all** your current clients. Keep full and open communication going with each of your clients at all times.)

Personality clash
I hold totally to the belief that the consultant owes their loyalty and their best efforts to the individual who hires their services. If you find the behaviour of a client is intolerable to you, discuss it openly, focusing on the behaviour, not the personality, and if the problem cannot be resolved try to have a qualified member of your team or network complete the assignment.

Mistakes we all make

In 1989 not one of the major firms who so confidently sell their crystal-ball-gazing facilities to all-comers predicted the length or depth of the recession. That was left to quirky individuals whose forecasts were patronized or pulverized according to style by the big six. What is worse for some of their ex-employees was that as the recession bit deeper they failed to recognize that the market for consultancy continued to grow. Thus, according to a report by Keynote Publications, an estimated one in ten lost their jobs at a time when they could have been working at full stretch.

I mention this not to crow over the major practices, but simply as an indication that we all make mistakes and the mistakes that consultants make invariably affect the lives of others. By recognizing and avoiding the most common pitfalls we can do much for our own status and reputation and a good deal more to protect our clients and their businesses.

Failing to understand that the client does not want change

In recent months there has been a tendency for consultants to concern themselves over what they are called. There is a feeling that as salespeople increasingly are referred to as 'consultants', and as more and more early retirers take on part-time jobs, often in their old function, yet call themselves 'consultants', those who see themselves as being at the core of the profession want a new title. A favoured title is 'change agent', and I believe that the simple pleasure that the profession is beginning to take in its use is symptomatic of the problem. It is easy to assume that the client wants 'change'. Why else would they bring in, at considerable expense, a change agent?

The simple fact is that not only do clients not necessarily want change in the form in which it would be recognized by the average consultant, their motivation for hiring external expertise is to justify the status quo. Of course, they seldom say that. As a consequence the consultant slips into 'creative mode' and proposes changes so radical that we would only expect someone who is paying for the privilege even to contemplate them.

Meeting resistance, the consultant proposes yet more extravagant changes which in turn are rejected or avoided and a crazy game of 'let's waste more money' ensues, until either client or consultant succumbs from exhaustion. The consultant should always ask the client at the earliest opportunity:

> *'In an ideal world, if I could devise a strategy which would enable you to achieve your goals without major change, would you prefer that, or do you really want to see changes in the organization?'*

The client's answer should be sensitively probed to ascertain, as far as possible, their real feelings. Where appropriate, an instrument which measures readiness for change, such as Harrison or Huczynski, should be used and its results carefully analysed.

Changing a subsystem only

When change is necessary it is almost invariably far reaching. To change only part of an organization often means that some other part works a little less well than it did before. Consultants need to be acutely aware of the effect of their actions and advice. One of the major shortcomings of customer-care programs has been that their sheepdip approach has been highly successful in changing motivation without addressing the need to change skills. Few things are more destructive of commitment than a passionate desire to achieve without the competence to make necessary and effective changes. Conversely, TQM is successful where it is recognized that it is total or it is nothing.

Every consultant should review their work in the light of effects throughout the organization. If one department's pleasure is another's pain, we have failed our client and our profession. If we create the dream without giving the means for fulfilment, we are storing up frustration.

A school in the North East of England has as its motto: 'God does not give us a dream unless he also gives us the strength to achieve it'. Consultants are often accused of wishing to play God. This is our opportunity to do so constructively.

Attempting 'bottom-up' change only

It is not true that people always resist change. Many advantageous changes we initiate for ourselves. We get married. We have children. We change jobs or careers. But we recognize that all change, no matter how attractive, has its price. What is more, the price is often paid during the process of change. The benefits lie at some time unspecified in the future. We get suspicious, therefore, when change is apparently promoted as being good for us lesser mortals, but either unnecessary or undesirable for those who sit on high.

Worse, experience tells us that where others prescribe change, but do nothing to change themselves, they are seldom committed to making change work and so they reverse it at the appearance of the first problem. That being so, we might as well let this go by with as little involvement as possible because, like the buses of my youth, there will be another one along in a minute.

A client sent for me because he had a problem. The TQM system was not working. The history went like this.

Initially, with the help of consultants, the company had installed quality circles. Middle management had not been convinced of the usefulness of the system and ignored employees' suggestions. The approach died slowly and quietly. Top management continued to demand quality, so they implemented the Juran approach. Different consultants were engaged. They liked the 'people bits' of Juran's ideas, but were less enamoured of statistical process control (SPC). What they did not like they ignored. But, 'what cannot be measured cannot be managed'. The system failed.

New consultants were hired to teach SPC. Unfortunately they didn't see it as part of their responsibility to tie in their program to what was being attempted on the factory floor through the dying Juran system. Another avoidable death of a good system. If Juran doesn't work, Crosby will, decreed top management. Crosby quality workshops were held and management held their breath. Nothing happened. Everyone thought: 'Why bother? There'll be another one along...'

I was destined to be that other one. My advice was painful. Painful to me, that is: I was turning away income.

> *'By now you and your people are probably the world authorities on what causes systems to fail. Capitalize on that. Forget about gurus, don't let a consultant near the place. Start with the CEO and the board, and develop a system which meets your company's needs by cascading workshops down through the organization. Be sure that the system is owned by those that have to make it work, and let me know how you get on.'*

They got on fine. I got no fee.

One other brief point about bottom-up change. If you decide that it is necessary, in the light of changing experience, that I change the way I do things, while you do things as you always did, that suggests to me that I got it wrong while you got it right. Fair enough, except that all the time I was apparently getting it wrong, nobody told me and from my perspective I seemed to be doing a pretty good job. What the hell were you doing meanwhile? I just don't think it's worth bothering.

Unbalanced use of process

> *'I'm a process consultant, I don't get involved with content.'*

True, but process is only useful to the extent that it facilitates achievement of client's goals. Too many consultants become so entrenched in process that they forget that the client needs to succeed in the real world today. Process, like candy, is dandy, but only to the extent that it deals with the problems as they are right now. And if liquor is quicker in meeting your client's needs, maybe you should lay your candy process aside for a while and join your client at the bar.

Agree outcomes and measure your effectiveness against them. A smart process which will be forgotten before it is useful serves no purpose. Consultancy is about outcomes and only, in the final analysis, about outcomes.

Creating change overload

Changing only a subsystem is equalled in fatuousness only by attempting to change everything at once, bringing the business to a halt while everyone plays musical chairs. The effective consultant is an competent planner and an able definer of priorities. The job is to facilitate change, not to develop anarchy.

Assess with care:

- ❏ The overall change strategy.
- ❏ The key priorities.
- ❏ Client resources and needs.
- ❏ Seriousness, urgency and growth potential of any problems.

Then produce a plan which is feasible, attracts the commitment of those who must make it work, and has minimal adverse effect on the day-to-day business of running the business.

Creating change for its own sake

Don't.

Imposing our own values

Consultants are, or ought to be, people of strong conviction. That is not an excuse for imposing our beliefs on others. If you cannot live with the values of the organization in which you are asked to do work and your client is not proactively seeking to redefine those values, you must ask yourself if you are the right person for the job.

Consider the following on the question of belief:

'A man who has no belief which he would die for has nothing to live for.'   *Martin Luther King*

But:

'To believe something is to believe that it is true: therefore a reason-able person believes each of his beliefs to be true: yet experience has taught him to expect that some of his beliefs, he knows not which, will turn out to be false. A reasonable person believes, in short, that each of his beliefs is true, and some of them are false. I for one, would expect better of a reasonable person.'   *WV Quine*

Beliefs lie at the core of values. An effective consultant seeks to impose neither, but holds the first tentatively and the second courageously.

Inappropriate attachment to client

I have said before that the consultant's first loyalty is to their client, the person within the organization who has hired them. This does not mean, however, that the consultant must protect the client at all costs. Client and consultant have an overriding responsibility to the organization which is paying both of them. In the often quoted situation where the consultant establishes that it is the client, or the client's behaviour, which is the cause of the problem, the consultant's responsibility is, to me at least, obvious.

They must, sensitively and sympathetically, cause the client to confront the problem and their role in it. And then, as joint prob-lem solvers, consultant and client must devise and monitor a plan to change the problematic behaviour. Should the client refuse to face up to their part in the problem, the consultant must make it clear to the client that they have no alternative but to face up squarely to both problem and proposed solution in their report and that they must insist, in this situation, that their report be made to the board.

Failure to be sufficiently candid

Without being obnoxious, it is incumbent on the consultant to provide factual, complete and objective findings to the client.

If the Lords of Appeal choose to interpret product liability legislation as governing the provision of professional services, failure to report the whole story could become a breach of legislation. That would make inappropriate tact a potentially expensive self-indulgence.

Failure to recognize their own resistance to change

I always feel a trace of fellow feeling when I hear Ken Dodd shout, 'I have a lot to give, and by God you lot are going to get it.'

It is natural to believe that what has been the foundation of past success will continue to work for us in the future, and if it isn't working this time to keep doing it, only harder.

John Grinder gives as one of the few 'rules' governing the therapeutic practice of neurolinguistic programming:

> *'If something is not working do something different. If something is not working it is almost certain that something else, almost anything else, will be better.'*

Consultants and other professionals need constantly to be adding to their store of knowledge and their repertoire of interventions. As a friend Peter Thomson says: 'We, more than anyone else, need to commit ourselves to life-long learning.'

That way we will not fear the need to change our approach.

Losing professional detachment

A major advantage, sometimes the only obvious advantage, which we bring to the client organization is that we come from outside. We are not part of the problem. If we choose to reject the role of unbiased observer, we take on the role of a participant with all the subjectivity and hidden agendas which that implies. We must constantly ask ourselves: 'Am I becoming excessively involved?'

We must care, but we must protect our client's interest by being passionate about outcomes, not routes to achievement.

Not seeking help when out of our depth

Sadly, some who perform with apparent success as consultants are happy and effective in the game of 'just doing enough'. I can understand, but not sympathize with, the one-man band who, conscious of the need to feed the kids and pay the mortgage, decides to 'take a chance'. I have neither understanding nor sympathy for the major consultancy which elects to send into the client premises inexperienced, insufficiently trained 'consultants', cheap to employ, expensive to hire, 'on a long leash'.

But at bottom both are equally culpable. Build a network. Ensure equitable rewards for all and always give your client the best service available at any price by bringing in the right level of expertise as it is needed.

Assuming that my particular brand of change is always the answer

Avoid force-fitting client problems to your solutions. Develop your abilities so that you can build solutions specific to needs from the ground up. If you feel that you must have a 'product' to survive in a competitive environment, and there are many who do, try to devise, alone or with colleagues, a range of flexible approaches which can be adapted to each situation.

And I have to say it again, predetermine and agree outcomes on which you will be judged. That way you will avoid inappropriate process 'just because it's there'.

SOAP BOX – EMPOWERMENT

Why are empowerment initiatives so seldom capable of delivering the massive benefits that are routinely promised? What goes wrong is that the 'let my people go' school of empowerment takes too little heed of what we know about human behaviour. First, people are simply fussy when it comes to being empowered. Most want to be in control of what they perceive as their job. They do not necessarily want to take on something which they believe the boss is being paid to do – and that may well include setting the rules and developing the game plan.

Second, people like to know what is expected of them, and they often want to know in detail.

Next there are, at the extremes, two very human responses to unexpected freedom. Some are paralysed like rabbits in the head-lights, others turn liberty into licence and enjoy an orgy of idiosyncratic behavioural chaos.

Fourth, but not really finally, the behaviour of supervisors often says more clearly than words, 'We're handing out freedom, but don't reach out for it if you value your job'. And, following delayering, down-sizing and other delights, how many people want to put their job on the line for the doubtful benefit of greater responsibility and greater risk?

But empowerment isn't just important in a volatile business world – it's vital. We need to tap into the human resourcefulness which exists in abundance in all organizations. We need to align the aspirations and behaviour of all our people, and we need to do it fast.

Get your clients to:

❑ Prepare for empowerment with care.
❑ Find out how much freedom people want and can manage.
❑ Walk the talk of what's expected at every level in the business.
❑ Establish clear limits and ensure they are applied fairly.
❑ Discourage confidence which outruns competence.
❑ Celebrate and reward success.
❑ Ease off the brakes a little more when people show that they are ready.
❑ Expect problems and support those who have difficulties.

16

Loving Them to Death Is Not Enough

TO A DEGREE THIS BOOK HAS SAILED UNDER FALSE COLOURS. IT HAS been presented as guide for and about professional advisers. Let me confess. What *High Income Consulting* is about, from cover to cover, is client service. If you are a one-man band you must learn to play the tunes which will delight the client. If you are part of a massive 'strategy boutique', it is no less incumbent on you to create, consistently and for all time, client delight.

Size of operation is finally no protection against the awesome power of the market. Eventually those who fail to delight the customer falter – and unless they learn, and learn quickly, they fall. Ask IBM or GM: they learned and are still around to talk about it, but it was a lesson which cost them jointly more than $30 billion.

The days of the satisficer in this business are coming to a welcome, though too long delayed, close. I know nothing of the politics or personality of Ross Perot's associate, supporter and rival Richard Lamm, but when he states that his vision is to make 'American politics a bullshit-free zone', I get a strong sense of fellow feeling. It may baffle brains in the short term and the short term may be longer than we would wish, but even in the consultancy business which has traditionally not only produced bullshit, it has been sold it at a profit, the great clean-up is coming and you have a golden opportunity to wield a broom.

Not just 'have a nice day'

Having graciously been called, by an US critic in reference to one of my other books, 'the most friendly guru', I don't undervalue the need or effect of being a nice guy, but believe me, being a nice guy won't cut it for you if you give lousy service. Let me digress a little and tell you a story.

A management consultant of considerable charm and winning ways was invited to serve a client company which was in clear danger of going belly up.

He put on his best bedside manner, listened with equal measures of care and concern to what the client said of his corporation's plight and, reaching behind him to where he kept all his off-the-shelf panaceas, he wrote up a good dose of downsizing. Smiling soothingly, he treated the patient. Sadly, things got worse. People in the organization lost their confidence and commitment and losses continued to mount.

As becomes a doctor, the consultant kept his composure and his charm in equal measure. He carefully explained that his treatment should not be applied as the unthinking cutting of heads. What was needed was careful, well-planned and expensive delayering. They delayered. People costs fell, all other costs rose, revenues plummeted. Our nice-guy consultant, pocketing his payment, continued to smile and soothe.

Diagnosing corporate amnesia and incipient corporate Alzheimer's, he indicated a strong dose of empowerment to free the system and release an outburst of creative energy. It failed. The consultant collected his fees and remained a nice guy.

Business process reengineering in a massive dose would certainly do the trick. It didn't – the corporation went under and sank without a trace.

Our nice-guy consultant was devastated. He wept sincere, sympathetic tears as he turned to a colleague. 'Such a tragedy,' he said, 'and just when I have worked out a hundred other ideas to try.'

Client delight must be, as Deming said, 'every time and for all time'. It is not and never was a product of fads or fallacies – these lead to foul-ups. Client delight does not come from building good client rapport, important as rapport is. Client delight comes from organizing the business in such a way that it becomes a necessary outcome of the way things are done in the practice.

Background research into customers' views

This section calls on the findings of many recent published and unpublished research projects. It identifies findings which all the projects have in common, regardless of the country of origin, the research methodology and size and type of business. In short, these findings are relevant to all of us, whatever our business. I use the words 'client' and 'customer' interchangeably on the grounds that to most of us I suspect that 'client' rather than 'customer' is simply a way of 'professionalizing' the business.

All the research which I have studied shows that the customer is less impressed by what I have called 'have a nice day' approaches to customer care than by evidence that the company is organized to meet and exceed customer expectations.

❓ ❑ In what ways is your business organized to delight the client?

❑ What are you going to do better than you do now?

❑ What are you going to do better than the competition?

The customer has little faith in customer satisfaction surveys and the like, which are perceived as being part of a bureaucratic approach to the marketplace. The same is true in respect of the retail customer or consumer when it comes to Charter Marks, and even ISO9000 means little or nothing. Most people have slight understanding of what such awards mean and are not impressed by them. Customers and clients are impressed by the way that your operation is designed regularly to exceed their expectations.

> ❑ **What do you do to enable your client to communicate easily with you – when you are a one-person operation and often away from home and office?**

Clients and customers are more interested in how the company markets itself and how its systems appear to work. Cues and clues which they look for are as follows.

Image and reputation

Much of what has gone before has been aimed at low-cost ways of building your reputation and image. In creating consistent client delight you need to have the client willing to try your services. You need, in Jay Abraham's phrase, to practise 'risk reversal' to facilitate the granting of the first opportunity to delight the client.

In marketing services it is neither necessary nor desirable to offer reduced prices or money-back offers.

Your fee level should be presented by you and received by your client as an indicator of excellence. John Fenton, perhaps the UK's leading sales trainer, always teaches that price is not an objection, it is a benefit. For example, if the client said to him that, say, Tom Lambert is cheaper, John would reply: 'Tom Lambert, yes, he's a first-rate trainer who knows exactly what his services are worth. We also fully understand the value of ours.' What is essential is that your claims are credible and that the client can use your services with total confidence. That can only come from marketing to build your status and reputation and designing your operation to back your image of excellence every time.

? ❏ Have you and your company developed a brand image for quality strong enough to have the 'person in the street' believe that they are being offered a quality product or service even when a new product or service is brought to the marketplace?

❏ Do **all** employees who come into contact with the customer create an impression of professionalism and specific knowledge of the customer need?

❏ Do they appear to be competent?

❏ Are they approachable?

❏ Do they actively encourage, through their customer-facing behaviour, the customer to express fully what they think and how they feel?

❏ Does the firm have an established reputation for fair dealing? If the business is a new one, which image-building techniques can be applied at once to get speedy results?

❏ Are top management known by name and accessible? (Think of Bill Gates.)

❑ Do other customers invariably speak well of the company? (Remember the 11 to 4 ratio. It is claimed that if a customer is delighted with the service they receive, they tell four people. If they are dissatisfied, they tell eleven.)

❑ Do you ask for, and receive, referrals with absolute confidence every time? Do you get unsolicited referral business?

Relationship

I said that being a nice person is not enough. I also stressed, however, that the personal relationship is important – but it really goes far beyond 'have a nice day'.

❑ Does the company stress to the customer, from the initial meeting, that what they are seeking is a long-term relationship?

❑ Is their behaviour congruent with any such claim? (For example, I used to advise a group of car dealers who never pushed the sale in respect of a new customer. They always indicated that since their intention was a long-term relationship or no relationship at all, they were not prepared to consider selling a car until mutual liking and understanding were developed. The customer never suggested that this was a waste of time and was not denied acess to product, only to order forms.)

❑ Are company employees loyal to the firm in their behaviour and their statements? How do you know?

❑ Does the firm reciprocate their loyalty? Are you known as a good employer? How do you recognize and reward loyalty? What do you do that others don't?

❑ Is the customer made to feel that they belong, that they are 'part of the team'?

Awareness

Clients demand that we demonstrate an awareness of their individual and, from their perspective at least, unique needs and wants. Never assume that needs and wants are the same thing. And if they are different, remember that the want will assume more importance in the client's eyes than the need – unless and until you can show them otherwise. Anyone can sell successfully once by supplying a want. Consistent client delight will only come from making needs into wants, satisfying the need and then going the extra mile.

❑ Do all employees show a sympathetic understanding of customer problems? What is your evidence for your answer?

❑ Are they sensitive and tactful when they respond and do they proactively offer help? If you are employing a large number of people, or work with a group of associates under a single banner, how do you know?

Systems

Businesses, even small businesses, are of necessity complex. In a one-person operation there are always a range of necessary activities competing for our time. Fortunately, a combination of technology and ingenuity enables us to create systems which save time and effort. When designing such systems, however, it is essential to focus on the needs of the client. Most of us will have had some experience of making a simple and reasonable request of some company where we have spent, or are thinking of spending, our limited resources of cash, only to be told that the system is against us: 'I'm sorry, sir. The computer does not give me that information.' We don't like it and neither does anyone else.

?
- ❑ Are those systems with which the customer comes into contact apparently designed to make the customer's life easier? What could be improved?

- ❑ Are systems designed to meet high expectations without becoming depersonalized? How do your customers see the difference between efficiency and effectiveness?

- ❑ Is what is promised consistently delivered?

- ❑ Are employees empowered to satisfy the customer on the spot? Is there a delighted customer at the end of every transaction? How do senior managers keep in touch with what is going on?

The characteristics of a client-driven practice

Recent research covering a wide range of businesses in many countries has shown that certain detailed characteristics are common to all companies which are seen by their customers as being truly 'customer friendly'. Or, in the formal words of one client report:

> *'Based on international benchmarking research the following characteristics are shown by longditudinal studies to be highly correlated with a company's ability to succeed in satisfying customer needs over an extended period. Factor analysis indicates that the characteristics tend to fall into clusters. That indicates that the organization which strongly shows any characteristic in a group is more likely to demonstrate the others.'*

On the basis of this growing body of research, I took the key indicators of structuring and developing the business to ensure the consistent delight of the customer and developed a short organizational self-test. Clients who have used it in their businesses have been delighted by the results which their committed workforce have enthusiastically helped to put in place – their customers are, needless to say, even happier. You are welcome to use this tool with your clients at no cost other than this: use this test in your own practice, large or small, before you unleash it on a client. If you are a one-man band please don't assume that you can write it off as being for big firms only. Even when you do everything in the business yourself, you need to ensure that it is focused on delighting the client and that you structure and leverage every activity towards this end. Any weakness means that your client suffers.

Use this test to make it easy to pinpoint where your organizational strengths lie, and where you have room, as a business, for improvement. Plan to build on and promote your strengths in the marketplace while mitigating or eradicating your weaknesses internally.

CUSTOMER DELIGHT QUESTIONNAIRE

For each characteristic, rate the extent to which the statement is true of your organization today, using the following scale:

1 – Not at all true
2 – True to a small extent
3 – Moderately true
4 – True to a great extent
5 – True all the time without any reservation

Think carefully about each question and complete them all, giving your honest opinion. This questionnaire is confidential, you need not put your name on it.

Vision and commitment

1. Our organization is totally committed to the idea of creating delighted customers at the end of every transaction. ☐

2. We seek consistently to do things right first time, every time. ☐

3. Executives always demonstrate by their actions their personal commitment to customer satisfaction. ☐

4. Our driving intention is always to exceed customer expectations in those things that matter most to them. ☐

5. We promote and reward employees on the basis of their demonstrated commitment to customer care. ☐

6. Everybody in our organization has confirmed their personal commitment to total quality. ☐

7. Satisfying customer needs always takes precedence over satisfying our own internal needs. ☐

8. We reward with praise or tangible benefits every example of exceptional customer service.

9. When mistakes are made we focus on problem solving and not the apportionment of blame.

10. We communicate fully to customers our intention to give them superior service.

Your score

× 2 = (your percentage score)

Client/customer relationships

1. When it comes to selling we play a consultative role with our customers.

2. In advertising, selling and promotion we avoid promising more than we are able to deliver.

3. We know the attributes of our products which customers value most.

4. Information from customers is fully utilized in designing our service and product offering.

5. We strive to be the leader in our industry in terms of customer retention.

Your score

× 4 (your percentage score)

Client/customer problems

1. We monitor all customer complaints. ☐

2. We regularly ask customers to give us feedback on our performance. ☐

3. Customer complaints are analysed to identify quality or service problems. ☐

4. We identify and eliminate internal procedures which cause customer problems. ☐

5. We refuse to live with convenient internal policies or procedures which fail to give added value to our customers. ☐

Your score ☐

× 4 (your percentage score) ☐

Client/customer understanding

1. We know how our customers define 'quality'. ☐

2. We provide opportunities for all employees, whatever their function, at some time to meet with customers. ☐

3. We clearly understand what our customers expect of us. ☐

4. Our key managers clearly understand our customers' requirements. ☐

5. Our top team has frequent contact with customers. ☐

Your score ☐

× 4 (your percentage score) ☐

Making it easy for clients and customers to do business with us

1. We make it as convenient as possible for our customers to do business with us. ☐

2. Employees are encouraged to go 'above and beyond' to serve customers well. ☐

3. Employees are told, as clearly as we know how, what they are free to do on their own authority to satisfy customers. ☐

4. We make it easy for customers to complain to us if they believe that they have cause. ☐

5. We do everything reasonable to resolve customer complaints quickly. ☐

Your score ☐

× 4 (your percentage score) ☐

Empowerment

1. We treat all employees with respect at all times. ☐

2. Employees at all levels have a good understanding of our products and services. ☐

3. Employees who work with customers are supported with resources to enable them to do the job well. ☐

4. At all levels of the organization employees are empowered to act on their own judgement to make things right for a customer. ☐

5. Employees feel that they are part of an exciting enterprise. ☐

Your score ☐

x 4 (your percentage score) ☐

Training and development

1. Decisions are pushed down to the lowest levels in the organization capable and qualified to make them. ☐

2. No lower-level employee is expected to make a decision for which they lack either the skills, knowledge, experience or confidence to ensure a good outcome. ☐

3. Managers are trained in the complexities of developing the autonomy of the workforce. ☐

4. Employees at all levels make at least some significant decisions about their own work. ☐

5. Employees are cross-trained so that they can support and fill in for each other when necessary. ☐

Your score ☐

× 4 (your percentage score) ☐

Business and organizational growth

1. Instead of competing with each other, functional groups cooperate to achieve shared goals. ☐

2. We study the best practices of other companies to see how we may do things better. ☐

3. We work continuously to improve our products and processes. ☐

4. When a new product or service would meet a known customer need, we bust a gut to make it available to them. ☐

5. We have a comprehensive quality policy throughout our organization. ☐

6. We recognize and respect the needs of the internal customer at every level. ☐

7. Our employees understand that quality means consistently meeting customer need at lowest cost, and they strive to reduce costs without damaging customer service. ☐

8. Our employees value and use creativity to provide exceptional service and build profitability. ☐

9. The key values of the organization are known to and owned by all. ☐

10. We invest in the development of innovative ideas. ☐

Your score ☐

× 2 (your percentage score) ☐

Employee attitude to quality

1. Every employee fully understands that total quality requires them consistently to meet internal and external customer needs at the lowest possible cost. ☐

2. Every employee recognizes that they have a personal role to play in the marketing of our products and services and actively seeks to create, identify and satisfy customer needs at a profit. ☐

Your score ☐

× 10 (your percentage score) ☐

Scoring this test could not be more simple. If you fail to score 100 per cent in any section, as marked by any member of your team, you have an opportunity to improve either your organization or your communication – because if you've got the business right and your employees can't see it, they have to be told, in the customer's interest.

If you, the professional, decide to use this test as part of the offering which you make to your client, that, as I have said, is fine – adapt and adopt should be the watchword of consultants. Think how much more powerful your sales pitch will be, however, if you are able to say:

'I know that this will work because I use it in my own business, which is why I am able to guarantee that all of my clients will be delighted with my work.'

A note to senior management

The future of your business is a function of your ability to delight and go on delighting your customers. The 'have a nice day' school of customer care is not enough to succeed with an increasingly knowledgeable market. Any score of less than 100 per cent in any section of the questionnaire means that you are missing an opportunity to dominate your chosen sectors. If, however, you can achieve and sustain a score of 100 per cent in every section, no matter how quickly the business environment changes, you are leading an organization which has the capacity to be, and continue to be, a world leader.

Why not use additional copies of this instrument and plot your organization's progress by completing it every six months, until you are fully satisfied with your standards of excellence?

Belief is an important factor in achievement. Even when you have near unanimity and most people are consistently scoring the firm at 100 per cent, take any 'deviants' seriously. They too serve your customers.

❑   Do all of your customer-facing staff take every opportunity to ask the delighted customer for referral business? If the customer is truly delighted rather than merely 'satisfied', there is no reason why they should not ask and every reason why they should do so with courtesy and confidence.

The ideal consultancy

Those who know me, or have read the first edition of this book, will know that I am totally committed to client delight. Sadly, I have tried for a number of years to change the shape of the consultancy business in the interests of the client by inappropriate means. I pinned my hopes on global certification. I should have known better.

I should have understood that the short-term thinking and immediate self-interest of those who run the show, both in the major consultancies and the professional bodies which they dominate, would not be assailable by ethics or argument. As Gary Hamel and CK Prahalad have made plain in their blockbuster *Competing for the Future*, the only way to change the shape of an industry is by developing a new competitive strategy which works. That is what we are doing with Psynergy.

Psynergy is a new-style consultancy. It gives the client a better service than that offered by the major companies at less cost. It brings together a group of top consultants, businesspeople, business authors and academics who share a clear set of business values. What makes us different is that, first and foremost, the client knows that what they see is what they get.

We employ no 'green beans', so those who appear and work in the client premises are the principals nominated by the client. There are no surprising Monday mornings when the client arrives to see a group of uncommunicative bright young graduates rushing around the building with clipboards and unbounded energy.

Second, our team includes top researchers from top universities, but we only pay for them when we use them. In the

Knowledge Age we have access to leading thinking without carrying the fixed costs. Similarly, our offices throughout the world are as small as we can get away with and still give the level of service which will act as a benchmark for others, so we are highly competitive in our fee structure. But that isn't all.

We believe in outcomes rather than activity. We are therefore, with the proviso that we do not fund the client's business (see Chapter 6), happy to predetermine outcomes and be paid mainly on results. Even where a straightforward daily rate is preferred, the client gains substantially. We have no spare bodies hanging around an office waiting for assignments. Our people are top professionals and that means that they are busy professionals. We must, for there is no way that we can afford to hang around the client corporation till kingdom come, transfer our skills and abilities to the client so that they are truly autonomous at the earliest possible moment and at the lowest possible cost. But that does not mean that we leave the client circumscribed by partial knowledge. We regularly update all clients on what is happening in the world of business and management theory at 'exploratoria' in which clients are helped to decide whether the latest ideas would help them, whether they could implement them on their own, or whether they need help.

In short, we give our clients what they want, to the degree that they need it, and deliver it through the individual or team of their choice. At the same time, we develop human resourcefulness in their organization to the highest possible level and we provide the emergent knowledge and challenge which will enable our clients to get ahead and stay ahead. All of this we do at a daily rate which is never cheap, but always competitive.

I believe that this is the future of the profession and I look forward to hearing that you are working in similar or, better yet, even more client-centred ways.

SOAP BOX – WHERE THE MONEY IS

In recent years there has, very properly, been a great deal of emphasis on the triumphs of the emerging Asian economies. It is at least as important that those of us who care to think strategically remind ourselves, from time to time, of where the real money still is.

If we consider GDP at purchasing power parity, so that we compare apples with apples, the US alone (GDP $6.9 trillion) accounts for more than 20 per cent of the world's total economic output. By adding Japan ($2.6 trillion), Germany ($1.7 trillion), France ($1.2 trillion) and Britain ($1.1 trillion), no less than 41 per cent of total world GDP is accounted for. Throw in Italy ($1.1 trillion) and Canada ($0.6 trillion) and we are up to 46 per cent. The remainder of the G10, the Netherlands ($0.3 trillion), Belgium ($0.2 trillion), Switzerland ($0.2 trillion) and Sweden ($0.2 trillion), bring the total GDP close to 50 per cent of all of the world's economic activity.

Consultants should look for opportunities in emerging markets and should be interested in growth wherever it occurs. We would all be wise, however, to be careful not to throw away still healthy babies with the bathwater.

Afterword

I have relied on the best research and information I know of and I stand by my every deduction or extrapolation. The success of the first edition and the success of those who have taken the lessons into the workplace give me total confidence. In the first edition, however, I expressed a concern which I want to repeat here.

It may seem to the astute reader that I have, at times, exceeded my brief of seeking to help the good consultant become the successful consultant, and that I have strayed into trying to turn the good consultant into the better consultant. *Mea culpa*.

The future of the consultancy profession is bright. The market continues to grow. The need for professional services will probably far outstrip any forecast yet made. But growth has a drawback.

A growing market attracts incomers. The more the opportunities are recognized, the more the competition is attracted. In the end there is only one route to success and that is quality. Quality must be the main characteristic of everything we do. Quality of action builds, in the long term, an unassailable reputation and image. This book has shared with you the quality secrets of the best and most successful in a profession. I hope it has done more. It has identified safe and certain short cuts from which you may select your personal route.

If you have gained from this book just one thing to improve your reputation and enhance your personal status, your chances of success are significantly increased. If you have found several, your success is certain.

Here's to that success!

Part IV

The Consultant's Toolkit

Proven Tactics For Building Your Practice

Marketing

1. The so-called 'window of opportunity' is open only briefly as an organization's priorities change. When a potential client recognizes the need for the services which you supply, yours must be the name they know. Your marketing, therefore, must be consistent and indirect, aimed specifically at making you well known to **all** your prospective clients.

2. Indirect methods of marketing bring clients to you, clamouring for you to serve them. Indirect methods include:
   - ❑ Public speaking engagements to suitable audiences.
   - ❑ Developing and delivering seminars.
   - ❑ Being prominent in professional or trade associations.
   - ❑ Writing books and/or articles for trade journals.
   - ❑ Publishing your own newsletter.
   - ❑ Writing 'letters to the editor'.
   - ❑ Using the press effectively to promote you.
   - ❑ Being listed in directories.

3. Your overall marketing strategy should be aimed at becoming well known in your field.

4. The tactics which you select must be consistent with building

your image and reputation and must be comfortable for you to perform.

5. Marketing must be regular and consistent. Even when you are 'fat, dumb and happy', still discipline yourself to marketing a minimum of 15 to 20 per cent of your time.

6. Consistent and effective marketing is the only way to smooth out the peaks and troughs of business.

7. Mailing brochures to potential clients 'cold' seldom brings a response and is prohibitively expensive. Only mail to those for whom you have identified a need which your services can meet.

8. Watch and read the news specifically as a market-development exercise. Look consistently for opportunities to serve.

9. Avoid using a CV to promote your services to business. Personnel departments have become the 'bin' into which unsolicited CVs are automatically dropped by directors and line management. If your offer is not specific to the personnel function you have little hope of attracting business. Worse, the use of a CV says 'Give me a job', and that is not the image for a professional to convey.

10. If you elect to advertise, do so only when there are many buyers in the market. Advertising professional services is difficult and if you choose to use it to stimulate a flagging market it is ruinously expensive and ineffective. Advertising must turn prospects into buyers. No prospects, no buyers.

11. If you do advertise, try to do so through a 'knowledge product' which may also bring you some revenue: something like a booklet, or the subtle advertising of a paid-for newsletter.

12. When speaking in front of groups of potential clients, be sure to give each person something which they will take away and to which they will refer and so keep. This excludes brochures almost by definition. Some information from a survey you have completed, a brief note on some new legislation, a list of sources of information or a little psychometric self-test are the kinds of things audiences keep.

13. Make sure that your contact details are clear on all pieces you hand out, and format them to go easily into handbags or pockets.

14. If you promote an information product through advertising, always charge for it. People with no real interest in your services will send for 'freebies': a small charge produces qualified leads.

15. When you see an item in print which you believe is of interest to a potential client, photocopy it and send it to them with a handwritten note. To make most effective use of time, write the notes when watching TV or travelling by train or air. This will keep those who could use your services, or refer you to others, thinking of you and a little indebted to you.

16. Regard lifelong learning as a critical part of your marketing strategy. The more knowledgeable you are, the more ideas you have to exploit and the easier it is for you to find material for articles and talks.

17. Don't be afraid of becoming a guru. Comment on trends and happenings in your chosen field to the press. Once they start to use your written pieces or calls, there is a snowball effect as they begin to turn to you for comment.

18. Ally yourself in the public mind with the decision makers in the field that you serve. Comment on what important people

are saying or doing and you will rapidly become seen as one of the 'movers and shakers'.

19. Demand of yourself that each day you think of three ideas to promote your practice. They may not all be viable, but your enthusiasm and energy will remain high and the exercise is good for the brain.

20. Always be prepared to walk away from bad business. Bad business includes those who do not pay you on time (or ever), those who fail to appreciate your services, and those who will damage rather than enhance your image if you are associated with them.

21. So that you can afford to walk away when client business is lean, build static income. Charge for your newsletter, having tested its value. Write little booklets. Franchise your successful seminars.

22. If small and impoverished clients come to you, serve them by encouraging them to build a little consortium who, by sharing the cost and rewards of your services, can afford you.

23. When you write a sales letter or brochure, concentrate on communicating, not impressing. Check everything for readability. If an intelligent nine-year-old would have difficulty understanding, most clients will.

24. Add a handwritten postscript to letters. In spite of its overuse by the direct mail pros, it still gets read.

25. Use your PS to direct your reader back into the main text. 'PS: John Harley of Megabucks estimates savings of one zillion in the first year using this approach.'

26. If you decide to offer seminars to existing or potential clients,

approach them as an entrepreneur rather than an educator. Select your subject as one which you could do off the top of your head while standing on it. Keep costs and handouts to a minimum. You can always develop fancy materials when you know that it is worthwhile from a healthy and potentially profitable response.

27. Always have available two or three short talks which you could give to audiences of prospective clients at the drop of a hat. Association secretaries who can turn to you in an emergency are friends indeed.

28. Consider holding free of charge client meetings or clinics a couple of times a year and invite existing or prospective clients. Take a theme which relates to your field: 'The avoidance of litigation', 'New technologies and how they affect your profit potential', 'Current thinking in quality circles'. Or simply run profit improvement clinics. Bringing people together to discuss matters which are important to them under your leadership will enable you to identify the major problems and issues, show something of what you can do and build your reputation at a stroke. It will also enable those who have used your services to tell each other and interested prospects how good you always are.

29. Schedule half a day each month to call prospects. Don't try any hard sell. Just say hello and pass on some piece of information which may be of interest. Ask what the important issues are at present by way of natural conversation. Ring off earlier rather than later: they will call you or stop you ringing off if they see a need for your services right now. It's an easy way to keep in touch without pressure and to be the name that they think of when the need arises to buy in your expertise.

30. When awards, unusual or prestigious assignments or honours come your way, let people know. Write a short press release

and mail a handwritten note to existing and old clients. Send a slightly more formal note to prospective clients to let them know what they are missing until they hire you. People like to tag on to success. Your successes make you valuable to know, and from a fee perspective just plain valuable.

31. If your business needs dictate that you must do some cold calling on prospective clients, avoid being seen as 'another salesperson'. Ask for the interview to get information for an article that you are writing. Write the article. Send a pre-publication copy to your prospect and ask for their comments and approval of any quotes. When the article is printed send, if possible, 20 photocopies that your prospect may pass on to their friends and business contacts. The prospect's desire to have their name seen in print can interest other influential people in your article and your services.

32. Don't go overboard on the cost and quality of your marketing and promotional bumf. (Short for 'bum fodder' – did you know?) Try to match where possible the quality in general use by your clients. They will feel comfortable with that.

33. When making a speech or presenting a proposal to a senior group, prepare a short introduction for your host or the chair-person which provides relevant information. They may not use it, but if they do not only are you in control, but someone else is doing some subtle selling on your behalf and that adds credibility. Some professional speakers are prepared to live with the waffling introduction they often get, but they write and insist on the script for thanking them at the end of their presentation. How's that for practical cheek?

34. Always accompany press releases with a photograph. It is esti-mated that the attachment of a good photograph increases the chances of publication by up to 30 per cent.

35. If you use a photograph, have an 'executive portrait' taken by a good professional. This is one of those areas where economy will not pay.

36. Market your services as highly specialized added value to your competitors. Find a niche where they are weak. Fill it and have them knock on doors for you as part of their offering. Most successful professionals subcontract and associate work counts for almost 16 per cent of the business.

37. If you have difficulty finding the time for all activities, never reduce the time spent marketing. Subcontract if you must some of your fee-earning activities, but do your marketing. It is that important.

38. By way of research, survey past and current clients to assess their future needs and establish the services which you should be planning to provide. In your survey, determine the value that they would put on any new service and reconsider your fee structure if they value it particularly highly.

39. Use surveys as the basis of press releases and consider selling them to business or commerce.

Networking

1. Networking, if done effectively, ensures an adequate flow of business and a quality service to the client, because the professional is not forced to accept business which others are better qualified to fulfil.

2. To network effectively, only work with those whom you trust, respect and who share your values.

3. Make it worthwhile for others to pass business to you. Pay at

least 25 per cent to the 'finder' of the business.

4. The client remains the client of the finder. With 25 per cent of the fee the finder can afford to spend one day in four looking after the client, ensuring that satisfaction is maintained and identifying further opportunities to serve.

5. Position yourself as the leader of the network and lay down the ground rules.

6. Don't spend time in unproductive networking. If business flows only one way, or not at all, leave them to it. Spend your time marketing yourself, build your reputation and be choosy when selecting from those who clamour to work with you.

7. When working with associates or subcontractors, always have a written agreement and include a non-competing clause stopping them from soliciting further business direct from your clients. (And vice versa, of course.)

Sales

1. When you meet your client for the first time, it is important that you understand and project the appropriate relationship. If they are to buy your expertise it is essential that you should be in all things but your specialism their peer. In your specialism you are their superior.

2. Approach the sales meeting as your assessment of whether you are able and willing to serve this client. You are a surgeon, not a salesperson.

3. Make sure that your client understands and accepts from the start that your purpose is to identify whether you are able to help. To do that effectively means that you have a number of

questions which you need to ask.

4. Control the conversation by asking questions and listening carefully to the answers. An effective salesperson spends more than 60 per cent of the time on a sales visit listening rather than talking.

5. Listen to understand what the client thinks and, most importantly, what they feel.

6. Use questions intelligently. Open questions first and most to help the client to talk freely. Closed questions next and less to clarify your understanding. Leading questions with subtlety and least to build agreement. Progress questions frequently during your presentation of your proposal to ensure that the client accepts and understands what you are offering. Closing question preferably only once to agree to the assignment.

7. If you are constantly asked for references, assume that your sales techniques need improving.

8. Communicate to your prospective clients very clearly that you only take assignments to which you can be totally committed. They really will want you all the more if they think that you are not begging for the job, and your insistence on work worthy of your total concentration will set at rest any concerns they may have about the standard of service which you will provide if you take the work.

9. Make it clear by the way that you get down to business that your time is valuable and you don't waste it. Remember that in due course the client will be paying for it.

10. Concentrate your attention on the client's problem and what you can do to resolve it. Avoid giving a long and unnecesssary history of your firm. If the client wants to know they will ask.

11. When making an appointment to see a client, steer a middle path between being too available and too busy. Too available and they will try to take advantage of your hunger for business. Too busy and they will suspect that you will give inadequate time to their problem.

12. Plan your response to any request for references. I would prefer to hear a professional say: 'I will be happy to ask one of my existing clients to contact you after our discussion. I never reveal anything about my client's business, not even their names, to a third party without their specific permission, so I must check with them first.' Above all, don't get flustered and don't offer the name of anyone who has not given you recent permission to use them. And remember, if you are asked for references most of the time you ought to consider how persuasive your sales approach is.

13. When talking of your past successes, do not try to impress by mentioning clients by name. Clients worry about what consultants say about them to others. Put their minds at rest by avoiding the tendency to drop names which so easily becomes a tendency to gossip.

14. Ask some prospects if you may record your discussion with them. Not only will it provide a perfect form of note taking, but it will teach you a lot about your sales skills.

15. If you do take notes, do so only after getting permission and keep them short. If you write pages it will be a distraction to the client from the important content of your discussion.

16. If you feel at the first meeting that you will have a personality conflict with this client, turn down the assignment.

17. Never exaggerate and oversell. Be specific about what you can achieve and tell the client what they must provide in order

that you may be successful.

18. Make sure that you always explain to the client why they can be confident that the following will not happen. Research shows that clients fear that the consultant will:
    - ❑ Prove to be incompetent.
    - ❑ Overcharge.
    - ❑ Spend too little time on the job.
    - ❑ Operate beyond management's control.
    - ❑ Make the organization dependent on the consultant for the future.
    - ❑ Disclose sensitive and confidential information.
    - ❑ Force-fit the problem to the consultant's standard solution.
    - ❑ Diagnose the problem inadequately.
    - ❑ Overestimate needs.
    - ❑ Assume that this problem is 'exactly like' others.
    - ❑ **Talk too much and fail to listen.**

19. Clients are tired of being sold to by angels and served by donkeys. That is, they are sick of major consultancies which use subject experts to sell and then send in inexperienced people wearing 'L' plates to do the job. They are beginning to demand WYSIWYG (what you see is what you get).

20. Avoid at all costs running down your competition. If the client is in danger of using Barrelmaker and Juvenile and you believe that they would make a dog's breakfast of the assignment, don't say so. Explain how your service offers unique advantages.

21. Each client believes that their problem is unique. Always talk of your experience with 'somewhat similar problems'. If you find yourself about to say 'exactly like', bite your tongue.

22. Even if their problem is 'exactly like', it isn't to them.

23. Before spending time with a prospect, be sure that you are talking to the MAN – one who has:
    - ❑ **Money** to pay for your services.
    - ❑ **Authority** to sign the contract.
    - ❑ **Need** for what you have to offer.

24. Follow up on sales calls, but don't create a feeling of pressure. Provide some extra information as the reason for your call.

25. If by mischance your first contact is not with a decision maker, don't be hesitant about insisting that you talk to the MAN yourself. The chances are remote of anyone, no matter how well intentioned, selling your services as well as you can.

26. If you are selling to a committee, try to talk to individuals separately and establish each decision maker's needs and expectations.

27. If the decision is to be made by the board of directors, make yourself available for the board meeting at which your proposal will be discussed. If they have questions they will prefer to get their answers from you direct.

28. When building information, only ask questions which are relevant and to which you do not already have the answers. If you know the answer and seek to show off your knowledge, ask: 'Is it still true that...?' Better yet, don't waste time.

29. Never leave without agreeing the prospect's next action. It may be to sign the contract; it may be to acquire some information. Never walk away from a vacuum.

30. Take responsibility for contact. If your next conversation is to be by telephone, make sure it is you that does the calling.

31. Much is said about dress. It is generally accepted that the best

form of dress for a salesperson is that which the customer is comfortable with. If your client is formal you should mirror their formality. If in doubt, dress up just a little.

32. Research shows that when a client is being sold to their mind follows a specific route. If you can satisfy the questions implicit in each step of the thought process, you will help the client buy rather than having to sell and that is more comfortable for both of you.

33. The questions are:
    - ❑ Does this person recognize that it is my situation which is important?
    - ❑ Do they understand that I already have a point of view and I value it, although I may be persuaded to change it?
    - ❑ Are they making it clear to me how I will benefit?
    - ❑ Are they really making clear what they offer?
    - ❑ Will the idea give me what I want?
    - ❑ Are they avoiding undue pressure?

34. If you are able to convince your client step by step that the answer to each question is 'yes', they will buy.

35. Avoid smart-alec closing techniques. If you want the assignment and you have demonstrated your ability to meet the client's needs, you are entitled to the contract. Just ask for it – and then shut up until the client says 'yes' or raises an objection.

36. Welcome client objections. When they express a concern to you they are still interested in what you have to say. They are inviting you to convince them.

37. Before closing be satisfied that you have made it absolutely clear to the client:
    - ❑ How they will benefit from your services.
    - ❑ Why they personally will gain from working with you.

❏ How much they will benefit.
❏ When they may expect to enjoy the first results.

Client care

1. Look for ways to provide unusual added value. Above all, look for ways to reduce the client's risk in using your services for the first time. Consider using what Jay Abraham calls 'reverse risk marketing' – if you are really good at what you do you have nothing to fear.

2. Tape your conversations with clients and give them the tape. They will have something tangible and if you have helped them to look at their business more analytically or in unusual depth they will appreciate having the full information.

3. Spend about 30 minutes per client per week identifying good ideas in their interests and send them a note or mini-proposal.

4. Keep in touch with clients and supply them with clippings and other pieces of information which may be of value to them whenever the opportunity occurs.

5. Sometimes, rather than accept an assignment from a client, show them how they could achieve the results they seek by using their own resources.

Fees

1. Establish your fees professionally in the following way:
    ❏ Decide on your value as a salaried employee.
    ❏ Add your best estimate of your overheads, including 'perks' and your salary on days you will not be billing direct to clients.

❑ Add a suitable profit margin to enable you to invest in the growth of your business.

2. Always be prepared set your fees on the value of services provided rather than just time expended. Do not underestimate your salary value.

3. Assume the risk, and profit opportunity, by expressing your fees as a fixed price rather than an open-ended daily rate. You will attract more business and if you are effective you will be more profitable.

4. Never cut your fees to win business. It gives the impression that you are 'flying a kite' and invites clients to see how far they can beat you down.

5. Where possible, protect your cash flow by having travel expenses, hotels etc. billed direct to the client.

6. Some clients prefer that you 'lose' expenses in a daily allowance which is added to your *per diem* charge. As long as you are properly reimbursed it matters little how.

7. Avoid billing for small items like telephone calls and the odd photocopy or postage stamp. Clients can be irritated by what they see as penny-pinching avarice. Add these to your overheads and thus into your *per diem* rate.

8. Some clients expect to be charged for the first meeting. If you propose to charge, make this clear from the outset, give value for money and use the opportunity to clarify your terms and conditions.

9. If the client cannot afford your total costs, look with them for those parts of the assignment which they could do themselves. You will find more often than not that they suddenly find

some 'flexibility' in the budget if they really have been sold on using you and you will usually do the complete job on your terms.

10. Used-car salespeople claim that it is not good policy to quote a neatly rounded figure as your fixed-price fee. Their experience leads them to believe that $30,000, say, is best received by the client when rounded up: $31,623 is seen as precise and accurate costing with all the fat trimmed.

11. Charge for all services, particularly diagnosis or need analysis. Clients may try to persuade the unwary that it is in their interests to do the diagnosis for free to get a fat contract thereafter. Diagnosis is usually the part that requires the maximum skill: do that for free and the client can usually manage the rest themselves.

12. Resist all blandishments to 'do this at a cut price to show what you can do, and charge your full fee for future work'. Not only may there not be future work, but even if there is the client will expect their 'usual discount'.

13. Don't price products like services. If your work for one client produces products which you can sell to many others, it is unacceptable greed to charge your development costs anew every time.

14. Do not leave it too long in an inflationary economy to raise fees. Too big a jump in costs could kill your business. Better to raise fees a little somewhat more often.

15. When you have to raise fees, use it as a marketing ploy. Advise existing clients early and offer the old fee rate for new jobs started within a given time of your announcement.

16. Ask for retainers where it is obvious that the client has a long-

term need for your services.

17. When you have retainers or long-term contracts, build in a cost-of-living clause so that your income retains its value.

18. Ask for upfront payments. You will be surprised how ready some clients are to fund the early stages of your work if they value your services.

19. Take a pride in your prices: let them properly reflect the value of your services and products.

20. When faced with the price objection 'Doolittle and Drink are cheaper!', the renowned sales consultant John Fenton used to reply, 'Well, they're an excellent company and I have no doubt that they have worked out to the penny what their service is worth. What I'm offering is...' I don't think John lost much business.

Brochures and proposals

1. Delay using a brochure until the pressure of time forces it on you. For as long as possible write an individual letter for each client showing how you are uniquely qualified to solve their problem.

2. When you write a brochure, make it factual not sales bumf.

3. Say what you have achieved in a range of situations, the special skills and knowledge that you brought to bear and the benefits to your clients (quantified where possible) of using your services.

4. Spice lightly with those details from your CV that you cannot bear the world to remain ignorant of and you're there.

5. If desirable, write a separate brochure for each sector or client group that you serve, using cases relevant to their forecast needs.

6. Use nine-year-olds to test for readability.

7. A good brochure makes the potential client want to talk to you. That means it must raise as many questions as it answers, but they have to be the right questions.

8. Provide some useful information, but never quite enough.

9. Always write a proposal, even when the client does not ask for one.

10. A good proposal is essential to accurate costing and it helps you to clarify the job in your mind.

11. Proposals are intended to sell your services. If you have been employed in an organisation where proposals are designed primarily to satisfy a senior partner's view of what is 'proper', you may need to rethink your proposal-writing skills or lose business.

12. If you are an engineer or scientist, think carefully about writing proposals which sell rather than inform.

13. A proposal should state:
    ❑ **What** you will do, but not how you will do it.
    ❑ Unique **skills** or **knowledge** which you will apply.
    ❑ The **benefits** which the client will gain.
    ❑ **When** you will complete each part of the assignment.
    ❑ **How much** your intervention will cost.
    ❑ Your **terms and conditions** of doing business.
    The rest is padding.

14. Be careful to write proposals, not recipes. Recipes can be too easily handed to another to cook.

15. Do not include the contract or letter of agreement in your proposal. Clients dislike anything which indicates that you are taking them for granted.

16. If you are invited to present your proposal verbally, prepare as carefully as you would for an important speech. Check the room and equipment as a matter of course and find out all that you can about your audience.

17. When by mischance a good proposal fails to get you the business, recycle it. Take out of it all references to the would-have-been client and send it to the CEOs of the other major players in the industry with a letter which reads: 'I have recently conducted research into some of the major issues which your industry is currently facing. The enclosed briefly covers some of my conclusions and recommendations. I would welcome an opportunity to discuss them...'

Contracts

1. Always work to a contract.

2. Regard a contract less as a legal document and more as a method of communication.

3. Contracts may be a short letter or a long legal document.

4. All contracts should include the following:
   - ❑ What you will do.
   - ❑ What your client will provide.
   - ❑ When and how you will be paid.
   - ❑ Who owns the rights to the outcome of your work,

particularly intellectual rights to 'products'.
- ❑ Circumstances under which you can bring in 'subcontractors'
- ❑ Circumstances under which the client can reassign the contract.

5. The contract should only be reassignable in the event of your death.

6. Do not try to limit your liability through the contract. It looks bad, and it won't wash in court anyway.

7. You should write the contract. If your client has a legal department and insists that they write it, expect them to try to tie you in to some totally unrealistic outcome. Get it put right before you sign.

8. Spell out your payment terms in the contract. Don't assume that because you provided a copy of your standard terms with the proposal the matter is settled. Clients have their standard terms too and they may be at variance.

9. Use the contract as a marketing tool. 'We seem to be agreed, shall I draw up a draft contract?' is a beautiful trial close.

10. Make your clients aware that you always insist on a contract. It raises your credibility and gives them a sense of security.

Process and administration

1. Client employees will either see you as a threat or a potential saviour. Remove the threat by having your client introduce you fully to staff, explaining your role.

2. Remove any threat which your client may feel by explaining up front how you will work for and through them.

3. Ensure that you and your client meet frequently to discuss progress and invite early and open expression of any concerns which they may have.

4. Never let your relationship with the client become adversarial. Your role is to serve the client first and only. If you cannot do that, either sort out your problems or walk.

5. If you elect to walk, ensure that a competent colleague or associate is available to take your place. Never leave the client dangling.

6. Respond to all correspondence within seven days. If it takes you that long to provide a detailed answer, acknowledge receipt of the letter in the interim.

7. Always return telephone calls within 24 hours wherever you are, and whatever you are doing. Maintain daily contact with your office and home.

8. In addition to using libraries for self-development and research, spend half a day at least twice a year wandering around a good university library and just see what is available. You will add greatly to your process skills with a little imagination.

9. Be aware that you will need to play different roles at different stages of an assignment (facilitator, problem solver, developer, catalyst etc.).

10. Plan your withdrawal from an assignment with as much care as you planned your entry. How will you ensure the client's ability to carry on your work?

11. Collect your fees at the agreed time or stop work until you are paid. It is not a matter of 'trust' but of business. You can only reasonably trust those who live up to their promises.

12. To turn down work without complications, simply say that it would create a conflict of interest. By definition to discuss your reasons further would be a conflict of interest, so you can leave with dignity whatever the reason.

13. Always ensure that the client accepts ownership of the problem and does not pass that ownership to you. They must continue to implement the solution after you have gone.

14. Try always to provide your client with more alternatives than were initially apparent. The quality of implementation of solutions often hinges on the attractiveness of the solution to the client.

15. **Always be open to new forms of process. Professionalism is, or should be, a matter of personal growth for professional and client.**

Glossary *126 Terms*

Ability: Technically this is the sum of the qualities, competences, access to power or influence, proficiencies, experience, talents and manual dexterities that enable individuals to perform a task effectively in a given time.

Ability tests: Psychometric or practical tests to determine what the individual can already do, as opposed to their potential. (*See* Aptitude tests.)

Achievement motivation (N-Ach.): One of the three motives which McClelland's research identifies as driving leadership behaviour. N-Ach. is the desire for personal achievement and, because of the personal bias, is more relevant to the entrepreneur than to the organizational leader. (*See* Affiliation motivation and Power motivation.)

Acquisition cost: The total cost of acquiring an asset, including interest paid on loans, fees to lawyers and accountants, additional equipment, training and so on. The important thing to remember is that the acquisition cost is invariably greater than, and sometimes much greater than, the purchase price.

Action learning: To overcome the problems of transfer of what is learned in the classroom to the workplace, Reg Reavans designed an approach which installed learning by dealing with real business problems and teaching only what was required at the time at which it was needed. An effective precursor of life-long learning: just in time, action learning is used as the methodology for some part-time MBA programs.

Action research: Social or organizational research in which the researcher's presence is recognized as potentially affecting the observed outcome. Research in which the observer intentionally acts as catalyst or change agent. (*Contrast with* the Hawthorne effect.)

Activity based costing (A C): A means by which all costs are allocated to the business activities which generate them in order to ensure that budgets are effectively applied to processes which generate revenues and profits. Recently Tony and Jeremy Hope have refined this concept to direct management attention to those 'investments' which lead directly to customer delight. (*See* Hope and Hope, 1995.)

Activity based management (A M): Using ABC (*above*) as a means of ensuring that what delights the customer and gives a return in profit, sales and referrals gets done.

Added value: Formerly and formally, the amount by which the income of a business exceeds the cost of its inputs. More recently taken to mean the additional, customer-delighting benefits or services offered by the customer-centred business.

Affiliation motivation (N-Aff): The drive to lead in order to nurture, build warm relationships and be liked by one's followers.

Alternate forms: A test of the reliability of a psychometric test. Any test presented in different formats should lead to identical results.

Aptitude tests: Generally, psychometric tests designed to enable the skilled user to predict the potential on-the-job performance of an individual.

Arousal: Technically, the activation of the sympathetic nervous system recognized as mild anxiety and 'butterflies in the stomach'. Some level of arousal is an essential contributor to peak performance (eustress). Excessive or minimal arousal is commonly referred to as stress (burnout or rustout).

Aspirational reference group: Any workgroup which enjoys sufficient status to make outsiders wish for membership. (*See* Status hierarchy.)

Assets: Plant, machinery, buildings, land etc. Anything which is owned by the organization and which is leveraged to produce a profit. People are not the primary assets of a business, they are not owned and are therefore not assets at all. People should be perceived neither as assets nor as a resource, but as pools of human resourcefulness which they can apply, at their own volition, to the welfare of the business if they choose to do so.

Assumptions: Based on our previous experience we create a belief system which is at the same time rational and irrational. We create assumptions where we lack facts or where we extrapolate from facts into an unknown and unknowable future. Since our assumptions drive personal and organizational behaviour to a major degree, it is wise to specify what assumptions are being made.

Auschwitz (survivor) syndrome: The pattern of reactions first recognised by Lifton in many of those who have survived an ordeal or trauma. Aspects of the syndrome include chronic anxiety, brooding on the event, withdrawal and loss of morale. Recent research suggests that major and repeated downsizing leads to such effects in a demoralized workforce.

Authoritarian: Autocratic leadership based on issuing orders and commands and tightly controlling the reward and sanction systems. Historic authoritarian behaviour bodes ill for the successful implementation of an empowerment program.

Balance sheet: A 'snapshot' freezing in time a statement of what the company owns (assets), what the company owes (liabilities) and what would be left for the owners if the company were to sell what it owns and pay its debts (equity or net worth).

Behaviourism: A once modish, much castigated school of psychology which gave rise to the 'greatest management principle' that what is rewarded gets done.

Benchmarking: A catch-up strategy aimed at identifying the best performers in the marketplace and adapting and adopting their behaviours. (*See* Leapfrogging.)

Boston Consulting Group matrix: The division of the product/service range into 'cash cows', which need little investment, but provide high revenue streams; 'stars', which need major investment during development but which are defined as the cash cows of the future; 'questionmarks', which may become stars given sufficient investment; and 'dogs', which have either 'had their day' and reached the end of their useful lifecycle, or which never made it and which justify no further investment.

Brainstorming: A creative group session to generate ideas. Brainstorming is a short activity, bound by formal rules including the capturing of all ideas, no evaluation until after the session and a specific role for the chairperson. It is far more than a *laissez-faire* ideas dump.

Brand: The identity given to a product or corporation through its name, design and marketing strategy. Key brands include Coca-Cola, Sony, McDonald's and Rolls-Royce.

Bureaucracy: Maligned as an organization in which strict rules and procedures are strangling originality, entrepreneurial flair and creativity, bureaucracy is an organizational form which flourishes in a period of minimal change and collapses in periods of volatility. (*See* Handy, 1992.)

Business cycle: The movement of a business over time from birth through growth and maturity to decline. Change is increasingly important to organizations in the modern world because, unless the business is effectively reborn every day, decline comes at a frightening pace.

Business plan: A comprehensive written statement indicating where the business is going over the next three to five years.

Business process reengineering: Redesigning a company's processes from first principles to produce dramatic improvements in cost, quality and service. Up to 80 per cent failure rate does not necessarily reflect on the concept as much as on the implementation. The publication of Hammer and Champy's *Reengineering the Corporation* (1993) started a bandwagon rolling which was boarded with alacrity by many of the incompetent. Those interested in the concept should consider going back to first principles by carefully reading Hammer and Champy's book.

Capital employed: The total funds, both fixed and working capital, which are used in the business.

Cash flow: The net volume of cash coming into a business in a specified time.

Catastrophe theory: Mathematical theory which shows that minor and gradual changes to the causes of behaviour can lead to drastic and sudden change. The last straw.

Change: In business change should be the process of moving from the present position to an improved situation. Consultants, who are generally in the change business, too often promote change when it is far from obvious how the new situation will be an improvement on the present. It is not true that people automatically oppose change. Not only does novelty have an appeal which some find difficult to resist, most people can readily be persuaded that change, any change, is inevitable and desirable. Thus the ever-growing market for fads, fallacies and futilities – and the bus queue syndrome.

Change agent: Internal or external consultant who acts as a catalyst for change.

Chaos theory: A mathematical theory concerning non-linear equations which is far too complex for any but specialists to relate to organizational behaviour.

Charismatic power: Leadership power resulting from perceived unique personal attributes or abilities.

Climate: The ambience of the business which results from the shared belief in values, myths, required behaviours, history and rules.

Cluster: A group of customers sharing certain relevant characteristics.

Coach: The individual who supports the implementation of new learning by acting as role model, guide, emotional support, resource provider, observer, monitor and provider of feedback. Recent research (Xerox Corporation, Joyce, Lambert and others) suggests that without effective coaching less than 2 per cent of what is learned is transferred to the workplace.

Co-determination: The involvement of the workers or their representatives in the strategic process. Approaches vary from the German model of 'worker directors' to Japanese attempts to have all workers at every level feed ideas into the general flow of explicit and implicit information. (*See* Nonaka and Takeuchi, 1995.)

Cognitive dissonance: A psychological theory developed by Leon Festinger which says that where an individual's beliefs and actions are in conflict one or other will be changed to reduce the discrepancy. Particularly loved of salespeople who use it to demonstrate that, although the grass may start out greener on the other side, the customer can readily be made to see their grass as getting greener by the second. (*See* Cialdini, 1993 or Lambert, *The Power of Influence*, 1996.)

Competitive advantage: The ability to identify, create and satisfy customer need better than your competitors at minimum cost. (For a unique and simple tool *see* Lambert, *Key Management Solutions*, 1996.)

Conative dimension: The likelihood that an individual will act on their expressed attitudes and beliefs. (*See* Kolbe, 1993.)

Conditioned response: Tendency to repeat behaviours previously rewarded and avoid behaviours previously punished. The consultant should be aware that if a behaviour is internally rewarded through, for example, congruence with the actor's value system, the addition of an external reward will reduce internal motivation.

Conformity: The tendency to go along with others even when those others are transparently wrong. One of the major concerns about the inappropriate use of teamwork or consensus. In most situations the best decisions are made by individuals working alone. (*See* Consensus decision making.)

Consensus decision making: Consensus should be looked for when the situation is a novel one in which previous experience is not a useful guide to current action and where key knowledge may be spread within the group.

Consortium: An alliance of companies to bid for a specific major contract which no one of them could hope to obtain alone. A key means by which relatively small companies can enter huge new markets, for example infrastructure works in South East Asia.

Contingency theory: There is no one way to organize a business. The effective organization depends on the people, the culture, the products or services, the location, the market, the political, legal and economic situation and so on. All forms of organization have had their successes. (*See* Bureaucracy.)

Convergent thinking: A thinking style which is aimed at reaching the single right answer through logic and which rules out creativity or intuition.

Corporate governance: The rules, procedures and codes of conduct which ensure that the business is conducted ethically at every level. An important emerging market for specialist consultants.

COST analysis: A psychologically sensitive and therefore superior alternative to SWOT analysis. (*See* Lambert, *Key Management Solutions*, 1996.)

Culture: At its simplest, 'the way things are done around here'.

Culture audit: A comprehensive analysis of the 'hard' and 'soft', current and historic determinants of the way things are done in the organization today. Hard factors include mission statements and policies and procedures, while soft factors include rituals, myths, stories, feelings and beliefs.

Delayering: The removal of complete layers of management in the expectation of reducing costs and speeding communications. Frequently the loss of experience combined with a greatly increased span of control can lead to disaster in corporations which have failed to prepare those below the excised layer of management to work with less supervision.

Delphi technique: A means of achieving group consensus. Each member of the group puts a proposal or decision in writing. An 'honest broker' writes a summary of each and returns them to the group who use them as a basis for their decision. It is argued that a summary, written in a uniform style by an individual with ostensibly no axe to grind, speeds the decision-making process and leads to a more rational decision.

Demand characteristics: Aspects of a situation which will exert pressure on individuals to behave in a way which can be pre-determined through an analysis of the circumstances.

Diary method: Study of work practices based on a written record of what people do – minute by minute, hour by hour, day by day.

Differentiation: Identifying the unique offering which the firm makes to the marketplace. Some argue that all mission statements should include the words 'what makes us different'.

Discourse analysis: Study of human experience and attitudes based on what they say and how they say it. 'I work for Megabucks Corporation!' as opposed to 'I only work for Megabucks'.

Distribution mix: The combination of channels which the company uses to get its products to the marketplace. A marketing consultant should advise that channels are audited from time to time to identify which offer the best levels of profit and customer satisfaction.

Divergent thinking: Intuitive, creative thinking involving non-rational conceptual leaps. In the Knowledge Age the stuff of tacit knowledge.

Dominance: In a highly competitive global marketplace the aim should be for sustainable strategic dominance of the industry or of carefully chosen niches.

Double bind: Catch 22, a problem from which there is no means of escape because alternatives cancel each other out.

Double blind: An experiment in which those who complete the evaluation have no knowledge of who among the subjects received special treatment and who were members of the control group.

Downsizing: A radical reduction and restructuring of the business either by a process of delayering or by concentrating on the core business and the disposal of all peripheral activities.

Drive theories: Theories of human motivation based on the idea that behaviour is directed towards the reduction of inner needs. Needs lead to tensions which lead to action.

Economies of scale: The, sometimes mistaken, belief that the more which is produced the lower the unit cost and, therefore, the greater the competitiveness and the higher the profit.

Emotional blocking: The inability of a worker to perform complex tasks not because of lack of ability, but because of anxiety.

Empathy: The ability to share another's feelings without necessarily sharing either their experience or their beliefs.

Empowerment: Building human resourcefulness by the planned and carefully monitored freeing of individuals at every organizational level to take their own decisions. Usually fails when a 'let my people go', proselytizing approach is ideologically implemented without adequate preparation of the workforce or testing to see if they want to be empowered.

Entrepreneur: Risk taker who founds and develops new enterprises. (*See also* Intrapreneur and Achievement motivation.)

Excellence: Not a cult invented by Tom Peters and Bob Waterman, but a reality without which no company can expect to perpetuate itself. The difficulty is that winning teams have a tendency to freeze. That is, corporations which dominate the markets of today are likely to assume that the same degrees of excellence will suffice in tomorrow's markets. This belief can be fatal.

Expert power: According to French and Raven, the degree of leadership power which comes from being an acknowledged expert. (*See* Lambert, *The Power of Influence*, 1996.)

Expert systems: Computer programs which summarize the opinions of experts to allow the less qualified to make decisions based on the best available advice.

Extraversion: The degree to which behaviour is outgoing and sociable.

Face validity: The likelihood that, as a result of its appearance, a subject will take a training instrument or psychological test seriously. The testee's view of whether the test is likely to measure something worthwhile and provide meaningful information.

Factor analysis: Identification, through statistical analysis, of intercorrelations of major clusters of data which are caused by a single common factor.

Factoring: The sale of a company's debtors at a discount to improve cash flow.

Feedback: Informal or formal responses to people concerning the quality of their performance. Research shows (Seward and Gers, 1984 and ongoing) that effective peer feedback can help to raise the transfer of learning after training from less than 13 per cent to better than 90 per cent.

Field theory: A psychological theory, developed by Kurt Lewin, which claims that behaviour is as much directed by the psychological environment as it is by personality.

Fireworks strategy: Launching a change program with a large number of more or less dramatic activities. A means of getting the whole organization's attention in one big bang.

Fixed capital: That part of funding tied up in premises, plant and equipment etc. Things which cannot be quickly turned into cash.

Force field analysis: A technique to promote change by identifying the key factors working against it and reversing or weakening them. (*See* Lewin, 1948.)

Four 'P's of marketing: 1. Product: branding, design etc. 2. Price, 3. Promotion and 4. Place. All four are extremely important, but the importance of place should not be underestimated. For many products, particularly consumer durables and fast-moving consumer goods, convenience comes second only to price as a factor in the purchasing decision.

Frustration–aggression hypothesis: Theory that the frustration of attempts to achieve a key goal is the basic cause of aggressive behaviour.

Gantt chart: A planning tool. In simple terms a timeline showing the temporal relationship between events.

Gestalt: A psychological approach based on the idea that experience is holistic and cannot usefully be reduced to its component parts.

Glass ceiling: The invisible barriers which stop women and minorities from attaining top positions in US and European organizations. The ceiling is showing a few, but not yet enough, cracks.

Globalization: Both the ability to move resources, cash and operations to any point on the globe at short notice and the development of marketing strategies and products which, contrary to normal marketing theory, are transferable into any market (McDonald's, Coca-Cola).

Glocalization: Either type of globalization implemented with due concern for local differences of culture, behaviour or expectation.

Groupthink: Inappropriate social consensus leading to decisions which are far removed from reality.

Hawthorne effect: Until recently regarded as a well-established psychological effect where it was assumed that observing any group at work led to an increase in performance. More recent thinkers (Furnham and others) suspect that it is not that simple. In any workplace there are so many variables that it is almost impossible to keep all but the subject of study unchanged. Any act of observation is therefore liable to create a change in circumstance.

Human resource management: An attempt to move away from old-fashioned, box-ticking, rule-promoting personnel management. It has seldom worked.

Ideology: Political, cultural or philosophical beliefs which direct behaviour without regard for relevance to the real world.

Image: The way a corporation or organization is seen by the public and its customers. The difficulties in changing an image can be such that it may be more effective to 'sell' the image you have than try to establish a new one. For example, scruffy, untidy business premises can be promoted as evidence of the lowest possible prices.

Infiltration strategy: Gradual change of marketing strategy, organizational structure, products, services etc. without announcement, each change being made, and market tested, one small step at a time.

Information power: Within an organization power flows to he, or she, who knows.

Innovalue: A Taiwanese concept of getting innovations, particularly in terms of design and enhanced performance, into the marketplace quickly at minimum cost.

Instrument: A practical device, similar in format to a psychometric test, used for analysis, training or action.

Internal locus of control: The belief that important life events are caused by one's own abilities, motives, attitudes, shortcomings etc. rather than external circumstances.

Intrapreneur: An employee who actively seeks to leverage everything which the company does to build revenues and profits.

Introversion: A tendency toward introspective, self-contained behaviour.

IQ: A number thought by some to indicate intelligence.

Joint venture: An alliance between two or more companies specifically to enable them to enter a new market or develop a new product.

Just in time: Originally a Japanese concept, now widely adopted, it aims at reducing stockholding and associated costs by having components delivered to manufacturing plants only as they are needed in production.

Klynveld Peat Marwick Goerdeler: Since 'K's are scarce, I thought you might like to know what KPMG stands for.

Knowledge Age: A development of the Information Age in which tacit knowledge (hunches, intuition, feelings etc.) is combined with explicit knowledge (data, information etc.) to produce the basis of decision making and action.

Knowledge workers: Increasingly valuable workers whose continually developing knowledge plays a key role in giving the organization its competitive edge.

Lateral thinking: An approach to problem solving which deliberately rejects conventional wisdom, points of entry or standardized solutions. Invented and developed by de Bono. The inability to name, and therefore think about, completely new concepts is overcome by the use of the nonsense word 'po'. (*See* de Bono, 1984.)

Lean enterprise: A company which combines close relationships with suppliers, distributors and customers with its constantly developing internal expertise to build continuously enhanced value.

Leapfrogging: A strategy aimed at overtaking competition and creating the future shape of the industry. (*See* Hamel and Prahalad, 1994.)

Legitimate power: Power and influence within and over a group which results from holding a relatively higher position in the formal hierarchy.

Levitt diamond: The concept that change in any major area of the business, people, technology, task, organizational structure etc., automatically produces change, not necessarily anticipated, in all the other key areas.

Linguistic determinism: The idea that thinking is constrained by language. (*See* Lateral thinking.)

Liquidity: The firm's ability to pay its short-term liabilities. Current assets should at least equal current liabilities, with a short-term loan facility covering the delay in turning debtors into cash.

Make or buy: The decision whether to make a component or outsource it. This decision is dependent on variables other than simply relative unit cost, including availability and continuity of supply.

Marginal cost: The cost of producing just one extra unit.

Market penetration: The percentage of all potential customers for a product or service who have actually bought it.

Market sector: A group of customers with shared characteristics whose needs are analysed from first principles with the intention of developing a product or service to satisfy those needs.

Market segment: A group of customers who are identified as potential buyers of our existing or planned product or service.

Market share: The percentage of buyers of a product or service who choose to buy that offered by the company.

Marketing: An integrated effort by everyone in the business to create, identify and satisfy customer wants and needs at a profit. If it does not involve everyone, if it does not seek to create need, and if it does not generate a profit it may be pretty, but it ain't marketing.

Mission statement: A living document, used daily, to move the organization towards its strategic goals, provide challenge and ensure that the values and ethics of the business are translated into the day-to-day treatment of all stakeholders.

Motivation: The internal needs which drive or energize behaviour. Most, if not all, readers will be familiar with Maslow's hierarchy of needs. Some recent psychological research has raised the intriguing possibility that the desire for control is even more basic than the desire for food, water and sex. If this is borne out by further research, the new approach of perception dynamics would appear to be even more potent than its inventor realizes.

Neurolinguistic programming (NLP): The study of how language and paralanguage affect thinking and behaviour. Consultants specializing in NLP have a delightful name for themselves. If I were an NLP specialist I would be a 'NLPer'. (If you don't get it try reading aloud.) (*See* Dilts, 1990.)

Niche strategy: Identifying and serving a small segment of the market with such a high level of excellence that the segment is effectively closed to competition.

Non-verbal communication: Used loosely to categorize all interpersonal communication other than the meaning of words. Strictly the expression means only communication that does not involve language in any form. Claims that the non-verbal aspects of communication account for 93 per cent of the transfer of meaning are extremely doubtful. Words retain immense power.

Objectives: Medium-term goals which are:
- ❑   Specific – they say precisely what is to be achieved
- ❑   Measurable

❑ Achievable
❑ Realistic – they can be achieved either with existing resources or with resources which can be acquired
❑ Timely.

Occupational testing: A combination of ability, aptitude and personality tests usually administered as the basis of career guidance.

Organizational development: The improvement of organizational and interpersonal effectiveness through workshops and on- and off-site planning activities.

Outsourcing: Purchasing goods or services from outside the business. Increasingly coming to refer to the purchase from external sources of services which were previously provided by internal departments, e.g. personnel, accounts receivable (debtors).

Overheads: Costs not allocated directly to the manufacture of a product or the provision of a service.

Paradigm: The framework of ideas, theories and assumptions implicitly adopted by a group at a specific time. This might be seen as intellectual groupthink.

Peer group coaching: Found by Gers and Seward to be a major factor in increasing the transfer of learning from training room to the workplace.

Perception dynamics: A behavioural science developed by Robson (unpublished research 1991–97, available from Ian Robson, Perception Dynamics Ltd, Claygate, Esher, Surrey KT10 0TG, UK) in which team behaviours are modified by aligning and changing perceptions, particularly the perception of the locus of control.

Personal construct theory: A theory developed by Kelly (1955) which suggests that people are not the passive recipients of experience, but rather 'scientists' who create theories of the world and test them against observation, prediction and experience. Personal constructs are explored through the use of repertory grid technique.

Phases of change: Usually given as denial, resistance, exploration and advocacy. This is a gross oversimplification: each change is a highly idiosyncratic process with a range of basic similarities of highly variable strength.

Power motivation (N-Pow.): The desire to lead in order to get things done in an organizational setting. According to McClelland's research the essential motive of the effective business leader. (See Lambert, *Key Management Solutions*, 1996)

Pricing strategy: Pricing for long-term competitive advantage rather than short-term profit.

Probability: The mathematical likelihood that an event will occur. (*See* Huff, 1978.)

Productivity: The single most important factor in corporate and national economic success. The output produced in a period of time divided by the resources used.

Psychological contract: The implicit understanding between an individual and their employer relating to how they will be treated. Downsizing has caused a dramatic reappraisal of the psychological contract, with a number of undesirable results.

Public relations: The sum of media relations, employee relations and community relations.

Referent power: Power which an individual is able to wield over or within a group because the group has adopted them as a role model and seeks to follow their behaviour.

Relationship marketing: Understanding the customer so well that their needs are met to a consistent standard of excellence which turns customers into advocates.

Reliability: A measure of the degree to which a psychological test would give the same results if taken by the same person on different occasions. Tests with low retest reliability are unlikely to provide worthwhile information. (*See also* Validity.)

Repertory grid technique: A technique which is useful for the exploration of how:
- Individuals interrelate within an organization
- Departments and divisions interrelate
- Different products are perceived
- A range of competitors are perceived etc.

The technique can also be used to identify those aspects which are important to individuals and groups. (*See* Fransella and Bannister, 1977.)

Reverse engineering: Analysis, usually by breaking down, of a competitor's product to see how it was made and what it cost to make.

Reward power: The influence which results from having the ability to manage the reward/sanctions system within a group.

Risk analysis: An assessment of the likelihood of being paid for work carried out.

Self-fulfilling prophecy: A prediction which is realized, not because of prescience, but because the predictor acts in such a way that the result becomes inevitable. If I declare that an individual is an idiot and then insist on treating them as if they were, they will probably behave like one regardless of their capacity or intelligence.

Self-image: A negative self-image is often the result of a limiting belief system. Incongruence between the real self and the self-image is a common cause of neurotic behaviour, anxiety and stress.

Self-inventory: A self-evaluation device in which the subject checks off those characteristics or personality traits they believe to be characteristic of themselves. The information given is then usually fed back to the donor by a trainer or consultant as if that person were some modern Delphic oracle.

Seven 'S's: A proven framework for thinking about the structure of organizations first introduced and developed by McKinsey and Co:
- ❑ Structure: how the business is currently organized
- ❑ Strategy: How the company chooses to achieve its goals
- ❑ Systems: Formal and informal procedures
- ❑ Skills: Competences of the organization
- ❑ Style: How the top team and other members of management present themselves to the workforce and how the workforce presents itself to the world
- ❑ Superordinate goals: The philosophy and values which underpin all activities.
- ❑ Staff: the quality of all the people; directors, management and employees.

Situational leadership: A leadership approach which is highly sensitive to the changing needs, competence and confidence of the team. (*See* Hersey and Blanchard, 1993.)

Stakeholder theory: The belief that an organizational strategy – or political program – should be designed to satisfy the needs of all who have a stake in the system. In business usually stockholders, employees (including management at all levels), suppliers, distributors and the community in which the business operates. (*See* Plender, 1997.)

Status hierarchy: An unfounded belief that some functions in an organization are intrinsically more important than others due to either a concept of 'glamour' (marketing is seen as more glamorous than production) or because one initiates work for another (research chemists are perceived as being superior to production chemists).

Status power: Power to influence the group which results from the conferral of status on an individual by the group. There is no set reason why status is conferred. It may be a reflection of the age, appearance, ability or seniority of the individual – or none of these.

Strategic alliance: An alternative to setting up greenfield sites in new markets or acquisition, a strategic alliance is the sharing of information, methods, marketing and finance between complementary businesses. Research suggests that approximately 50 per cent of strategic alliances are major successes for both partners, 30 per cent fail totally and the balance meet the needs of one partner more than the other.

Strategic business unit (S U): An autonomous profit centre within a conglomerate or corporation. Widely used to place responsibility as close as possible to the market and, less widely used, to protect the parent company in the event of the failure of a subsidiary. (The latter is a strategy promoted and possibly invented by de Savary.)

Strategic fit: The degree to which a company's strategy is consistent with its capabilities. (*See* Ansoff, 1971 – old, but still mindstretching.)

Stress: Technically a non-specific response to a situation, stress is usually taken to mean 'burnout' caused by overwork. Stress in the form of 'rustout' is as likely to result from underactivity. Not all stress is harmful. (*See* Arousal.)

SWOT analysis: An overused and often ignored qualitative analysis of where the company stands and what it faces. (*See* COST analysis.)

Tacit knowledge: The beliefs, feelings, hunches and guesses of the workforce.

Task orientation: A leadership approach which relates better to the structure of rules, deadlines and objectives than to the social needs of groups. Fleischmann, Bales and others argue that the effective leader balances social and task behaviour or creates space for the informal leader.

Telecommuter: An executive or other employee who works from home, optimizing the use of on-line communications. (*See* Kinsman, 1987.)

Time to market: There is increasing evidence that market success is enjoyed more by those businesses which get their innovations quickly into the marketplace and, where necessary, improve them in the light of experience than by those who seek to perfect their offering through protracted R & D testing and development. There are obvious exceptions, e.g. pharmaceuticals, but for consultants Shenson always advised that market testing is better and cheaper than market research. (*Compare* Taiwan's concept of Innovalue.)

Total quality management: Now and for all time consistently delighting the customer at minimum cost. Remember Deming's dictum; 'What can't be measured can't be managed'. (*See* Deming, 1988.)

Transactional leadership: A leadership style which responds to current events.

Transformational leadership: A leadership style which seeks to evolve with the organization and which is strategic in focus. Transformational leadership is aimed at long-term change and is driven by a clear vision.

Unique selling proposition: The key, unique benefit which differentiates the product or service from any offered by competition.

Validity: A measure of the degree to which psychometric tests actually measure what they are supposed to measure. A surprising number used in business fail the various tests of validity. (*See also* Reliability.)

Values: The 'ought tos' of the organization. The beliefs that are shared and will get the whole business to the barricades should the need arise. In the ultimate, those beliefs which according to Martin Luther King are so strongly held that they are, at the same time, what make life worthwhile and are the only things worth dying for.

Vision: A concise, but clear, inspirational statement of where the organization is going.

Working capital: That part of funds used for day-to-day trading, working capital includes cash, accounts receivable (debtors) and stocks. Things which, in theory at least, can be quickly turned into cash.

Zero based budgeting: Ignoring historical information and developing budgets on a clean piece of paper as if the firm were a new start-up each year. A sort of business process reengineering for finance departments, but a much older and better-tested concept.

Zero-sum game: A situation in which if I win, you can do nothing other than lose. A non-zero-sum game is a set of circumstances in which a win–win outcome is possible, i.e. one in which both sides can win.

Bibliography

As always, this is a somewhat idiosyncratic collection of books which I believe will provide the consultant with effective and reliable tools of the trade, or will noticeably widen the perspective brought to the client workplace. I recommend any book by Charles Handy or Peter Drucker without reservation.

Abraham, RH and Shaw, CD, *Dynamics: The Geometry of Behaviour*, Ariel, 1984

Adair, John, *Effective Team Building*, Pan, 1987

Ansoff, Igor, *Corporate Strategy*, Pelican, 1971

Argyle, Michael, *The Anatomy of Relationships*, Penguin, 1985

Argyle, Michael, *Bodily Communication*, Routledge, 1993

Argyle, Michael, *The Psychology of Interpersonal Behaviour*, Penguin, 1994

Austin, JL, *How To Do Things With Words*, Oxford University Press, 1962

Axelrod, Robert, *The Evolution of Cooperation*, Penguin, 1990

Bandler, Richard, *Frogs Into Princes*, Real People, 1979

Bandler, Richard and Grinder, John, *The Structure of Magic* (in two volumes), Science and Behaviour, 1975

Belbin, R Meredith, *Management Teams: Why They Succeed or Fail*, Butterworth Heinemann, 1991

Bennis, Warren, *On Becoming a Leader*, Business Books, 1989

Berger, LA and Sikora, MJ, *The Change Management Handbook: a Road Map to Corporate Transformation*, Irwin, 1994

Blanchard, Kenneth and Peale, Norman Vincent, *Power of Ethical Management*, Mandarin, 1990

Burgess, Anthony, *A Mouthful of Air: Language and Languages Especially English*, Hutchinson, 1992

Burrus, Daniel, *Technotrends*, HarperBusiness, 1993

Cialdini, Robert B, *Influence*, Morrow, 1993

Clarke, L, *The Essence of Change*, Prentice Hall, 1994

Courtis, John, *Marketing Services*, Kogan Page, 1988

Coward, Rosalind, *Our Treacherous Hearts: Why Men Get Their Own Way*, Faber, 1992

Crainer, Stuart, *The Financial Times Handbook of Management*, Pitman, 1995

Crainer, Stuart, *Key Management Ideas*, Pitman, 1996

Crawley, John, *Constructive Conflict Management*, Nicholas Brealey, 1992

de Bono, Edward, *Lateral Thinking for Management*, Pelican, 1984

Deming, W Edwards, *Out of the Crisis*, Cambridge University Press, 1988

Dilts, J, *Changing Belief Systems with NLP*, Meta, 1990

Economist Books, *Pocket Strategy*, 1994

Economist Books, *Pocket World in Figures* (annual)

Economist Books, *Pocket Britain in Figures* (annual)

Economist Books, *Pocket USA* (annual)

Economist Books, *Pocket Asia* (annual)

Economist Books, *Pocket Europe* (annual)

Economist Books, *Pocket Latin America* (annual)

Engel, James F, Blackwell, Roger D and Miniard, Paul W, *Consumer Behaviour*, Dryden, 1990

Erickson, Milton H (ed. Sydney Rosen), *My Voice Will Go With You: The Teaching Tales of Milton H Erickson*, Norton, 1982

Farb, Peter, *Word Play*, Cape, 1974

Frager, Robert and Fadiman, James, *Personality and Personal Growth*, HarperCollins, 1984

Fransella, Fay and Bannister, Don, *A Manual for Repertory Grid Technique*, Academic Press, 1977

Furnham, Adrian, *All in the Mind*, Whurr, 1996

Furnham, Adrian and Gunter, Barry, *Business Watching*, ABRA, 1994

Furnham, Adrian and Oakley, D, *Why Psychology?*, UCL, 1995

Galbraith, Jay R, *Designing Organizations: An Executive Briefing on Strategy, Structure and Process*, Jossey-Bass, 1995

Galbraith, Jay R and Lawler, Edward E, *Organising the Future: New Logic for Managing Complex Organisations*, Jossey-Bass, 1993

Galbraith, John Kenneth, *The Anatomy of Power*, Hamilton, 1984

Galbraith, John Kenneth, *Affluent Society*, Deutsch, 1985

Galbraith, John Kenneth, *New Industrial State*, Penguin, 1991

Galbraith, John Kenneth, *Money: Whence It Came, Where It Went*, Penguin, 1995

Gardner, Howard, *Frames of Mind*, Heinemann, 1983

Gates, Bill, *The Road Ahead*, Viking, 1995

Gilley, Jerry W and Eggland, Steven A, *Marketing HRD Within the Organisation*, Jossey-Bass, 1993

Goldberg, Steven, *Why Men Rule*, Open Court, 1993

Goldsmith, James, *The Trap*, Macmillan, 1994

Grinder, John, *TranceFormations*, Real People, 1981

Hackman, Richard, *Groups That Work and Those That Don't: Creating Conditions for Effective Teamwork*, Jossey-Bass, 1990

Hackman, Richard and Oldham, John, *Work Redesign*, Addison Wesley, 1980

Hamel, Gary and Prahalad, CK, *Competing for the Future*, Harvard Business School Press, 1994

Hammer, Michael and Champy, James, *Reengineering the Corporation: A Manifesto for Business Revolution*, Nicholas Brealey, 1993

Hampden-Turner, Charles, *Charting the Corporate Mind: From Dilemma to Strategy*, Blackwell, 1990

Handy, Charles, *Understanding Organisations*, Penguin, 1992

Harre, Rom (ed.), *Motives and Mechanisms: An Introduction to the Psychology of Action*, Methuen, 1985

Hersey, Paul, *Selling: A Behavioural Science Approach*, Prentice Hall, 1988

Hersey, Paul and Blanchard, Kenneth, *Management of Organizational Behaviour*, Prentice Hall, 1993

Hope, Tony and Hope, Jeremy, *Transforming the Bottom Line*, Nicholas Brealey, 1995

Huff, Darrell, *How to Take a Chance*, Penguin, 1978

Hunt, John W, *Managing People at Work*, McGraw Hill, 1992

Jay, Ros, *The Essential Marketing Sourcebook*, Pitman, 1996

Johnson, H Thomas and Kaplan, Robert S, *Relevance Lost, The Rise and Fall of Management Accounting*, Harvard Business School Press, 1987

Johnson, Mike, *Managing in the Next Millennium*, Butterworth Heinemann, 1995

Jonker, J, *Toolbook for Organizational Change*, Pba, 1996

Kenichi, Ohmae, *The Borderless World*, Collins, 1990

Keyes, Daniel, *The Minds of Billy Milligan*, Bantam, 1981

Kinsman, Francis, *The Telecommuters*, Wiley, 1987

Koch, Richard, *The Financial Times Guide to Strategy*, Pitman, 1995

Kolbe, Kathy, *Pure Instinct*, Times, 1993

Krugman, Paul R, *Development, Geography and Economic Theory*, MIT Press, 1991

Krugman, Paul R, *Rethinking International Trade*, MIT Press, 1994

Krugman, Paul R, *Peddling Prosperity: Economic Sense and Nonsense in the Age of Diminished Expectations*, Norton, 1995

Krugman, Paul R, *Pop Internationalism*, Norton, 1996

Lambert, Tom, *The Power of Influence*, Nicholas Brealey, 1996

Lambert, Tom, *Making Change Pay*, Technical Communications, 1996

Lambert, Tom, *Key Management Solutions*, Pitman, 1996

Leavitt, Harold J, *Managerial Psychology*, University of Chicago, 1978

Lipnack, J and Stamps, J, *The Teamnet Factor*, Oliver Wight, 1993

Mann, Nancy R, *The Keys to Excellence*, Prestwick Books, 1987

Mant, Alistair, *Leaders We Deserve*, Robertson, 1983

McKenna, Eugene F, *Psychology in Business*, LEA, 1987

Midgley, Mary, *Women's Choices: Philosophical Problems Facing Feminism*, Weidenfeld and Nicholson, 1983

Midgley, Mary, *Beast and Man: The Roots of Human Nature*, Methuen, 1990

Mole, John, *Mind Your Manners*, Nicholas Brealey, 1995

Moore, Robert and Gillette, Douglas King, *Warrior, Magician, Lover*, Harper, 1990

Moore-Ede, Martin, *The Twenty Four Hour Society*, Piatkus, 1993

Morgan, Gareth, *Imaginization: The Art of Creative Management*, Sage, 1993

Naisbitt, John, *Megatrends Asia*, Nicholas Brealey, 1996.

Nonaka, Ikujo and Takeuchi, Hirotaka, *The Knowledge Creating Company: How Japanese Companies Create the Dynamics of Innovation*, Oxford University Press, 1995

Obeng, Eddie, *All Change! The Project Leader's Secret Handbook*, Pitman, 1994

Ostrander, Sheila, *Cosmic Memory*, Souvenir Press, 1992

Owen, Hilary, *Creating Top Flight Teams*, Kogan Page, 1996

Penn, Bill, *Be Your Own PR Expert*, Piatkus, 1992

Peters, Tom, *The Tom Peters Seminar*, Macmillan, 1994

Peters, Tom, *The Pursuit of Wow*, Macmillan, 1995

Pfeffer, Jeffrey, *Competitive Advantage through People*, Harvard Business School Press, 1994

Plender, John, *A Stake in the Future*, Nicholas Brealey, 1997

Popcorn, Faith, *The Popcorn Report*, Arrow, 1992

Price, Frank, *Right Every Time*, Gower, 1990

Quek, Swee Lip, *Business Warfare*, Temple House, 1995

Quinn, Pat, *The Secrets of Successful Low Budget Advertising*, Heinemann, 1987

Quinn, Pat, *The Secrets of Successful Copywriting*, Heinemann, 1988

Reed, Evelyn, *Sexism and Science*, Pathfinder, 1978

Romaine, Suzanne, *Language in Society*, Oxford University Press, 1994

Scheele, Paul R, *The Photoreading Whole Mind System*, Learning Strategies Corporation, 1993

Seligman, MEP and Garber, J, *Human Helplessness: Theory and Research*, Academic Press, 1980

Sewell, Ron, *Fly With the Geese*, Sewell International, 1995

Shank, John K and Govindarajan, Vijay, *Strategic Cost Management*, Free Press, 1993

Sheldrake, Rupert, *The Rebirth of Nature*, Century, 1990

Shenson, Howard L, *How to Develop and Promote Successful Seminars and Workshops*, Wiley, 1990

Shenson, Howard L, *The Contract and Fee Setting Guide for Consultants and Professionals*, University Associates, 1990

Shtogren, John A (ed.) *Models for Management; The Structure of Competence*, Teleometrics International, 1980

Sun Tsu (trans. Cleary, Thomas), *The Art of War*, Shambala, 1988

Sutherland, Stuart, *Irrationality: The Enemy Within*, Penguin 1994

Suzuki, DT, *Essays in Zen Buddhism*, Hutchinson (Rider), 1985

Tannen, Deborah, *You Just Don't Understand*, Virago, 1992

Tannen, Deborah, *That's Not What I Meant: How Conversational Style Makes or Breaks Your Relations With Others*, Virago, 1992

Tannen, Deborah, *Talking 9 to 5*, Virago 1995

Thurow, Lester, C, *Head to Head: The Coming Economic Battle Among Japan, Europe and America*, Nicholas Brealey, 1993

Thurow, Lester C, *The Future of Capitalism: How Today's Economic Forces Will Shape Topmorrow's World*, Nicholas Brealey, 1996

Trompenaars, Fons, *Riding the Waves of Culture*, Nicholas Brealey 1993

Walsh, Ciaran, *Key Management Ratios*, Pitman, 1996

Westen, Drew, *Psychology: Mind, Brain and Culture*. Wiley, 1996

Wilson, Edward O, *On Human Nature*, Harvard University Press, 1978

Wrong, Dennis H, *Power: Its Forms, Bases and Uses*, Harper, 1980

Seminars for Professionals

THE RANGE OF PUBLIC PROGRAMS OUTLINED BELOW ARE A SAMPLE OF the range which I offer. They should not be taken to be exhaustive or even realistically representative of the programs and workshops that can be presented.

Entrepreneurial/intrapreneurial success and style – 1 day

This seminar is based on the use of proven instruments and individual counselling. It enables the participant to produce a personal successs strategy by meeting the following **objectives**.

On completion of the seminar the participant will implement a personally congruent strategy to:

❏ Achieve entrepreneurial success.
❏ Be a successful intrapreneur.
❏ Assess entrepreneurial style and success factors, build on strengths and mitigate weaknesses.
❏ Manage behaviour to build exceptional client/corporate relationships.
❏ Exploit personal and group entrepreneurial and intrapreneurial strengths.

High income consulting masterclass – 2 days

Objectives: on completion of the seminar the participant will understand the following, select those proven strategies which are congruent with their desired professional image and preferred personal behaviours and implement them effectively:

❑ How to price services for maximum profit and income.
❑ How to build your image and have clients come to you.
❑ How to avoid giving away your services for free.
❑ How to generate 'static' income.
❑ When to use and how to write contracts.
❑ Nine low-cost/no-cost ways to win professional exposure.
❑ The five **key** factors of consulting success.
❑ How to flourish in all economic circumstances.
❑ How to get more and better referral business.
❑ Professional liability and what to do about it.
❑ How to turn the first client meeting into a contract.
❑ How to write business-winning proposals.
❑ Advertising and direct mail strategies.
❑ Using the press and the media.
❑ How to make networking pay.
❑ How to get advanced payments and retainers.
❑ Collecting your fees.

Internal consultancy teams will learn how to build their status, reputation and results within the corporate environment.

The power of influence – 3 days

This can be presented as a fully interactive program, in two modules, each of five days. The ten-day format allows considerable opportunities for practice and feedback and is usually conducted for corporate clients, cascading down from top management to customer-facing staff.

The three-day program is more than a concept overview with

some time built in for threat-free practice. To gain optimal benefit from the three-day program participants are strongly advised to
bring with them a specific example of a real-world sales/influence
opportunity that they can work on.

Objectives: on completion of the seminar the professional will:

❑ Understand and apply the psychological determinants of
influence.
❑ Build commitment of peers, superiors, subordinates and customers to their ideas.
❑ Sell their services/ideas in a manner appropriate to the role and
status of a professional adviser or leader.
❑ Identify the internal or external 'client's' principal objectives
and relate their services directly to the achievement of 'client'
goals.
❑ Overcome totally and for all time any fear of failure or rejection.
❑ Manage 'difficult clients' positively and build a uniquely constructive 'client' relationship.
❑ Understand why women have a cultural advantage when influencing behaviour and developing relationships and use that
knowledge effectively and ethically to influence others.

How to select, manage and control consultants and other professionals – 1-day workshop

Aimed directly at the needs of the manager, director or government official who needs to make an informed choice:

❑ Whether to engage the services of a professional adviser, and if
so:
❑ How to select the best available at the most reasonable cost.
❑ How to manage and control the intervention.

Objectives: on completion of this workshop the client will:

❏ Establish when to use and when not to use external advisers.
❏ Identify the right professional adviser at the right price.
❏ Ensure effective control of the assignment is maintained at every stage of the job.
❏ Ensure an appropriate and speedy return on any investment in professional services.

In addition to the above programs, I design and deliver seminars on creativity, strategic dominance, problem solving, decision making, managing change, making training work, facilitation skills, coaching and mentoring, motivation and leadership etc.

For more complete information you can talk to me on (+44) 01525 713503 or fax me on the same number. My e-mail address is 100435.771@compuserve.com and my business addresses are:

Beaumont Lambert International   Psynergy Ltd
51 Mill Lane   37 Gower Street
Greenfield   London
Bedford   UK
UK   WC1E 6HH
MK45 5DG